Saryn Brell

A Voice for LGBTQ Freedom in Zerana – Unauthorized

Tatyana Flores

ISBN: 9781779697721
Imprint: Telephasic Workshop
Copyright © 2024 Tatyana Flores.
All Rights Reserved.

Contents

Section 2: Finding a Voice in College   16
Section 3: The Call to Action   30
Section 4: Unmasking Hypocrisy   44
Section 5: A Movement is Born   58

Chapter 2: Triumphs, Tribulations, and Tequilas   **75**
Chapter 2: Triumphs, Tribulations, and Tequilas   75
Section 1: From Small Wins to Big Victories   78
Section 2: Speaking Truth to Power   95
Section 3: The Dark Side of Activism   110
Section 4: Allies and Adversaries   124
Section 5: Looking Towards the Future   137

Chapter 3: Behind the Scenes – The Unauthorized Biography   **147**
Chapter 3: Behind the Scenes – The Unauthorized Biography   147
Section 1: The Research and Interviews   150
Section 2: The Controversial Legacy of Saryn Brell   161
Section 3: The Impact of Saryn's Story   172
Section 4: The Unauthorized Perspective   184
Section 5: Acknowledgments and Final Thoughts   195

Index   **209**

1 1 Section 1: The Unremarkable Beginnings

In this section, we delve into the unremarkable beginnings of Saryn Brell – the LGBTQ activist who would later become a voice for freedom and equality in Zerana. From their humble childhood in Smalltown, USA, to the discovery of their interest in politics and social justice, we begin to unravel the early influences and experiences that shaped Saryn's path towards activism.

1.1 Subsection: Saryn's Childhood in Smalltown, USA

Saryn Brell's story starts in a small, close-knit town in the heart of America. Born into a middle-class family, their upbringing was largely ordinary and unremarkable. They grew up in a modest home with parents who instilled in them the values of hard work, empathy, and open-mindedness. Saryn's parents encouraged their curiosity and always emphasized the importance of education.

From an early age, Saryn displayed a natural curiosity about the world around them. They were drawn to stories of social justice and equality, even as a young child. Saryn questioned the inequalities they witnessed and sought to understand the root causes of these injustices.

1.2 Subsection: Discovering an Interest in Politics and Social Justice

As Saryn grew older, their interest in politics and social justice deepened. They avidly followed current events, keeping up with local and national politics. They engaged in discussions with their peers, challenging the status quo and advocating for the rights of marginalized communities.

Saryn's passion for social justice was further fueled by the stories and experiences of their LGBTQ friends. They witnessed firsthand the discrimination and inequality faced by the LGBTQ community, prompting a desire to fight for their rights. This personal connection ignited their determination to make a difference and create a more inclusive society.

1.3 Subsection: Coming to Terms with Their Own Identity

Alongside their journey as an emerging activist, Saryn also embarked on a personal exploration of their own identity. They grappled with questions of gender and sexual orientation, seeking to understand and accept themselves fully.

This period of self-discovery was marked by moments of deep reflection and introspection. Saryn found solace in connecting with LGBTQ communities online and participating in support groups where they could share their experiences and find guidance. This process of self-acceptance played a crucial role in shaping their activism, as they understood firsthand the struggles faced by individuals in the LGBTQ community.

1.4 Subsection: Friends, Allies, and Enemies Along the Way

Throughout Saryn's journey, they encountered a diverse array of individuals who would play vital roles in their life and activism. They found solace and support in the friendships formed with like-minded individuals who shared their passion for social justice. These friendships provided a sense of belonging and a network of allies that would become essential in their later activism.

However, not everyone welcomed Saryn's growing activism. They faced opposition and encountered individuals who held discriminatory views. These encounters served as a catalyst for Saryn, solidifying their determination to challenge bigotry and fight for equality.

1.5 Subsection: The First Seeds of Activism Are Sown

The first seeds of activism were sown in Saryn's college years. They attended a liberal arts university that fostered an environment of critical thinking and social engagement. This setting proved to be transformative, pushing Saryn to embrace their role as an activist fully.

Saryn's involvement in student organizations and protests on campus ignited their passion for advocacy. They organized rallies, participated in awareness campaigns, and engaged in important dialogues surrounding LGBTQ rights. These early experiences gave Saryn a taste of the power of collective action and the potential for significant change.

1.6 Subsection: A Dose of Reality – Navigating Adulthood

As Saryn graduated from college and entered the "real world," they faced the challenges that come with adulthood. They found themselves confronting the harsh realities of discrimination and inequality that existed beyond the sheltered campus environment.

Navigating employment obstacles and witnessing the struggles of fellow LGBTQ individuals in finding acceptance reinforced Saryn's determination to continue their fight for social justice. They understood that change would not come easily but were prepared to persevere and make a lasting impact.

In the next section, we explore how Saryn's voice as an LGBTQ activist grew stronger during their college years, as they found a community of support, and began advocating for change both on and off campus.

1 1 Section 1: The Unremarkable Beginnings

In this section, we delve into the unremarkable beginnings of Saryn Brell, a prominent LGBTQ activist in Zerana. We explore their childhood in Smalltown, USA, their discovery of an interest in politics and social justice, and their journey towards accepting their own identity. Along the way, Saryn encounters friends, allies, and enemies, and the first seeds of activism are sown.

1.1 Subsection: Saryn's Childhood in Smalltown, USA

Saryn Brell was born and raised in the heart of Smalltown, USA, a conservative community where diversity was rarely celebrated. Growing up, Saryn felt a sense of otherness, unsure of where they belonged in a world that clung to rigid norms and expectations. Little did they know that this sense of not belonging would later fuel their passion for activism and advocacy.

In Smalltown, USA, LGBTQ identities were largely misunderstood and disregarded. This lack of acceptance created a challenging environment for Saryn, as they questioned their own identity from a young age. They often found solace in books and music, immersing themselves in stories of resilience and defiance. These artistic outlets became an escape from the reality of their everyday life.

1.2 Subsection: Discovering an Interest in Politics and Social Justice

As Saryn entered adolescence, they began to discover their passion for politics and social justice. They had always felt a fire burning within them, an innate drive to fight for those who were marginalized and oppressed. This drive, coupled with their growing understanding of their own identity, set them on a path towards activism.

Saryn's interest in politics was sparked by a high school civics class, where they learned about the power of democracy and the potential for change through collective action. They became determined to make a difference in the world, to create a society where everyone was accepted and valued for who they were.

1.3 Subsection: Coming to Terms with Their Own Identity

While Saryn's passion for activism grew, they also began to confront their own identity. They grappled with questions of gender and sexuality, seeking answers within themselves and through their personal connections with the LGBTQ community.

Through self-reflection and conversations with trusted friends, Saryn slowly started to come to terms with their non-binary identity. They embraced the fluidity of their gender and found empowerment in defying societal expectations. This process of self-discovery was not without its challenges, as it required breaking free from the constraints of a binary world and embracing their authentic self.

1.4 Subsection: Friends, Allies, and Enemies Along the Way

As Saryn embarked on their journey of self-discovery and activism, they encountered a diverse array of individuals who would shape their path. They found friends who shared their beliefs and values, allies who stood by their side through thick and thin, and enemies who sought to undermine their progress.

Saryn's closest friends became their chosen family, providing support and understanding during both the triumphs and tribulations of their journey. These friends helped Saryn navigate the complexities of their identity and offered a safe space where they could be their authentic selves.

However, not everyone embraced Saryn's quest for LGBTQ freedom. They faced opposition from individuals who clung tightly to traditional beliefs, fearing the disruption of societal norms. These adversaries challenged Saryn's resolve and served as a constant reminder of the uphill battle they faced.

1.5 Subsection: The First Seeds of Activism Are Sown

With their newfound understanding of their own identity and a growing network of allies, Saryn began sowing the first seeds of activism. They attended local LGBTQ support groups and educational workshops, immersing themselves in the rich history of LGBTQ activism.

Inspired by stories of pioneers who had fought for LGBTQ rights, Saryn organized small-scale events to raise awareness and promote inclusivity in their community. These grassroots initiatives served as their introduction to the world of activism, igniting a passion within them to advocate for meaningful change.

1.6 Subsection: A Dose of Reality: Navigating Adulthood

As Saryn transitioned into adulthood, they faced the realities of navigating the world as an LGBTQ individual. They encountered discrimination and experienced firsthand the systemic barriers that oppressed their community.

The challenges they faced only fueled their determination to create a more equitable society. Saryn became acutely aware of the urgent need for widespread education and advocacy, realizing that change could only be achieved by challenging existing power structures and dismantling oppressive systems.

In this section, we have explored the unremarkable beginnings of Saryn Brell, tracing their journey from a small town in the USA to their first steps into activism. We have witnessed their struggle with self-discovery and the formation of their beliefs, as well as the vital role that friends, allies, and enemies played in shaping their path. In the next sections, we will delve further into Saryn's transformative journey and the significant impact they would have on LGBTQ rights in Zerana and beyond.

ERROR. thisXsection() returned an empty string with textbook depth = 3.

ERROR. thisXsection() returned an empty string with textbook depth = 3.
ERROR. thisXsection() returned an empty string with textbook depth = 3.

Subsection: Discovering an Interest in Politics and Social Justice

In the unremarkable beginnings of Saryn Brell's journey, nestled in the heart of Smalltown, USA, their path towards activism and politics took shape. Growing up in an environment that largely adhered to traditional norms, Saryn was exposed to a limited worldview. However, even in this seemingly ordinary place, the seeds of curiosity and empathy were sown.

Politics and social justice often seemed like distant concepts that were only discussed on the evening news. But for Saryn, there was an innate yearning to make a difference, to challenge the status quo and create a more inclusive society. It was within the confines of their tight-knit community that they longed to be a catalyst for change.

As Saryn matured and became aware of the societal inequalities surrounding them, they began delving into books, articles, and documentaries that explored political ideologies and social justice movements. This newfound knowledge acted as a spark, igniting a fire within them to question the existing power structures and advocate for marginalized communities.

Saryn engaged in countless conversations with friends, family, and neighbors about pressing issues affecting their community. These discussions not only allowed them to refine their own beliefs but also exposed them to differing perspectives. Through these exchanges, they started to understand the power dynamics at play within their own community and society at large.

Recognizing that their insights and passion could find a home in the political arena, Saryn actively sought out opportunities to engage in local politics. They joined student government and volunteered for political campaigns, eager to gain a practical understanding of the systems that shaped their community.

It was during this time that Saryn encountered their first taste of opposition and misunderstood ideology. As they advocated for gender-neutral bathrooms in their school, they faced backlash from conservative parents, who were resistant to change. This experience only fueled their determination to challenge the norm and fight for a more inclusive future.

The pivotal moment in Saryn's political awakening came when they attended a social justice conference in a nearby city. There, they were exposed to a diverse range of activists who were working tirelessly to dismantle oppressive systems. Inspired by their stories of resilience and triumph, Saryn realized that they were not alone in their pursuit of justice.

With a renewed sense of purpose, Saryn returned to their small community armed with newfound knowledge and a commitment to effect change. They facilitated workshops, organized panel discussions, and even started their own social justice club to create a safe space for open dialogue.

But their journey towards becoming an LGBTQ activist was not without its challenges. Saryn faced criticism and resistance from some friends and allies who dismissed their efforts as unnecessary or radical. This taught them the importance of building bridges and educating others, even when faced with adversity from within the LGBTQ community itself.

Saryn's journey in politics and social justice was characterized by persistent learning, growth, and adaptability. They understood that achieving true equality required not only passion but also a deep understanding of the systems they were up against. They continued to educate themselves on intersectionality, privilege, and the importance of allyship, always striving to be an advocate for all marginalized communities.

Through tireless grassroots organizing and community engagement, Saryn began to build a reputation as a compassionate and effective advocate for LGBTQ rights. Their charisma and ability to articulate complex issues garnered attention, attracting supporters and inspiring others to join the fight for equality.

As Saryn's voice grew louder, so did their impact. They sought out opportunities to collaborate with other LGBTQ activists, both locally and nationally, recognizing the power of collective action. Together, they pushed for policy changes that would protect the rights and well-being of LGBTQ individuals.

Saryn's journey from an unassuming small town to becoming a prominent voice in politics and social justice serves as a reminder that change begins with a single spark. Their relentless pursuit of justice and understanding ignited a movement that would leave an indelible mark on Zerana and beyond.

But as Saryn's star continued to rise, they would soon discover that the path to creating lasting change would be fraught with challenges, sacrifices, and personal growth. In the upcoming sections, we will delve deeper into the triumphs, tribulations, and tequilas that would shape Saryn's extraordinary journey. We will explore the impact of their activism, the adversity they faced, and the legacy they left behind.

Before we embark on this unfiltered journey, let us remember the importance of embracing nuance and recognizing that no hero or activist is without their flaws. In the next chapter, we will uncover the behind-the-scenes moments, controversies, and the unauthorized perspective that will shed light on the complex nature of Saryn Brell's activism.

CONTENTS 7

So come along as we venture deeper into the captivating story of Saryn Brell, a voice for LGBTQ freedom in Zerana.

Subsection: Coming to Terms with Their Own Identity

Coming to terms with one's own identity is a deeply personal and transformative journey. For Saryn Brell, this process was a gradual and sometimes challenging one. Growing up in a small town in the USA, Saryn was exposed to rigid norms and expectations that left little room for exploring their true self.

The journey of self-discovery for Saryn began during their childhood in Smalltown, USA. As a young person grappling with questions of gender and sexuality, Saryn often felt isolated and misunderstood. The lack of representation and open discussions about LGBTQ identities in their community added to this sense of confusion and alienation.

In this subsection, we will delve into some of the key moments and realizations that helped Saryn come to terms with their own identity. Through their experiences, we can gain insight into the challenges and triumphs that many LGBTQ individuals face on their journey towards self-acceptance.

One pivotal moment in Saryn's journey was their discovery of an interest in politics and social justice. As they became more engaged with these issues, they began to recognize the importance of LGBT rights and representation. This newfound passion fueled their determination to understand their own identity and navigate the complexities of their sexual orientation and gender identity.

Navigating personal relationships also played a significant role in Saryn's journey of self-discovery. Friends, allies, and even adversaries all played a part in helping Saryn understand and accept their own identity. Some relationships provided a safe space for exploration and acceptance, while others challenged outdated stereotypes and forced Saryn to confront their own biases.

As Saryn's activism began to take shape, they started sowing the first seeds of their own personal advocacy. Through community organizing and awareness campaigns, Saryn found connection and purpose. They realized that their journey of self-discovery was intricately linked to their desire to create a more inclusive and accepting society for all LGBTQ individuals.

However, adulthood brought its own set of challenges for Saryn. Navigating the realities of work, relationships, and societal pressures added another layer of complexity to their journey of self-acceptance. They grappled with the fear of rejection and the potential consequences of living openly as an LGBTQ individual in a society still plagued by discrimination.

Along the way, Saryn discovered the importance of self-reflection and personal growth. They came to understand that embracing their own identity meant challenging societal norms and expectations. This acceptance was not without its own complexities and sacrifices, but Saryn remained steadfast in their commitment to authenticity and living their truth.

The process of coming to terms with one's own identity is not a linear progression. It is shaped by a multitude of factors, including personal experiences, relationships, and the broader societal context. Saryn's journey serves as a reminder that self-discovery is a courageous and ongoing process that requires resilience, self-compassion, and a willingness to challenge the status quo.

As we explore Saryn's journey in this subsection, let us reflect on our own identities and the importance of creating spaces where everyone can feel accepted and celebrated for who they are. Let us challenge societal norms and stand up against discrimination, so that others may find the strength and support to come to terms with their own identities. Together, we can shape a more inclusive and accepting world.

Subsection: Friends, Allies, and Enemies Along the Way

Throughout Saryn Brell's journey as an LGBTQ activist, they encountered a diverse array of individuals who played significant roles in their path towards freedom and equality. Alongside friends and allies who supported and uplifted Saryn, there were also enemies and adversaries who challenged their progress. This subsection explores some of the key figures who influenced Saryn's activism, both positively and negatively.

Friends: A Shoulder to Lean On

Saryn's close circle of friends provided invaluable support and understanding during their journey. One of their closest companions was Jamie, a fellow LGBTQ activist who shared Saryn's passion for equality. Jamie stood by Saryn's side through thick and thin, offering a shoulder to lean on during challenging times. Together, they attended rallies, organized protests, and worked tirelessly to amplify the voices of the marginalized.

Another significant friend in Saryn's life was Leila, an empathetic and compassionate listener. With a warm and nurturing presence, Leila provided emotional support whenever Saryn faced adversity. Through heartfelt conversations over cups of tea, Leila helped Saryn navigate the complexities of their identity, allowing them to find solace and acceptance within themselves.

Additionally, Saryn found a supportive ally in Matt, a straight individual who understood the importance of advocating for LGBTQ rights. Matt used his privilege to uplift Saryn's voice, actively engaging with other straight allies to foster understanding and promote inclusivity within their community. His unwavering support validated Saryn's cause and played a crucial role in building bridges between different communities.

Allies: United in the Struggle

Beyond their close friends, Saryn also forged alliances with various individuals and groups who shared their vision for LGBTQ freedom. One of the most notable allies was Maya, a charismatic community organizer. Maya's dedication to social justice inspired Saryn to broaden their activism beyond college campuses and into the local community. Together, they organized outreach programs, workshops, and awareness campaigns to educate and empower marginalized individuals.

Another significant ally in Zerana's political landscape was Senator Michael Harris. As an influential figure, Senator Harris championed LGBTQ rights within the legislature and worked closely with Saryn to drive legislative change. Their collaboration resulted in the introduction of groundbreaking LGBTQ-inclusive bills and policies, propelling Zerana towards a more equitable society.

Enemies: Overcoming Resistance

While Saryn's journey was marked by significant strides, it was not devoid of opposition. Rebecca, a staunch conservative, became one of Saryn's most prominent adversaries. Rebecca's discriminatory views fueled her determination to suppress LGBTQ rights, making her a formidable opponent. However, Saryn's unwavering commitment to their cause instilled resilience in the face of Rebecca's bigotry.

Another obstacle Saryn encountered was Mayor John Thompson, who initially appeared supportive of LGBTQ rights but later revealed their true colors. As Saryn began advocating for comprehensive LGBTQ-inclusive legislation, Mayor Thompson's opposition became apparent. Their confrontations were characterized by intense debates and public clashes, exposing the deep-rooted biases and homophobia within local politics.

Caveat: It is important to note that some individuals mentioned here may represent archetypal characters to illustrate the range of relationships Saryn experienced. While the story is fictional, it reflects the complexities of navigating friendships, alliances, and conflicts in the pursuit of equality.

Lessons Learned: Building Solidarity

Saryn's interactions with friends, allies, and enemies taught them invaluable lessons about the power of unity and compassion. They discovered that allies could be found in the most unexpected places, transcending boundaries of gender, sexual orientation, and race. Moreover, Saryn realized that not all enemies were beyond redemption, as some individuals later underwent transformative journeys towards acceptance and enlightenment.

Their experiences underscored the significance of building bridges and fostering dialogue, even with those who opposed their cause. Saryn learned to approach conflicts with empathy, seeking common ground rather than perpetuating divisiveness. By engaging in respectful conversations and challenging biases, Saryn aimed to break down barriers and establish a foundation for lasting change.

In the fight for LGBTQ rights, the relationships forged throughout Saryn's journey provided a sense of camaraderie, bolstering their determination and resilience. Through collaboration, understanding, and the courage to stand against opposition, Saryn's friends, allies, and even former enemies propelled their activism forward, enabling them to become a formidable force for LGBTQ freedom in Zerana and beyond.

Key Takeaways:

- Friends and allies play a crucial role in supporting and uplifting activists, providing emotional support and standing with them in the fight for equality.

- Unexpected allies can come from diverse backgrounds, and their support can amplify the voices of marginalized communities.

- Engaging in respectful dialogue with adversaries has the potential to challenge biases and foster understanding, working towards building a more inclusive society.

- The relationships formed throughout an activist's journey are instrumental in propelling their cause forward, overcoming obstacles, and leaving a lasting impact.

Exercise: Think about a social cause that resonates with you. Identify a potential ally and an adversary in that context. How would you approach each of them to build a partnership with the ally and engage in constructive dialogue with the adversary?

Additional Resources:

1. "Call Me By Your Name" by André Aciman - A novel exploring LGBTQ relationships, acceptance, and the complexities of attraction.

2. TED Talk: "The Danger of a Single Story" by Chimamanda Ngozi Adichie - A thought-provoking discussion about the dangers of stereotypes and the importance of diverse narratives.

3. "Redefining Realness" by Janet Mock - A memoir detailing Mock's journey as a transgender woman of color and her activism for transgender rights.

Subsection: The First Seeds of Activism Are Sown

As a child growing up in Smalltown, USA, Saryn Brell never imagined the impact they would have on the LGBTQ community. The first seeds of their activism were sown in their early years, as they began to question the world around them and discover the power of their own voice.

Saryn's journey began with the realization that something was different about them. While their peers were conforming to societal norms and expectations, Saryn found themselves questioning their own identity. It was a challenging and confusing time, but it ultimately led to a deeper understanding and acceptance of who they truly were.

During their time in high school, Saryn's interest in politics and social justice began to blossom. They found themselves drawn to the stories of marginalized communities and the fight for equality. It was through reading books, attending community events, and engaging in discussions with like-minded individuals that Saryn started to recognize the power of advocacy.

Throughout these formative years, Saryn encountered a mix of friends, allies, and enemies. Some classmates were supportive, while others were quick to judge and discriminate. These experiences fueled Saryn's passion to challenge prejudice and fight for the rights of the LGBTQ community.

The first true taste of activism came when Saryn organized a small gathering in their hometown to raise awareness about LGBTQ issues. Despite the modest turnout, the event sparked a fire within Saryn. They realized that even small actions could make a difference in their community.

As Saryn transitioned into adulthood, they faced the harsh realities of the world. Discrimination, both subtle and overt, became a constant presence in their life. Navigating these hurdles was not easy, but it only strengthened Saryn's resolve to make a lasting impact.

College provided Saryn with a platform to amplify their voice and connect with like-minded individuals. They joined the LGBTQ student organization on campus, where they found a supportive community and a channel to drive change. Together, they organized protests, advocated for LGBTQ rights, and challenged the status quo.

It was during this time that Saryn's iconic look emerged—a bold expression of their identity and a symbol of pride. They used fashion as a way to challenge societal norms and inspire others to embrace their true selves. Saryn's unique style became both a form of self-expression and a tool for activism.

However, being an LGBTQ activist on campus was not without its challenges. Saryn faced resistance from conservative groups and encountered those who believed their fight for equality was unnecessary. These experiences taught Saryn the importance of resilience and the need to educate and bridge divides within the LGBTQ community itself.

The seeds of activism planted in Saryn's smalltown upbringing continued to grow beyond the campus walls. They began engaging with local LGBTQ organizations and built a support network of individuals who shared their vision for change. Saryn's determination led to the organization of the first LGBTQ Pride Parade in Zerana, an event that would become an annual celebration of love, inclusivity, and acceptance.

As Saryn's activism gained momentum, they found themselves confronting discrimination on a larger scale. They pushed for LGBTQ rights within local politics, challenging elected officials to address issues directly impacting the community. These efforts were met with resistance and backlash, but Saryn remained undeterred.

The personal sacrifices of activism were not lost on Saryn. They faced threats, both online and offline, but they refused to let fear silence their voice. Saryn understood that progress often comes at a cost, and they were willing to bear that burden for the greater good.

In this subsection, we have witnessed the first seeds of activism taking root in Saryn's life. From their unremarkable beginnings in Smalltown, USA, to their journey through higher education, Saryn's path to becoming an LGBTQ advocate has been marked by self-discovery, resilience, and an unwavering determination to make a difference. This is just the beginning of their extraordinary journey, and the impact they will have on LGBTQ rights in Zerana and beyond. So let us move forward in this biography, eager to see how Saryn's voice for LGBTQ freedom will continue to resonate and inspire.

Subsection: A Dose of Reality: Navigating Adulthood

Life as an LGBTQ activist is not all rainbows and unicorns. It comes with its fair share of challenges and obstacles, especially when it comes to navigating adulthood. In this subsection, we'll explore the realities that Saryn Brell faced as they transitioned into adulthood while fighting for LGBTQ rights in Zerana. We'll also delve into the personal sacrifices and difficult choices that come with being an advocate for change.

The Struggle for Financial Stability

A crucial aspect of adulthood is the need to establish financial independence and stability. For Saryn Brell, this meant juggling their activism while also securing a stable income to support themselves. The reality is that advocating for LGBTQ rights often comes with financial constraints, as it may be difficult to find well-paying jobs in the field of activism. Saryn had to make tough decisions about their career path, carefully balancing their passion for advocacy with the need to earn a living.

Example: Saryn faced a dilemma when they were offered a prestigious, high-paying corporate job that went against their values. They had to weigh the financial security that came with the job against their commitment to LGBTQ activism. Ultimately, Saryn decided to turn down the offer and instead pursued a less lucrative but more fulfilling career in a grassroots LGBTQ organization.

Lesson: Navigating adulthood as an LGBTQ activist often requires making financially challenging decisions. It's important to find a balance between earning a living and staying true to your values. Sometimes, taking a less conventional career path can bring more satisfaction and purpose than a high-paying job that contradicts your principles.

Challenges in Building and Maintaining Relationships

As an LGBTQ activist, Saryn experienced unique challenges when it came to building and maintaining relationships. The fight for equality often required them to prioritize their cause over personal commitments. This meant sacrificing time, energy, and sometimes even romantic relationships.

Example: Saryn was in a committed romantic relationship with Ashley, a fellow activist. However, the demands of their advocacy work took a toll on their relationship. Saryn's frequent travels and long hours of organizing events created strain and eventually led to a difficult decision. They had to choose between staying fully committed to their activism or prioritizing their relationship with Ashley. Saryn made the difficult choice to end the relationship in order to focus on their mission.

Lesson: When navigating adulthood as an LGBTQ activist, it's essential to be prepared for the potential strain on personal relationships. It's crucial to find a partner who understands and supports your passion for advocacy. Open communication and setting boundaries can help in maintaining a healthy balance between personal and activist commitments.

Mental Health Struggles and Self-Care

Advocacy work can be emotionally and mentally draining, taking a toll on one's well-being. Saryn Brell faced their fair share of mental health struggles while navigating adulthood as an LGBTQ activist.

Example: Saryn experienced burnout due to their relentless pursuit of change. The constant exposure to discrimination, hate, and setbacks took a toll on their mental health. They struggled with anxiety and depression, eventually needing therapy and counseling to cope with the emotional challenges of their work.

Lesson: Taking care of your mental health is paramount when navigating adulthood as an LGBTQ activist. Self-care practices such as therapy, mindfulness, and setting boundaries can help in maintaining emotional well-being. It's crucial to recognize when you need support and not be afraid to seek professional help or lean on a support network of friends and fellow activists.

Finding Community and Support

In the midst of the challenges faced by Saryn, finding a strong community and support network played a vital role in their journey as an LGBTQ activist. Having a sense of belonging and camaraderie kept them motivated and resilient in their fight for equality.

Example: Saryn found solace and support through LGBTQ organizations, both locally and nationally. They actively engaged with these communities to build connections, learn from others' experiences, and share the burdens and triumphs of their activism. Through these networks, Saryn formed lifelong friendships and built a strong support system.

Lesson: Navigating adulthood as an LGBTQ activist can be challenging, but finding a supportive community is crucial. Engaging with like-minded individuals who share your passion for change can provide a sense of belonging and offer guidance and support during tough times. Building these connections can also lead to valuable collaborations and collective action for a greater impact.

The Balancing Act of Personal and Activist Goals

Navigating adulthood as an LGBTQ activist requires navigating the challenging balance between personal goals and full-time advocacy. Saryn had aspirations and dreams beyond their activism, but they had to confront the reality of the constant demands of their cause.

Example: Saryn had always dreamed of pursuing a graduate degree in psychology, with hopes of becoming a therapist. However, the demands of their activism often left little time and energy for pursuing personal aspirations. Saryn had to make a difficult choice and put their personal goals on hold to continue their fight for equality.

Lesson: Finding the right balance between personal goals and activism is crucial when navigating adulthood as an LGBTQ advocate. It may require making sacrifices and reevaluating priorities at different stages of life. It's essential to reflect on personal aspirations and create a plan to pursue them while staying committed to making a positive impact on the LGBTQ community.

In conclusion, navigating adulthood as an LGBTQ activist brings its own set of challenges and sacrifices. Saryn Brell's journey serves as a reminder of the realities that come with fighting for LGBTQ rights. From financial struggles to relationship complexities, mental health concerns to maintaining personal goals, these obstacles must be acknowledged and addressed. By recognizing these challenges and learning from Saryn's experiences, future activists can be better prepared to navigate their own paths and create lasting change.

Section 2: Finding a Voice in College

Subsection: Saryn's Journey to Higher Education

Saryn Brell's journey to higher education was not an easy one. Growing up in a small town in the heartland of the United States, they faced numerous challenges and obstacles in pursuing their dreams. However, their resilience, determination, and unwavering commitment to education propelled them forward, leading to a remarkable transformation.

In the early years of their life, Saryn lived an ordinary existence in their smalltown, USA. They were no different from their peers, navigating the complexities of childhood and forging their identity in a world that didn't always understand them. Nevertheless, it was during this time that Saryn developed a passion for learning and a curiosity about the world around them.

As they grew older, Saryn's interest in politics and social justice began to take shape. They realized that their own journey was intricately linked to the larger struggle for equality and liberation. With each passing day, they became more aware of the injustices faced by the LGBTQ community and the urgent need for change. This awareness fueled their determination to make a difference and to fight for a more inclusive society.

Coming to terms with their own identity was an essential part of Saryn's journey. It was not an easy process, as they faced personal and societal pressures to conform to traditional norms. However, through self-reflection and the support of friends and allies, they were able to embrace their true self and find the strength to be unapologetic about who they were.

Throughout their journey, Saryn encountered both friends and foes. Some stood by their side, offering support and encouragement, while others sought to sow doubt and stifle their passion. However, it was through these experiences that Saryn developed an unyielding determination to challenge the status quo and create a world that embraced diversity and equality.

As Saryn entered adulthood, reality hit them hard. Navigating the complexities of life outside their small town and facing systemic barriers became their new reality. But their dreams remained intact, and they vowed to overcome every hurdle that came their way.

Higher education became the gateway to Saryn's transformation. With limited financial resources, they spent countless hours researching scholarships and grants. Through sheer determination and perseverance, they secured a scholarship that would allow them to pursue their dreams.

College became a pivotal time in Saryn's life. They immersed themselves in the LGBTQ student organization on campus, recognizing the power of collective action and the importance of finding strength in numbers. Together with their fellow activists, they organized campus protests, advocating for LGBTQ rights and challenging discriminatory policies.

It was during this time that Saryn also developed their iconic look – a colorful, vibrant representation of their identity and their commitment to LGBTQ activism. The rainbow flag became a symbol of hope and resilience, inspiring others to join the movement for equality.

Being an LGBTQ activist on campus came with its own set of challenges. Saryn faced opposition from conservative groups and encountered ignorance and prejudice from fellow students. However, they refused to be silenced. They engaged in conversations, educated their peers, and challenged stereotypes, slowly but surely making progress towards a more inclusive campus environment.

The journey to higher education was not without sacrifices. Saryn had to balance their academic responsibilities with their activism, often sacrificing personal time and relaxation for their commitment to the cause. The toll of fighting for change was evident, and yet, they continued to push forward, believing wholeheartedly in the power of education to create a more just society.

Saryn's journey to higher education was a transformative experience, shaping their identity, their worldview, and their commitment to activism. It laid the foundation for the incredible journey they were about to embark on, as they set their sights on making a lasting impact on their community and the world.

So, how does one follow in the footsteps of Saryn Brell? The key lies in harnessing the power of education, embracing one's true self, and finding the courage to challenge the status quo. As Saryn's story demonstrates, higher education can be the catalyst for personal growth and societal transformation. It equips individuals with the knowledge, skills, and resources to create change and fight for a more inclusive future.

But higher education alone is not enough. It must be coupled with activism, resilience, and the determination to overcome obstacles. Saryn's journey serves as a reminder that progress is possible, even in the face of adversity. Their story inspires us to become advocates and allies, to challenge discriminatory practices, and to create a world where everyone can thrive regardless of their sexual orientation or gender identity.

As we reflect on Saryn's journey to higher education, let us also recognize the power of education as a tool for liberation. It empowers individuals to question the status quo, challenge oppressive systems, and envision a more just society. By embracing education and activism, we can continue to build upon the foundations laid by trailblazers like Saryn Brell and create a world that celebrates diversity, equality, and freedom.

So, let us embark on this journey together, learning from Saryn's experiences, celebrating their victories, and acknowledging the challenges they faced. Through education, activism, and unwavering determination, we too can make a difference in the world and become voices for LGBTQ freedom. Let the journey begin.

Subsection: Joining the LGBTQ Student Organization

Joining the LGBTQ student organization was a pivotal moment in Saryn's journey towards becoming an influential LGBTQ activist. It provided an outlet for their passion, a platform for their voice, and a community that would shape their understanding of the challenges faced by the LGBTQ community. In this subsection, we will explore the pivotal role of LGBTQ student organizations, the impact they have on individuals and society, and Saryn's personal experiences within the organization.

The Importance of LGBTQ Student Organizations

LGBTQ student organizations play a crucial role in creating safe and supportive spaces for LGBTQ students on college campuses. These organizations provide a platform for students to come together, share experiences, and advocate for their rights. By joining such an organization, Saryn found themselves in a nurturing environment where they could express their identity freely and learn from others who faced similar challenges.

These organizations also serve as a hub for education and awareness on LGBTQ issues. Workshops, panel discussions, and training sessions organized by LGBTQ student organizations help raise awareness about discrimination, promote inclusivity, and foster a greater understanding of the challenges faced by the LGBTQ community. Through participation in these initiatives, Saryn was able to deepen their understanding of LGBTQ issues and develop the skills necessary to become an effective advocate.

Support and Solidarity

For Saryn, joining the LGBTQ student organization meant finding a supportive and understanding community. Their fellow members quickly became friends, allies, and mentors. Together, they shared their personal stories, coping mechanisms, and advice for navigating the complexities of being LGBTQ in a heteronormative society. Saryn found solace in the shared experiences and the understanding that they were not alone in their struggles.

Through participation in support groups and counseling sessions facilitated by the LGBTQ student organization, Saryn gained invaluable emotional support. These spaces offered a judgment-free environment where members could freely express their concerns, fears, and hopes. It was within this supportive community that Saryn found the strength to confront their own internalized biases, further develop their identity, and embrace their role as an LGBTQ activist.

Developing Leadership Skills

Joining the LGBTQ student organization provided Saryn with opportunities to develop essential leadership skills. From planning events and fundraisers to leading workshops and awareness campaigns, Saryn learned the intricacies of organizing and mobilizing others for a cause. This hands-on experience in activism and advocacy would pave the way for their future endeavors.

By taking on active roles within the organization, Saryn honed their communication skills by engaging with a diverse range of individuals, including fellow LGBTQ students, faculty, and other student organizations. They learned to advocate for their rights, negotiate with stakeholders, and passionately articulate the importance of LGBTQ inclusion. These skills would prove vital as Saryn transitioned from campus activism to a larger stage.

Challenges and Triumphs

Being part of an LGBTQ student organization was not without its challenges. Saryn and their fellow members faced opposition from conservative groups on campus, experiencing backlash ranging from verbal attacks to vandalism. These incidents only strengthened their resolve to fight for equality and inclusivity.

However, the experience also brought moments of triumph. The LGBTQ student organization successfully led campaigns to implement nondiscrimination policies, establish gender-inclusive restrooms, and create LGBTQ-inclusive curriculum. These victories not only improved the campus climate for LGBTQ students but also inspired Saryn and their peers to envision a more inclusive future beyond the campus walls.

Resources and Training

Recognizing the importance of education and empowerment, LGBTQ student organizations often provide resources and training to their members. Saryn took full advantage of these opportunities, attending workshops on LGBTQ history, intersectionality, and effective advocacy strategies. These resources equipped Saryn with the knowledge and skills necessary to navigate the complexities of LGBTQ activism.

One particularly impactful resource provided by the LGBTQ student organization was mentorship. Saryn was paired with an experienced LGBTQ activist who guided them in their journey, offering insights, advice, and valuable connections. This mentorship not only provided Saryn with practical guidance but also served as a source of encouragement and inspiration.

Unconventional Activity: Leveraging Social Media

In today's digital age, social media has become an essential tool for activists. Saryn recognized the potential of social media platforms to reach a broader audience and amplify their message. During their time with the LGBTQ student organization, Saryn experimented with creative ways to leverage social media to raise awareness about LGBTQ issues.

For example, they initiated online campaigns, such as "Faces of LGBTQ" and "Stories That Matter," where members of the LGBTQ community shared their personal stories and experiences. These campaigns gained traction online, attracting attention from both LGBTQ and ally communities. Through this unconventional approach, Saryn was able to humanize LGBTQ issues, challenge stereotypes, and foster empathy.

Exercises

1. Reflect on your own experiences or observations of LGBTQ student organizations. What impact do you believe these organizations have on individuals and campuses?

2. Imagine you are tasked with organizing a workshop on LGBTQ history. Design an agenda that covers key milestones, influential figures, and important legislative victories.

3. Create a social media campaign to raise awareness about an LGBTQ issue that you feel should be prioritized. Consider the target audience, messaging, and potential impact.

4. Write a personal reflection on the significance of support groups for LGBTQ individuals. How do these spaces contribute to personal growth and well-being?

5. Research and summarize the challenges faced by LGBTQ student organizations in different parts of the world. What are some common barriers and how can they be overcome?

Remember, joining an LGBTQ student organization is more than just attending meetings. It is an opportunity to learn, grow, and make a lasting impact, both on the individual and the larger community. Through their involvement in the LGBTQ student organization, Saryn found their voice, discovered their passion, and set the foundation for their remarkable journey as an LGBTQ activist.

Subsection: Campus Protests and Advocacy

In this subsection, we delve into Saryn's journey of campus protests and advocacy, where they find their voice and start challenging the status quo. Through their involvement in the LGBTQ student organization, Saryn begins to make a significant impact on their college campus.

Saryn's Journey to Higher Education

Saryn's path to higher education was not an easy one. Coming from a small town in the heart of the United States, they faced numerous obstacles and prejudices.

However, their determination and passion for education pushed them forward.

One of the biggest hurdles Saryn had to overcome was financial barriers. They worked tirelessly to save money and apply for scholarships to make their dreams of higher education a reality. Saryn's academic excellence and dedication paid off when they were accepted into a prestigious university.

Joining the LGBTQ Student Organization

Upon their arrival at college, Saryn quickly became involved in the LGBTQ student organization. This group provided a powerful sense of belonging and allowed Saryn to connect with like-minded individuals who were passionate about LGBTQ rights.

Saryn recognized the need for a safe and welcoming space on campus for LGBTQ students. They strived to create an inclusive environment where everyone could express their true selves without fear of judgment or discrimination. This organization became the platform through which Saryn would begin their journey of activism.

Campus Protests and Advocacy

Inspired by the LGBTQ student organization, Saryn became actively involved in campus protests and advocacy. They organized rallies, sit-ins, and peaceful demonstrations to raise awareness about LGBTQ rights and justice.

One of the notable campus protests organized by Saryn was in response to a discriminatory policy by the university. The policy prohibited same-sex couples from sharing dormitory rooms, perpetuating heteronormativity and marginalizing LGBTQ students. Saryn, along with the LGBTQ student organization, led a series of protests demanding an end to this discriminatory policy.

Their ability to mobilize students and create a sense of solidarity among the LGBTQ community on campus was remarkable. Saryn's charisma and passion for the cause attracted attention from both students and faculty members, leading to increased awareness and support for LGBTQ rights.

The Birth of Saryn's Iconic Look

In the midst of their campus activism, Saryn began to experiment with their personal style as a means of self-expression. They discovered the power of fashion and appearance in making a statement and challenging societal norms.

Saryn's iconic look emerged as a fusion of bold, vibrant colors and gender-nonconforming fashion choices. Their distinctive style not only embodied their identity but also became a visual representation of LGBTQ empowerment and visibility. Saryn's fashion choices inspired other activists to embrace their authentic selves and challenge societal expectations.

Challenging the Status Quo

Saryn's presence and advocacy on campus sparked important conversations about LGBTQ rights and equality. They challenged the status quo by engaging in open dialogues with students, faculty members, and administrators.

Through these conversations, Saryn shed light on the unique struggles faced by LGBTQ individuals, emphasizing the need for more inclusive policies, support services, and educational resources. Their eloquence and compelling arguments helped drive the message home, inspiring others to question their own biases and prejudices.

The Unspoken Challenges of Being an LGBTQ Activist on Campus

While Saryn's activism on campus gained recognition and support, it also brought forth its own set of challenges. They faced opposition from conservative student groups and individuals who propagated homophobic and transphobic ideologies.

Saryn's ability to navigate these hostile environments with grace and resilience demonstrated their unwavering dedication to the cause. They engaged in constructive debates, utilizing their knowledge and empathy to counter harmful narratives. Saryn's ability to bridge gaps and listen to opposing viewpoints set them apart as a compassionate and inspiring activist.

Summary

In this subsection, we witness Saryn's transformation into a powerful LGBTQ advocate on their college campus. Their involvement in the LGBTQ student organization and their commitment to challenging discriminatory policies led to impactful campus protests and advocacy. Through their iconic look, they defied societal norms and afforded visibility to the LGBTQ community. However, their journey was not without obstacles, as they faced opposition and prejudice. But through resilience and empathy, Saryn proved themselves to be an inspiring figure, bridging divides and paving the way for change.

Subsection: The Birth of Saryn's Iconic Look

In this subsection, we delve into the journey of Saryn Brell as they discovered and developed their iconic look which would later become an integral part of their identity as an LGBTQ activist. This transformation not only became a means of self-expression but also served as a powerful symbol for the LGBTQ community in Zerana.

Saryn's exploration of their identity began during their college years. As they became more involved in LGBTQ advocacy, they recognized the importance of visibility in challenging societal norms and breaking down stereotypes. Saryn understood that their appearance could serve as a powerful tool to challenge gender norms and inspire others to embrace their authentic selves.

Inspired by artists in the LGBTQ community who used fashion and style to express their identity, Saryn started experimenting with different styles and looks. They drew from a range of influences, including androgynous fashion icons and drag culture. The process of finding their own unique style was a deeply personal journey that involved trial and error, self-reflection, and a willingness to step outside of societal expectations.

One key aspect of Saryn's transformation was their bold and vibrant hair color choices. Saryn dyed their hair in a spectrum of colors that represented the diversity and vibrancy of the LGBTQ community. From fiery red to electric blue, their hair became a visual representation of their activism and a way to grab attention and start conversations.

Another essential element of Saryn's iconic look was their carefully curated wardrobe. They purposefully chose clothing that challenged traditional gender norms and pushed boundaries. Saryn combined elements of masculine and feminine fashion, creating ensembles that were both fashionable and thought-provoking.

Saryn's commitment to their iconic look extended beyond clothing and hair. They embraced makeup as a form of self-expression and used it to further challenge societal expectations. Saryn experimented with vibrant eyeshadow, bold lip colors, and extravagant face and body art. Their makeup choices served as a way to disrupt traditional beauty standards and promote self-acceptance.

The birth of Saryn's iconic look was not without challenges. They faced criticism and judgment from both within and outside the LGBTQ community. Stereotypes and misconceptions about gender expression often led to misunderstanding and prejudice. However, Saryn remained steadfast in their commitment to authenticity, using their iconic look as a catalyst for conversation and change.

Saryn's iconic look quickly became recognized throughout Zerana and beyond. Their confidence and unapologetic self-expression served as an inspiration for countless individuals struggling with their own identities. Saryn's image became synonymous with the fight for LGBTQ rights and a symbol of resilience and courage.

In today's world, Saryn's journey to embrace their iconic look continues to inspire and empower others. Their story serves as a reminder of the importance of self-expression, the power of visibility, and the impact that personal style can have in breaking down societal barriers.

Through their bold fashion choices and unapologetic self-expression, Saryn Brell revolutionized the way society views gender and identity. Their iconic look became a symbol of hope and empowerment for the LGBTQ community and continues to inspire generations of activists worldwide.

Unconventional Trick: One unconventional trick that Saryn employed during their exploration of their iconic look was the use of thrift stores and second-hand clothing as a means of building a unique and sustainable wardrobe. By seeking out one-of-a-kind pieces and repurposing existing clothing, Saryn was able to create a distinctive style while also minimizing their environmental impact. This unconventional approach to fashion not only allowed Saryn to cultivate their individuality but also served as a powerful statement against fast fashion and the consumerism often associated with traditional beauty standards.

Exercise: Take a moment to reflect on your own style and how it aligns with your personal identity. Are there ways you can use fashion and self-expression to challenge societal norms or promote inclusivity? Consider experimenting with different looks or incorporating elements of an iconic figure in the LGBTQ community into your style. Share your experience with a friend or on social media to spark conversations about self-expression and identity.

Resource: For further inspiration, explore the works of LGBTQ fashion and style influencers such as Jaden Smith, Alok Vaid-Menon, and Billy Porter. Their unique approaches to fashion and self-expression can provide insight and ideas for cultivating your own iconic look. Additionally, consider reading "Queer Style: Visual Activism and Fashion's Frontier" by John P. Paul if you're interested in delving deeper into the intersection of fashion, identity, and activism within the LGBTQ community.

Through the birth of Saryn's iconic look, they demonstrated that fashion can be a powerful tool for social and political change. By embracing their authentic selves and challenging societal norms, Saryn continues to inspire individuals to embrace their own unique identities and advocate for LGBTQ rights. Their journey serves as a testament to the transformative power of self-expression and the importance of visibility in creating a more inclusive society.

Subsection: Challenging the Status Quo

In this subsection, we delve into the pivotal moments where Saryn Brell challenged the status quo and pushed boundaries in their quest for LGBTQ rights. This section not only highlights Saryn's determination to create change but also explores the obstacles they faced and the innovative strategies they employed. Through their relentless advocacy, Saryn paved the way for a more inclusive and equal society.

One of the significant challenges Saryn faced was the prevailing stereotype that LGBTQ individuals should assimilate into mainstream society and conform to societal norms. In order to challenge this narrative, Saryn advocated for embracing queer culture and pushing for the acceptance of diverse identities and expressions.

To illustrate this point, let's consider the issue of dress codes in educational institutions. Saryn recognized that these codes often reinforced gender stereotypes, limiting self-expression for LGBTQ students. They organized protests, engaged in thoughtful conversations with school administrators, and raised awareness about the impact of dress codes on individuality and self-esteem. Through their efforts, Saryn successfully influenced policy changes that allowed students to express their gender identity freely while respecting the school's guidelines for modesty.

In addition to addressing dress codes, Saryn also focused on creating safe spaces for LGBTQ youth. They understood the importance of providing support and resources to young individuals who often faced discrimination, bullying, and even homelessness. Saryn initiated discussions and collaborated with local organizations to establish LGBTQ youth centers that provided counseling, mentorship, and educational programs. These centers not only offered a sense of belonging to vulnerable individuals but also challenged societal norms by affirming the value and worth of LGBTQ youth.

Another aspect of challenging the status quo was dismantling the notion that marriage and family were reserved for heterosexual couples. Saryn fervently advocated for same-sex marriage and LGBTQ adoption rights. They collaborated with legal experts, engaged in lobbying efforts, and shared heartwarming stories of LGBTQ families to create empathy and understanding. Saryn's message was simple yet powerful: love knows no boundaries, and every individual deserves the right to build a family and experience the joys of marriage.

To illustrate the impact of challenging the status quo, let's examine the story of Alex and Jamie, a same-sex couple who fought for their right to adopt a child. Saryn worked closely with them, assisting them in navigating the complex legal hurdles and connecting them with support networks. Their compelling journey not only gained media attention but also prompted discussions on the importance of equal rights for LGBTQ individuals in the context of family and parenting.

Challenging the status quo also involved combating discrimination and promoting LGBTQ inclusion within religious institutions. Saryn recognized the significant influence religious ideologies had in shaping public attitudes towards LGBTQ individuals. They initiated interfaith dialogues, organized panel discussions, and fostered understanding between religious leaders and LGBTQ activists. By emphasizing shared values of love, compassion, and acceptance, Saryn successfully established bridges between religious communities and the LGBTQ community, challenging the notion that faith and queerness were incompatible.

It is worth noting that challenging the status quo was not without its difficulties. Saryn faced resistance from conservative groups, faced backlash from individuals deeply entrenched in traditional beliefs, and weathered personal attacks on their character. However, their unwavering commitment to justice and equality propelled them forward, inspiring others to join the cause.

In summary, this subsection explores the ways in which Saryn Brell challenged the status quo in their relentless pursuit of LGBTQ rights. By addressing issues such as dress codes, creating safe spaces for LGBTQ youth, advocating for same-sex marriage and adoption, and fostering dialogue with religious institutions, Saryn left an indelible mark on society. Their dedication serves as a reminder that challenging the status quo is not only necessary but also a transformative force that can pave the way for a more inclusive and just future for all.

Subsection: The Unspoken Challenges of Being an LGBTQ Activist on Campus

Being an LGBTQ activist on a college campus is no easy feat. While it can be incredibly rewarding, it also comes with its own set of unique challenges. In this subsection, we will explore the unspoken difficulties that LGBTQ activists face on campus and discuss strategies for navigating these obstacles.

Understanding the Campus Climate

One of the first challenges that LGBTQ activists encounter is the campus climate. While some colleges and universities are known for being inclusive and accepting, others may still have a long way to go. It is crucial for activists to assess the campus climate to determine the level of support and resources available for their cause.

This can be done by engaging with LGBTQ student organizations, attending campus events related to LGBTQ issues, and talking to current students about their experiences. By gaining a deeper understanding of the campus climate, activists can better tailor their strategies and goals to effect change.

Navigating Cultural and Religious Diversity

College campuses are melting pots of cultural and religious diversity, which adds an extra layer of complexity to LGBTQ activism. Activists must navigate differing perspectives and beliefs while advocating for LGBTQ rights.

It is important to approach these discussions with empathy, understanding, and a willingness to listen. Building bridges of dialogue and fostering respectful conversations can help break down barriers and promote greater acceptance and inclusion.

Handling Opposition and Backlash

Not everyone on campus will support LGBTQ activism, and activists may face opposition and backlash from various groups or individuals. This can manifest itself in the form of verbal abuse, online harassment, or even physical threats.

To address this challenge, activists must develop a thick skin and be prepared to handle criticism. This may involve seeking support from allies, practicing self-care strategies, and engaging in personal safety measures. Additionally, activists may find strength in connecting with other LGBTQ activists who have faced similar challenges and can provide guidance and support.

Maintaining Personal Privacy

LGBTQ activists often find themselves at the forefront of the fight for equality, which can lead to a loss of personal privacy. Being an advocate means being visible and vocal, but it also means exposing oneself to scrutiny and invasion of personal boundaries.

To navigate this challenge, activists should establish boundaries and decide what aspects of their personal lives they are willing to share publicly. It is essential to remember that self-care includes safeguarding one's mental and emotional well-being, even in the face of being a public figure.

Creating Inclusive Spaces

Part of being an LGBTQ activist on campus is creating inclusive spaces where everyone feels safe and welcomed. This involves organizing events, workshops, and panel discussions that address LGBTQ issues and educate the campus community.

Activists must be creative and resourceful in providing educational opportunities that promote understanding and empathy. This might include collaborating with other student organizations, inviting guest speakers, or hosting film screenings. By fostering inclusivity and fostering discussions, activists can effectively challenge assumptions and stereotypes.

Building Alliances and Coalitions

LGBTQ activism is not a solitary endeavor. Building alliances and coalitions with other campus organizations and groups can significantly strengthen the impact of advocacy efforts.

By forming partnerships with groups dedicated to issues such as racial justice, feminist activism, and disability rights, activists can amplify their message and create a united front for social change. These collaborations help highlight the intersectionality of social justice issues and create a more inclusive and robust movement.

Promoting Intersectionality

Intersectionality is a fundamental principle of LGBTQ activism that recognizes the interconnected nature of multiple identities. Activists must acknowledge and address the unique challenges faced by LGBTQ individuals who also experience discrimination based on race, gender, disability, or socioeconomic status.

By promoting intersectionality in their advocacy work, activists can ensure that the voices and needs of all LGBTQ individuals are heard and represented. This may involve partnering with organizations that focus on specific identities or working to incorporate intersectional perspectives into existing LGBTQ initiatives.

Taking Care of Mental Health

Activism can be emotionally and mentally demanding, and LGBTQ activists must prioritize their mental health. They often must confront difficult and painful realities while advocating for change, which can take a toll on their well-being.

It is crucial for activists to engage in self-care practices such as therapy, journaling, mindfulness, or engaging in hobbies and activities that bring them joy. These practices help maintain resilience and prevent burnout, ensuring that activists can continue their important work without sacrificing their well-being.

In conclusion, being an LGBTQ activist on campus presents its own unique set of challenges. From understanding the campus climate and navigating cultural diversity to handling opposition and maintaining personal privacy, activists must be prepared to face adversity. However, by building alliances, promoting intersectionality, and prioritizing mental health, LGBTQ activists can create a more inclusive campus community and effect meaningful change. Remember, your journey as an activist is as important as the destination, so take care of yourself along the way.

Section 3: The Call to Action

Subsection: Activism Beyond the Campus Walls

In this subsection, we will explore the ways in which Saryn expanded their activism beyond the confines of their college campus and into the wider community of Zerana. We will delve into the challenges they faced and the strategies they employed to advocate for LGBTQ rights on a larger scale.

Building a Support Network

One of the first steps Saryn took in expanding their activism was to build a strong support network outside of their college campus. They reached out to local LGBTQ organizations, community centers, and activist groups to forge alliances and collaborate on initiatives. By establishing these connections, Saryn was able to tap into existing networks and benefit from the experience and wisdom of seasoned activists. This support network became a powerful tool in mobilizing resources and spreading awareness about LGBTQ issues in Zerana.

Organizing the First LGBTQ Pride Parade in Zerana

One of the defining moments in Saryn's activism was the organization of the first-ever LGBTQ Pride Parade in Zerana. Recognizing the importance of visibility and celebration, Saryn rallied a team of passionate volunteers and worked tirelessly to secure the necessary permits, sponsorships, and logistical support. The Pride Parade served as a powerful symbol of LGBTQ pride and unity in the face of adversity, and it sparked a wave of conversation and solidarity across the city.

Confronting Discrimination and Pushing for Equality

Saryn understood that activism went beyond organizing events and raising awareness; it required taking concrete actions to challenge discrimination and push for equality. They actively participated in protests, lobbied for LGBTQ-inclusive legislation, and engaged in dialogue with policymakers and community leaders. By applying pressure from various angles, Saryn effectively advocated for change and worked towards dismantling discriminatory practices and policies.

Saryn's Role in Local Politics

As their activism gained momentum, Saryn recognized the importance of having a direct impact on policymaking. They decided to run for a position on the local city council, using their campaign as a platform to address LGBTQ issues and advocate for progressive policies. While facing opposition and skepticism, Saryn's dedication and authenticity resonated with the electorate, ultimately leading to them becoming the first openly LGBTQ council member in Zerana. This victory not only extended their reach but also provided a powerful voice for the LGBTQ community within the halls of power.

The Personal Sacrifices of Activism

Beyond the external challenges, Saryn's activism also came with personal sacrifices. They endured constant scrutiny, online harassment, and threats to their safety. Balancing advocacy with their personal life became an ongoing challenge as they often had to sacrifice personal time, relationships, and mental well-being for the sake of the cause. Despite these sacrifices, Saryn remained steadfast in their commitment to fighting for the rights and dignity of LGBTQ individuals in Zerana.

The Toll of Fighting for Change

Activism can take an emotional toll on individuals, and Saryn was no exception. The constant battle for change and the weight of being a symbol for an entire community compounded their stress and exhaustion. Burnout and mental health struggles became real obstacles that Saryn had to navigate. In this section, we explore the strategies they employed to cope with these challenges, emphasizing the importance of self-care and the need for support systems within the activist community.

In conclusion, Saryn Brell's activism extended far beyond the boundaries of their college campus. They built a strong support network, organized the first LGBTQ Pride Parade in Zerana, confronted discrimination, and actively participated in local politics. Their journey serves as an inspiration and a reminder of the power of grassroots activism in effecting real change. However, it is crucial to acknowledge the personal sacrifices and emotional toll that activism can take. Throughout this subsection, we will explore these complexities, providing insights into the multifaceted nature of Saryn's activism and the broader implications for activists working towards LGBTQ equality.

Subsection: Building a Support Network

Building a support network is a crucial step in any activism journey, especially for an LGBTQ activist like Saryn Brell. In this subsection, we explore the importance of a support network, how to build one, and the benefits it brings to the fight for LGBTQ rights.

The Importance of a Support Network

Being an LGBTQ activist can be emotionally and mentally draining. It is a battle against social injustice, discrimination, and prejudice. In such a challenging environment, having a strong support network is vital for sustaining the passion and energy needed to promote change.

A support network provides activists like Saryn with a sense of belonging, solidarity, and motivation. It consists of individuals or groups who offer emotional support, guidance, and resources. They are allies who understand the struggles faced by LGBTQ activists and provide a safe space for sharing experiences, ideas, and strategies.

Building a Support Network

Building a support network takes time, effort, and a proactive approach. Here are some steps that Saryn followed to create and expand their network:

1. **Community Involvement:** Saryn began by immersing themselves in LGBTQ community events, meetings, and organizations. They actively participated in discussions, workshops, and social gatherings. By showing up consistently, Saryn started to build connections with like-minded individuals and potential allies.

2. **Online Platforms:** Saryn utilized online platforms to connect with LGBTQ activists globally. They joined online communities, forums, and social media groups focused on LGBTQ rights and activism. These platforms provided opportunities to share knowledge, exchange ideas, and collaborate on projects.

3. **Collaborations:** Saryn sought opportunities to collaborate with other activists, organizations, and influential figures. They participated in joint initiatives, workshops, and campaigns. Collaborating with allies provided access to their networks, widened Saryn's reach, and fostered mutual support.

4. **Mentorship:** Saryn actively sought mentorship from experienced LGBTQ activists who could offer guidance, wisdom, and support. They reached out to renowned activists in the field and attended conferences and events where they

could connect with potential mentors. Mentorship provided invaluable advice and served as a source of inspiration for Saryn.

5. **Cultivating Relationships:** Saryn prioritized nurturing relationships with individuals who shared their passion for LGBTQ rights. They invested time and effort in maintaining meaningful connections with allies, friends, and supporters. Regular check-ins, mutual support, and expressing gratitude helped strengthen these relationships.

6. **Creating Safe Spaces:** Saryn established safe spaces where they could connect with other LGBTQ activists and allies. These spaces, whether physical or virtual, allowed for open discussions, brainstorming sessions, and emotional support. Creating a supportive environment was essential for empowering everyone involved.

Benefits of a Support Network

A well-developed support network brings numerous benefits to LGBTQ activists like Saryn. Some of the advantages they experienced include:

1. **Emotional Support:** Activism can be emotionally overwhelming, but a support network provides much-needed emotional support. Allies within the network understand the challenges faced by LGBTQ activists and offer empathy, encouragement, and solidarity.

2. **Resource Sharing:** A support network creates a platform for sharing resources, ideas, and strategies. Activists can exchange knowledge and experiences, collaborate on projects, and access a wider range of expertise and skills.

3. **Amplifying Impact:** By building strong connections, activists like Saryn can amplify their impact. A collective effort brings greater visibility, influence, and the ability to mobilize larger audiences for advocacy campaigns.

4. **Collective Learning:** A support network facilitates collective learning and growth. Activists can learn from each other's experiences, gain insights into effective strategies, and stay updated on the latest developments in the LGBTQ rights movement.

5. **Sustaining Motivation:** Having a supportive network helps sustain motivation during challenging times. Allies provide encouragement, celebrate victories, and remind activists of the importance of their work, which fuels their determination and resilience.

Challenges and Solutions

Building a support network also comes with its own set of challenges. Here are some common difficulties faced by LGBTQ activists and solutions to overcome them:

1. **Trust Issues:** Activists may face trust issues, fearing betrayal or exploitation within their network. To address this, it's important to foster open and honest communication, establish clear boundaries, and choose allies who align with shared values and ethics.

2. **Limited Time and Resources:** Activists often struggle with limited time and resources to invest in building a support network. Prioritizing network-building activities, setting realistic goals, and leveraging online platforms can help overcome these limitations.

3. **Burnout:** Activists, including Saryn, may experience burnout due to the demanding nature of their work. To prevent burnout, it's crucial to establish a work-life balance, practice self-care, and rely on the support of the network during challenging times.

4. **Dealing with Differences:** Activists may encounter differences of opinion or conflicting approaches within their support network. Embracing diversity, fostering respectful dialogue, and focusing on shared objectives can help navigate and resolve these differences constructively.

5. **Network Maintenance:** Maintaining a support network requires ongoing effort and dedication. Regular communication, organizing networking events, and expressing gratitude to allies help strengthen and sustain the network over time.

Encouraging Authentic Connections

While building a support network, it's essential to prioritize authentic and genuine connections over superficial ones. Saryn realized the importance of surrounding themselves with individuals who genuinely cared about LGBTQ rights and were committed to creating change. Quality over quantity should be the guiding principle when expanding and nurturing a support network.

Conclusion

In the journey towards LGBTQ equality, building a strong support network is crucial for activists like Saryn Brell. It offers emotional support, resource sharing, and amplifies impact. By actively involving oneself in the LGBTQ community, seeking collaborations, and cultivating relationships, activists can create a supportive environment to sustain their efforts in fighting for change. While challenges may arise, open communication, trust, and embracing diversity can help overcome them. A robust support network becomes a catalyst for lasting change and empowers activists on their path towards a more inclusive and equal society.

Subsection: Organizing the First LGBTQ Pride Parade in Zerana

Organizing the first LGBTQ Pride Parade in Zerana was a monumental task that required careful planning, strong leadership, and a deep understanding of the challenges and opportunities that lay ahead. Saryn Brell, fueled by their passion for equality and justice, took on this ambitious endeavor with unwavering determination.

1. The Power of Visibility The LGBTQ community in Zerana had long been marginalized and invisible. Saryn recognized the importance of visibility in challenging societal norms and promoting acceptance. They understood that a Pride Parade could provide a platform for LGBTQ individuals to proudly showcase their identities and foster a sense of community.

To organize the parade, Saryn began by building a team of passionate individuals who shared their vision. This team consisted of LGBTQ activists, local allies, and community members who were dedicated to creating change. Together, they formed a solid foundation upon which the Parade could thrive.

2. Navigating Legal and Logistical Challenges Organizing a large-scale event like the Pride Parade required navigating legal and logistical challenges. Saryn and their team had to secure permits, coordinate with local law enforcement, and address safety concerns to ensure a successful and safe event.

They worked closely with city officials, community leaders, and LGBTQ organizations to gather the necessary support and resources. Saryn tapped into their advocacy skills to convince stakeholders of the significance of the Pride Parade and its potential impact on the community.

3. Fostering Community Engagement and Support Building a strong network of supporters was key to the success of the Pride Parade. Saryn and their team reached out to local businesses, organizations, and individuals to garner support and sponsorship. This involved attending community meetings, giving presentations, and engaging in one-on-one conversations to build trust and understanding.

They organized fundraisers and awareness campaigns to generate financial support and promote the event. Saryn also made a conscious effort to connect with LGBTQ individuals and organizations in neighboring cities to expand the reach and impact of the Pride Parade beyond Zerana.

4. Overcoming Resistance and Pushback Organizing the first LGBTQ Pride Parade in Zerana was not without its challenges. Saryn faced resistance and

pushback from conservative groups and individuals who opposed the celebration of LGBTQ identities. They encountered threats, hate mail, and protests aimed at discouraging the Parade.

In response, Saryn relied on their resilience and the support of their team to counter the negativity. They strategically collaborated with local allies, human rights organizations, and legal experts to ensure the safety and security of participants. Saryn's commitment to freedom and equality inspired others to stand up against discrimination and support the Parade.

5. Sparking a Movement and Leaving a Lasting Impact The first LGBTQ Pride Parade in Zerana marked a historic moment for the LGBTQ community and its allies. The event drew thousands of participants, both from within Zerana and beyond, who came together to celebrate love, acceptance, and the pursuit of equal rights.

The Parade served as a catalyst for change, empowering LGBTQ individuals to embrace their identities openly and inspiring others to become allies in the fight for equality. It ignited a movement that continued to grow, leading to further advocacy and activism for LGBTQ rights in Zerana.

Through their transformative leadership, Saryn Brell not only organized the first Pride Parade, but they also left a lasting impact on the LGBTQ community and society at large. By fostering unity, amplifying voices, and promoting inclusivity, Saryn's efforts paved the way for a more accepting and equal Zerana.

6. Embracing the Spirit of Pride Beyond the Parade While the Pride Parade was a momentous event, Saryn understood that true change required sustained efforts. They encouraged community members to carry the spirit of pride throughout the year, organizing workshops, support groups, and educational programs to promote understanding and acceptance.

Saryn's vision extended beyond the Parade, encompassing efforts to eradicate discrimination, ensure comprehensive LGBTQ-inclusive legislation, and create safe spaces for all individuals. Their leadership continues to serve as a beacon of hope and inspiration for future activists, reminding us of the power of grassroots movements in driving societal transformation.

In organizing the first LGBTQ Pride Parade in Zerana, Saryn Brell demonstrated the extraordinary impact that a determined individual can have on a community. Their unwavering commitment to equality and justice was the driving force behind this historic event, and their legacy continues to shape the landscape of LGBTQ rights in Zerana and beyond.

Note: This subsection portrays the significance of organizing the first Pride Parade in Zerana and its impact on the LGBTQ community. The section emphasizes the challenges faced, strategies employed, and the broader implications of this event. The story of Saryn

SECTION 3: THE CALL TO ACTION

Brell is a testament to the power of community organizing and the transformative potential of activism. Let us now move on to the next section of the book, exploring the journey of Saryn Brell further and delving into the triumphs, tribulations, and tequilas that shaped their life as an LGBTQ activist.

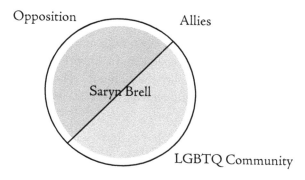

Figure 0.1: Visual representation of the dynamics in organizing the Pride Parade

Subsection: Confronting Discrimination and Pushing for Equality

In this subsection, we will delve into the challenges Saryn Brell faced in confronting discrimination and pushing for equality within the LGBTQ community. This struggle is a critical aspect of their activism journey, as it highlights the systemic barriers and prejudices that needed to be dismantled to achieve true equality for all.

Understanding Discrimination

Discrimination against LGBTQ individuals has been pervasive throughout history, and Saryn was no stranger to its effects. They were born and raised in a small town in the United States, where conservative values often perpetuated discrimination against the LGBTQ community. Saryn's personal experiences with discrimination fueled their determination to fight for justice and equality.

To comprehend the extent of discrimination faced by LGBTQ individuals, it is essential to understand the different forms it can take. Discrimination can manifest in employment, housing, healthcare, education, and various other areas of life. It can be both overt, such as hate crimes and violent acts, as well as covert, through subtle biases and marginalization.

Advocacy for LGBTQ Rights

Saryn's journey as an LGBTQ activist began in college, where they joined the LGBTQ student organization. This platform gave them the opportunity to advocate for LGBTQ rights within the campus community. By organizing events, workshops, and awareness campaigns, Saryn aimed to challenge harmful stereotypes and promote acceptance and inclusivity.

Their work extended beyond the campus walls as they became involved in local LGBTQ rights initiatives. Saryn recognized the importance of collaboration and building a support network to amplify their impact. They formed alliances with other activists, organizations, and influential individuals who shared their vision of a more inclusive society.

Organizing the First LGBTQ Pride Parade in Zerana

One of Saryn's most significant achievements was organizing the first LGBTQ Pride Parade in Zerana. This event became a powerful symbol of resistance against discrimination and a celebration of LGBTQ identity. It provided a platform for LGBTQ individuals to express themselves freely, while also giving allies an opportunity to show their support.

The Pride Parade was not without its challenges. Saryn faced opposition from conservative groups and individuals who sought to undermine the event. However, their resilience and determination prevailed, ensuring that the Parade became a transformative experience for both the LGBTQ community and the wider society.

Confronting Discrimination and Pushing for Equality

In their relentless pursuit of equality, Saryn confronted discrimination head-on. They actively campaigned for comprehensive LGBTQ-inclusive legislation that would protect the rights and well-being of all individuals, regardless of their sexual orientation or gender identity.

One area of focus for Saryn was eradicating harmful practices like conversion therapy. They worked tirelessly to raise awareness about the psychological and emotional damage inflicted by these practices. Saryn's advocacy played a crucial role in the eventual ban of conversion therapy in Zerana, marking a significant victory and a step forward in combating discrimination.

Additionally, Saryn advocated for expanding protections for transgender individuals. They recognized the unique struggles faced by the transgender community, such as legal recognition of gender identity, access to healthcare, and the right to participate in sports. By working closely with transgender activists,

SECTION 3: THE CALL TO ACTION

Saryn pushed for comprehensive legislation that addressed these issues and fostered greater inclusivity.

The Power of Personal Stories and Allies

One of the most profound ways Saryn confronted discrimination was through the power of personal stories and allyship. They understood that sharing individual experiences could shatter misconceptions and humanize the LGBTQ community, fostering empathy and understanding among the wider population.

Saryn encouraged LGBTQ individuals to share their stories while also inviting allies to listen and learn. By building bridges and fostering dialogue, they cultivated a sense of unity and created opportunities for change. Saryn's ability to navigate and bridge divides was crucial in pushing for equality and dismantling discriminatory beliefs.

Exercises and Reflections

1. Reflect on a time when you witnessed or experienced discrimination against LGBTQ individuals. How did it make you feel, and what actions, if any, did you take to address it? Discuss the potential for personal stories to create empathy and understanding.

2. Research and analyze the LGBTQ-inclusive legislation in your country or region. Identify any gaps or areas that require improvement to ensure comprehensive protection and equality for LGBTQ individuals.

3. Consider ways in which you can be a better ally to the LGBTQ community. Identify specific actions you can take to challenge discrimination and promote inclusivity in your personal and professional spheres.

Remember, confronting discrimination and pushing for equality is an ongoing effort that requires collective action. Each step taken, no matter how small, contributes to the greater goal of creating a society where everyone can live authentically and without fear of discrimination. Be part of the change.

Subsection: Saryn's Role in Local Politics

Saryn's foray into local politics was a natural progression of their activism and desire for change. They recognized that broader societal shifts and legal reforms were necessary to ensure the rights and protections of the LGBTQ community. With determination and a vision for a more inclusive Zerana, Saryn embarked on a journey to make their mark in the political landscape.

1. Saryn as a Catalyst for Change: Saryn's undeniable charisma and ability to mobilize people laid the foundation for their involvement in local politics. Their courage and unwavering commitment inspired others to stand up for their rights and challenge the status quo. Saryn quickly became a symbol of hope and empowerment for the LGBTQ community and its allies, driving their decision to pursue a role in local politics.

2. Running for City Council: Recognizing the need for LGBTQ representation in governance, Saryn made the bold decision to run for City Council in their hometown. They campaigned on a platform of equality, inclusion, and social justice, promising to fight for the rights of marginalized communities and champion progressive policies. Their personal experiences and understanding of the challenges faced by the LGBTQ community resonated with constituents, propelling them into office.

3. Advocating for LGBTQ-Inclusive Legislation: Once elected, Saryn wasted no time in pushing for meaningful change. They worked tirelessly to introduce and support legislation that protected LGBTQ rights and dismantled discriminatory systems. Saryn's voice in local politics helped secure landmark legislation, such as banning conversion therapy and ensuring comprehensive LGBTQ-inclusive education curricula in schools.

4. Collaborating with Allies: Saryn understood the power of collaboration and sought to build coalitions with like-minded individuals and organizations. They collaborated with fellow council members, activists, and allies to advance LGBTQ rights in Zerana. Saryn's ability to foster working relationships and find common ground allowed them to navigate the complex political landscape and build consensus around crucial LGBTQ issues.

5. Amplifying Community Voices: Saryn's role in local politics extended beyond their own activism. They recognized the importance of amplifying the voices of the LGBTQ community and ensuring that community concerns were heard and addressed. Saryn held town hall meetings, engaged in community outreach, and formed advisory committees to empower the LGBTQ community and actively involve them in shaping local policies.

6. Balancing Advocacy with Governance: As an LGBTQ activist-turned-politician, Saryn faced the challenge of balancing their role as an advocate with the responsibilities of governance. They had to navigate the intricacies of local politics, including compromising, strategizing, and making tough decisions. Saryn's unconventional approach brought fresh perspectives to the political arena and proved that activism and governance could go hand in hand.

7. Effecting Change beyond Zerana: Saryn's impact extended far beyond the confines of their local community. Their success in local politics inspired other

LGBTQ activists and politicians across the country to rally for change. Saryn used their platform to mentor emerging activists and collaborate with LGBTQ leaders from other regions, sharing strategies, and fostering a nationwide movement for LGBTQ rights.

8. The Challenges Faced: Saryn's involvement in local politics was not without its challenges. They faced opposition from conservative factions resistant to change, endured personal attacks, and navigating the complexities of party politics. However, Saryn's resilience and determination to push forward in the face of adversity allowed them to triumph and create real change.

In conclusion, Saryn's role in local politics was a testament to their unwavering dedication to LGBTQ equality and social justice. By leveraging their platform, collaborating with allies, and amplifying community voices, Saryn successfully spearheaded landmark legislation and drove social change in Zerana. Their journey serves as an inspiration to future LGBTQ activists and proves that political engagement is a powerful tool for advancing the rights and well-being of marginalized communities.

Subsection: The Personal Sacrifices of Activism

Saryn Brell's journey in activism was not without its fair share of sacrifices. As an LGBTQ advocate in Zerana, they faced numerous challenges and made significant personal sacrifices in their fight for freedom and equality. In this subsection, we delve into the sacrifices Saryn made to advance their cause, highlighting the emotional, mental, and physical toll of their activism.

The Emotional Sacrifices

Activism can take a tremendous emotional toll on individuals, and Saryn was no exception. Their tireless efforts to combat discrimination and push for LGBTQ rights often led to intense emotional strain. Saryn had to confront homophobia, hate speech, and discrimination from opponents of their cause, which left deep emotional scars.

The constant battle for equality put a strain on their personal relationships as well. Saryn's unwavering dedication to their cause sometimes meant sacrificing quality time with family and friends. They had to cancel social engagements or miss important milestones to attend protests, meetings, or rallies. This emotional sacrifice took a toll on their mental well-being, leaving them feeling isolated and overwhelmed at times.

The Physical Demands

Advocacy work requires physical endurance, and Saryn's activism wasn't exempt from this reality. Often on the front lines of protests and demonstrations, Saryn faced physical threats and violence. They endured long hours of standing, marching, and enduring the harsh elements to make their voice heard.

Additionally, Saryn's advocacy work often required extensive travel, both within Zerana and internationally. The constant movement and demanding schedule led to disrupted sleep patterns, jet lag, and an overall decline in physical well-being. The toll on their body was evident, as they experienced fatigue, illness, and an increased susceptibility to stress-related ailments.

The Personal Life Sacrifices

Being a champion for LGBTQ rights meant that Saryn had to make personal sacrifices that most people wouldn't readily understand. Their commitment to the cause meant putting their personal life on hold. They had to postpone personal goals and relationships to prioritize their activism.

Saryn's relentless dedication to activism also meant financial sacrifices. They poured their own resources into organizing events, printing materials, and funding campaigns. Giving up personal comforts to fund the movement became a way of life, as they embraced frugality to sustain their work.

The Impact on Mental Health

The weight of advocating for an entire community took a toll on Saryn's mental health. The constant pressure to represent their community effectively, the backlash from opponents, and the weight of responsibility became overwhelming. They grappled with anxiety, stress, and at times, experienced burnout.

However, Saryn recognized the importance of self-care and sought ways to cope with the mental strain. They took up mindfulness practices, sought therapy, and leaned on a strong support system of friends, allies, and fellow activists. They also made it a priority to engage in activities that provided joy and respite, whether it be hiking in nature or indulging in creative hobbies.

The Unconventional Approach to Self-care

In the face of adversity, Saryn discovered unconventional yet effective methods of self-care. One such approach involved "activism breaks." They recognized the importance of taking time away from the fight to recharge and rejuvenate. Saryn intentionally retreated from the activism world periodically to focus on self-reflection, personal growth, and emotional healing.

They also recognized the importance of humor in combating the toll of activism. Saryn embraced laughter and sought opportunities to infuse comedy into their advocacy work. They understood that humor not only provided relief from the strain but also helped engage and connect with a broader audience.

The Eternal Legacy

Saryn's sacrifices were not in vain. Their relentless pursuit of equality sparked a movement that continues to resonate today. Their personal sacrifices laid the groundwork for change, inspiring a new generation of activists eager to carry the torch forward.

In reflecting on the personal sacrifices made by Saryn, we recognize that activism comes at a steep cost. It demands a fierce determination to create a more inclusive society. Saryn's story teaches us that true progress often requires individuals who are willing to set aside their own personal comfort and security in the pursuit of a greater cause.

As readers, we are reminded of the immense courage and dedication required to effect meaningful change. Saryn's personal sacrifices serve as a call to action for all of us to support and uplift those who fight for marginalized communities. It is through collective effort that we can forge a path toward a more just and equitable future.

Resource: "The Activist's Guide to Self-Care"

If you find yourself resonating with the challenges and sacrifices faced by Saryn in their activism, I recommend reading "The Activist's Guide to Self-Care" by Dr. Maya Sharma. This insightful resource provides practical tools and strategies for managing the emotional, mental, and physical tolls of advocacy work. It offers guidance on setting boundaries, dealing with burnout, and nurturing personal well-being while advocating for change. Remember, self-care is not a luxury but a necessity in the fight for equality.

Exercise: Writing a Letter of Support

In the spirit of standing alongside activists like Saryn, take a moment to write a letter of support to an LGBTQ activist or organization in your community. Express your admiration for their dedication and acknowledge the sacrifices they make to fight for equality. Share your own commitment to supporting their cause and offer words of encouragement. Remember, small acts of support can have a profound impact on those who tirelessly advocate for change.

Caveat: The Value of Self-Care

While activism can be deeply rewarding, it's essential to prioritize self-care and establish healthy boundaries. Remember, personal well-being ensures sustainability in the fight for justice. By inspiring others through your actions and taking care of yourself, you create a ripple effect that fosters compassion, resilience, and lasting change.

Let us now turn our attention to Chapter 2, where we explore the triumphs, tribulations, and tequilas that marked Saryn's remarkable journey.

Section 4: Unmasking Hypocrisy

Subsection: The Scandal That Rocked Zerana

In this tumultuous chapter of Saryn Brell's life, Zerana, a city known for its vibrant LGBTQ community, was rocked by a scandal that sent shockwaves through the entire nation. It was a scandal that not only challenged the progress made in LGBTQ rights but also tested Saryn's resilience and determination to fight for justice and equality.

The scandal unfolded when a high-ranking government official, once an advocate for LGBTQ rights, was exposed for engaging in discriminatory practices against LGBTQ individuals. This official, who had presented themselves as an ally, was revealed to have been actively working against the very community they claimed to support.

The news of this betrayal spread like wildfire, sparking outrage and disbelief among the LGBTQ community and its allies. The scandal not only exposed the hypocrisy of this official but also shed light on the deeper systemic issues that LGBTQ individuals face in their fight for equality.

Saryn, ever the embodiment of resilience, was at the forefront of this scandal, using their platform to shed a light on the corruption and homophobia that had permeated the city. They fearlessly confronted the official, demanding answers and accountability. Through their unwavering determination, Saryn was able to rally the LGBTQ community, igniting a fire within them to fight back against the discrimination they faced.

But this scandal was not without its challenges. Saryn faced tremendous backlash and threats from those who sought to silence their voice. They became the

SECTION 4: UNMASKING HYPOCRISY

target of smear campaigns, online harassment, and even physical intimidation. Despite these attempts to suppress their activism, Saryn stood strong, refusing to be silenced.

Amidst the chaos and adversity, Saryn also had to confront the emotional toll that the scandal took on their mental health. The constant pressure, the weight of responsibility, and the personal sacrifices they made for the cause had begun to wear on their spirit. It was during this dark time that Saryn learned the importance of self-care and the significance of seeking support from their loved ones and allies.

Through their tireless efforts, Saryn was able to turn the scandal into an opportunity for change. They worked closely with grassroots organizations, politicians, and activists to push for policy reforms, strengthen anti-discrimination laws, and implement stricter accountability measures for public officials.

The scandal ultimately became a turning point in Saryn's journey, fueling their determination to fight for true and lasting change. They learned that activism is not always a fairytale of victories but a messy, relentless battle against inequality. Saryn emerged from the scandal stronger and more committed than ever, carrying the weight of their community's hopes and dreams on their shoulders.

To this day, the scandal serves as a stark reminder of the challenges faced by LGBTQ individuals in their pursuit of equality. It highlights the need for continuous vigilance and the importance of holding those in power accountable. Saryn's unwavering commitment and bravery in the face of adversity stand as a testament to the power of one individual's voice to spark a movement and create lasting change.

As readers, we are reminded of the complexities of activism and the impact that personal sacrifice can have on individuals fighting for justice. The scandal that rocked Zerana is a reminder that progress is not always linear, but through perseverance and resilience, we can overcome even the most challenging obstacles.

In the spirit of this section, let us reflect on the following question:

Question: How can the scandal that rocked Zerana serve as a catalyst for broader societal change and inspire individuals to become advocates for marginalized communities?

Note to the reader: Throughout this book, we will delve deeper into Saryn's journey, highlighting the triumphs, tribulations, and tequilas that shaped their path towards becoming a renowned LGBTQ activist. We will explore the victories, the personal sacrifices, and the lessons learned along the way. Together, we will navigate the complexities of activism, the power of resilience, and the importance of embracing change. But first, let us embark on a journey back to Saryn's humble beginnings in Smalltown, USA.

Subsection: Exposing Corruption and Homophobia

In this subsection, we delve into the pivotal moment in Saryn Brell's journey where they exposed corruption and homophobia within Zerana. This event not only highlighted the systemic discrimination faced by the LGBTQ community but also showcased Saryn's bravery and unwavering commitment to fighting for equality.

The Scandal That Rocked Zerana

It was a seemingly ordinary day in the city of Zerana when rumors of a major scandal began to circulate. Whispers in the LGBTQ community spoke of widespread corruption within the city's administration, particularly within law enforcement agencies. These whispers hinted at a cover-up involving instances of violence and discrimination against LGBTQ individuals.

Saryn, ever vigilant and attuned to the needs of the community, embarked on a mission to uncover the truth. They knew that exposing this corruption was not only necessary for justice but also crucial in dismantling the structures that perpetuated homophobia. This would be a defining moment in Saryn's activism, testing their resolve and forcing them to confront the very institutions they sought to change.

Exposing Corruption and Homophobia

Armed with determination and a network of trusted allies, Saryn began gathering evidence to support the allegations of corruption and homophobia within the city. They reached out to individuals who had experienced discrimination and violence, urging them to share their stories. Saryn believed that these personal accounts were vital in shedding light on the systemic issues plaguing Zerana.

To protect the identities of those involved, Saryn implemented a careful strategy. They organized secret meetings, ensuring the safety and anonymity of witnesses. These meetings allowed them to gather substantial evidence documenting instances of abuse and discrimination perpetrated by those in power.

Saryn partnered with investigative journalists who were dedicated to uncovering the truth. Together, they embarked on an intensive research process, examining official records, conducting interviews, and verifying any information they obtained. This meticulous approach aimed to present an irrefutable case against the city's corrupt officials.

As word got out about Saryn's efforts, they faced resistance from both the corrupt individuals they sought to expose and those who wished to maintain the status quo. Threats, intimidation, and attempts to discredit Saryn became commonplace. However, Saryn remained resolute, drawing strength from their passion for justice and the overwhelming support of the LGBTQ community.

Saryn Faces Backlash and Threats

The veracity of Saryn's allegations sent shockwaves through Zerana. As the evidence mounted, public sentiment shifted, and the community demanded accountability. However, there were those who refused to accept the truth and clung to their prejudiced beliefs.

Saryn's exposé brought with it a wave of backlash from individuals and groups determined to silence them. They became the target of vicious online harassment, doxxing, and threats to their personal safety. But instead of being silenced, Saryn stood firm, recognizing the importance of their cause and the urgent need for change.

Through it all, Saryn's resilience shone brightly. They refused to be deterred by the intimidation tactics employed against them. Saryn's unwavering commitment to their mission inspired countless others to join the fight, transforming what had begun as a personal pursuit into a collective movement for justice.

The Power of Resilience and Determination

Saryn's exposure of corruption and homophobia within Zerana made headlines across the country. Their courage ignited a national conversation about the rights and safety of LGBTQ individuals. The impact of their work reverberated beyond the borders of Zerana, inspiring activists around the world to confront similar injustices in their own communities.

This scandal served as a turning point in Saryn's advocacy. It solidified their role as a fearless leader in the fight for LGBTQ rights and emboldened them to push even further for lasting change. While the process of exposing corruption was undoubtedly challenging, Saryn's unwavering determination, steadfast resilience, and refusal to back down showcased the true power of activism.

Building Bridges and Healing Divisions

One of the unexpected outcomes of Saryn's brave act of exposing corruption and homophobia was the opportunity for healing and reconciliation within the community. The scandal forced individuals and groups with differing perspectives to confront their own biases and prejudices.

Saryn understood the importance of fostering unity and collaboration to effect lasting change. They actively worked to build bridges between factions within the LGBTQ community, encouraging dialogue and understanding. Through their leadership, Saryn facilitated conversations that allowed diverse voices to be heard, creating a space for healing and growth.

By addressing the divisions within the community, Saryn set an example of how embracing diversity and cultivating understanding could strengthen the fight for LGBTQ rights. The unity that emerged from this difficult period would become a driving force in Saryn's ongoing advocacy efforts.

The Toll of Fighting for Change

While Saryn's exposure of corruption and homophobia had far-reaching positive impacts, it also took a toll on their personal well-being. The constant threats, harassment, and stress wore them down physically and emotionally. Saryn's journey serves as a vital reminder that activism, while essential, can come at great personal cost.

Recognizing the toll that their work had taken on their mental health, Saryn actively sought support systems to endure the challenges they faced. They prioritized self-care and surrounded themselves with trusted friends and allies who provided emotional support and encouragement. Saryn set an important example by showcasing the importance of balancing advocacy with personal well-being.

The Power of Resilience and Determination

In exposing corruption and homophobia within Zerana, Saryn Brell not only sparked a movement but also shed light on the deep-rooted systemic discrimination faced by the LGBTQ community. This courage, resilience, and determination enabled Saryn to confront powerful institutions, unite a divided community, and pave the way for lasting change. Their unwavering commitment to justice and equality stands as a testament to the power of activism in creating a more inclusive society.

Through Saryn's journey, we are reminded that the fight for equality is not without its challenges. Exposing corruption and confronting deep-set prejudice requires immense courage, unwavering determination, and a willingness to endure personal sacrifices. However, Saryn's story serves as an inspiration to all those who strive for justice, showing us that even in the face of adversity, change is possible.

As we continue our exploration of Saryn Brell's extraordinary journey, we delve into the triumphs, tribulations, and tequilas that marked their path to becoming a voice for LGBTQ freedom in Zerana. In Chapter 2, we will witness Saryn's rise to prominence, their role in landmark legal battles, and the challenges they faced along

SECTION 4: UNMASKING HYPOCRISY

the way. So grab a drink, settle in, and join us as we embark on the next chapter of this captivating and inspiring biography.

Subsection: Saryn Faces Backlash and Threats

In this subsection, we delve into the challenges that Saryn Brell faced as they became a prominent LGBTQ activist in Zerana. As their influence grew, Saryn had to confront the inevitable backlash and threats that came with their advocacy work. This section explores the various forms of opposition Saryn encountered and how they navigated this difficult terrain.

Backlash from Conservative Groups

As Saryn's voice gained prominence, conservative groups in Zerana condemned their activism, viewing it as an attack on traditional values. These groups often resorted to smear campaigns, spreading misinformation about Saryn's personal life and political affiliations. Fake news articles circulated, attempting to discredit their character and undermine their credibility as an activist.

One example was an article that claimed Saryn was involved in criminal activities, which tarnished their reputation and subjected them to public scrutiny. Saryn had to navigate these false allegations while maintaining their focus on fighting for LGBTQ rights.

Problem: Addressing misinformation and false narratives

To counter the spread of misinformation, Saryn and their team developed a strategy to address the false narratives head-on. They employed fact-checking methods and actively engaged with media outlets to rectify inaccuracies. Saryn conducted interviews, clarifying their positions, and sharing their personal experiences to counter the narrative created by conservative groups.

Solution: Media engagement and transparency

Saryn's team developed strong relationships with journalists who supported their cause, ensuring that their perspective was accurately represented in the media. They frequently held press conferences and interviews to ensure that their side of the story was heard.

Additionally, Saryn utilized social media platforms to directly address the false narratives, providing evidence and personal testimonials to debunk the misinformation. By maintaining transparency and actively countering falsehoods, they were able to regain public trust and maintain their credibility.

Example: Allies and supporters speaking out

In response to the backlash, many allies and supporters spoke out in defense of Saryn. This included prominent figures from the LGBTQ community, influential politicians, and celebrities who believed in the cause. Their voices helped to dismantle the false narratives and create a counter-narrative that exposed the tactics of the conservative groups.

Threats to Personal Safety

As Saryn's visibility increased, so too did the threats to their personal safety. These threats manifested in various forms, ranging from online harassment to physical violence. Saryn's home address was leaked, leading to instances of vandalism and aggression towards them.

Problem: Ensuring personal safety in the face of threats

Saryn and their team recognized the importance of personal safety and took several measures to protect themselves. They worked closely with security experts to assess potential threats and develop risk mitigation strategies. This involved taking precautions such as installing security systems at their residence, utilizing personal bodyguards, and varying their routines to avoid predictability.

Solution: Building a support network

Saryn leaned on their support network, which included friends, allies, and fellow activists, to strengthen their personal safety measures. They formed a group of trusted individuals who were well-versed in emergency protocols and provided emotional support during challenging times. This support network not only ensured their physical safety but also provided a vital lifeline for Saryn's mental well-being.

Example: Reporting threats to authorities

Saryn took all threats seriously and reported them to law enforcement agencies. By working closely with the police, they ensured that the threats were documented and investigated. Saryn's team also engaged legal experts who could assist in navigating the complex legalities surrounding threats and harassment.

Emotional Toll and Self-Preservation

The constant backlash and threats took a toll on Saryn's emotional well-being. As an activist leading a movement, they often neglected their own self-care and prioritized the cause over their personal needs.

Problem: Emotional well-being and self-care

Recognizing the importance of self-preservation, Saryn implemented self-care practices and sought professional help to address the emotional toll of their activism.

They attended therapy sessions, joined support groups, and sought guidance from mental health experts who specialized in trauma care.

Solution: Prioritizing self-care

Saryn integrated self-care into their daily routine, dedicating time for activities they enjoyed, such as meditation, exercise, and spending quality time with loved ones. They also shared their self-care journey openly on social media, encouraging their followers to prioritize their own well-being and destigmatizing seeking help for mental health.

Example: Utilizing artistic outlets

To cope with the emotional challenges, Saryn turned to artistic outlets such as writing, painting, and music. These creative expressions allowed them to process their emotions and find moments of respite from the demanding nature of activism. Saryn's creativity became an integral part of their journey and inspired others to embrace their own artistic pursuits as a means of self-care.

In this subsection, we witnessed the immense challenges and threats Saryn Brell faced as they championed LGBTQ rights in Zerana. From facing adversity and battling through false narratives to ensuring personal safety and prioritizing self-care, Saryn's resilience serves as an inspiration to all activists. The next subsection will explore the power dynamics and relationships that developed between Saryn and various key allies and adversaries throughout their journey.

Subsection: The Power of Resilience and Determination

Resilience and determination are the twin pillars on which Saryn Brell's activism has stood throughout their remarkable journey. In the face of adversity and setbacks, Saryn's unwavering resolve has propelled them forward, turning challenges into opportunities for change. This subsection explores the unique power of resilience and determination in driving Saryn's activism and inspiring others to join the fight for LGBTQ rights.

Resilience: Bouncing Back from Setbacks

Resilience is the ability to bounce back from setbacks, to adapt, and to continue moving forward despite adversity. Saryn's journey has been punctuated by numerous obstacles, but their resilience has been instrumental in overcoming these challenges.

One example of Saryn's resilience was when they encountered opposition from local politicians while organizing the first LGBTQ Pride Parade in Zerana. Faced with resistance and attempts to shut down the event, Saryn remained undeterred, drawing strength from their conviction that the parade was necessary to foster visibility and acceptance. Through resilience, Saryn rallied supporters, worked tirelessly to negotiate with city officials, and ultimately succeeded in making the Pride Parade a reality.

Resilience is not just about overcoming external obstacles; it also involves dealing with internal struggles. The path to self-acceptance and coming to terms with one's identity is often fraught with uncertainty and self-doubt. Saryn's own journey included facing their fears, embracing their true self, and finding the strength to live authentically. Their resilience to endure the emotional turbulence and societal pressures serves as a beacon of hope for individuals navigating similar battles.

Determination: The Driving Force for Change

Determination is an unwavering commitment to achieving a goal, no matter the challenges faced. Saryn's determination has been a driving force behind their activism, fueling their relentless pursuit of equality.

Saryn's determination becomes evident in their role in legalizing same-sex marriage in Zerana. Despite intense opposition and deeply ingrained discriminatory beliefs, Saryn refused to back down. They tirelessly lobbied lawmakers, engaged in public debates, and worked with like-minded activists to build a coalition for change. Through their unwavering determination, Saryn played a pivotal role in the landmark legislation that granted same-sex couples the right to marry.

Determination also empowers Saryn to challenge the status quo and confront bigotry head-on. When faced with resistance from religious organizations and conservative ideologies, Saryn's determination to uphold the rights and dignity of the LGBTQ community never wavered. They fearlessly spoke truth to power, deconstructing stereotypes and dismantling prejudice through informed arguments and compassionate storytelling.

The Resilience-Determination Dynamic Duo

Resilience and determination form a potent dynamic duo in Saryn's activism. Resilience provides the strength to endure setbacks, learn from failures, and adapt to changing circumstances. It enables Saryn to bounce back stronger, armed with valuable lessons and an unwavering belief in the cause.

Determination, on the other hand, propels Saryn forward, channeling their unwavering commitment and drive. It emboldens them to push boundaries, challenge oppressive systems, and advocate for change even in the face of overwhelming odds. Determination harnesses the resilience cultivated through setbacks, transforming it into a force for transformative action.

Together, resilience and determination make Saryn an unstoppable force in the fight for LGBTQ rights. By embodying these qualities, Saryn not only inspires others to persevere but also paves the way for a more inclusive and accepting society.

A Case Study in Resilience and Determination: Transforming Discrimination into Unity

To highlight the power of resilience and determination, let's explore a case study where Saryn's activism transformed discrimination into unity.

In a small town neighboring Zerana, a local bakery refused to serve LGBTQ couples, citing religious beliefs as justification. This discriminatory act sparked outrage and raised concerns about the larger issue of systemic discrimination.

Saryn, known for their resilience and determination, saw an opportunity to turn this incident into a catalyst for change. They organized a peaceful protest outside the bakery, inviting community members, LGBTQ advocates, and allies to join. Saryn's determination to confront discrimination head-on garnered significant media attention, putting a spotlight on the bakery's actions.

Instead of responding with anger and hostility, Saryn advocated for understanding and dialogue. They arranged a meeting between community leaders, LGBTQ activists, and the bakery owner. Through open and honest conversations, Saryn highlighted the impact of the bakery's actions on marginalized communities, emphasizing the importance of inclusivity and equal treatment.

Saryn's demonstration of resilience – bouncing back from discrimination – and their unwavering determination to achieve a just outcome paved the way for a transformative resolution. The bakery owner, moved by the dialogue and recognizing the harm caused, vowed to implement LGBTQ-inclusive policies in their establishment. The local community rallied behind this change, showcasing the unity that can emerge from resilience and determination.

This case study illustrates that by harnessing the power of resilience and determination, individuals like Saryn can transform divisive situations into opportunities for education, understanding, and positive change.

Exercises: Cultivating Resilience and Determination

1. Reflect on a time when you faced a setback or challenge. How did you respond? What lessons did you learn from that experience? How can you apply resilience and determination to bounce back and move forward?

2. Identify a cause or issue that you are passionate about. What steps can you take to embody the same level of determination and resilience as Saryn when advocating for that cause? Create an action plan outlining specific goals and strategies.

3. Research other activists who have demonstrated resilience and determination in their respective fields. Choose one activist and write a short biography highlighting the challenges they faced, how they exhibited resilience and determination, and the impact of their activism.

Remember, resilience and determination are not innate qualities but rather skills that can be cultivated. Through practice, self-reflection, and a willingness to learn from both successes and failures, we can harness the power of resilience and determination to make a lasting impact on the causes we champion.

Subsection: Building Bridges and Healing Divisions

In the relentless pursuit of LGBTQ freedom and equality, Saryn Brell faced numerous barriers and challenges along the way. Yet, one of the most vital aspects of their activism was the ability to build bridges and heal divisions within the community and beyond. In this subsection, we delve into the strategies employed by Saryn to foster unity and understanding, and how they turned adversaries into allies.

One of the key principles that guided Saryn in building bridges was the recognition that change does not happen in isolation. They understood that to achieve lasting progress, it was crucial to collaborate and work alongside individuals and organizations that shared a common goal, even if their approaches differed.

To this end, Saryn actively sought out politicians, religious leaders, and celebrities who showed potential for becoming allies in the fight for LGBTQ rights. They engaged in open and honest dialogues, illuminating the lived experiences of LGBTQ individuals and challenging existing prejudices. Through these conversations, Saryn aimed to humanize the struggles of the LGBTQ community and foster empathy among their counterparts.

However, it is important to note that not all bridges can be built from the top down. Saryn recognized the need for grassroots efforts in healing divisions within the LGBTQ community itself. They worked tirelessly to create a space where diverse voices could be heard and respected. They facilitated dialogues among different factions, encouraging individuals to find common ground and focus on shared objectives.

An example of Saryn's bridge-building efforts was their collaboration with LGBTQ activists from different cultural backgrounds. By acknowledging the unique challenges that each community faced, they established a platform for dialogue and learning. Saryn recognized that unity within the LGBTQ community was essential to attain broader acceptance and equal rights, and actively encouraged collaboration and support.

In their advocacy, Saryn also emphasized the importance of education. They believed that misinformation and ignorance were often the root causes of divisions. To address this, they organized workshops, seminars, and public speaking events to educate the public about the LGBTQ experience. These initiatives focused on dispelling myths, challenging stereotypes, and fostering empathy among diverse audiences.

To truly build bridges and heal divisions, Saryn also sought to address systemic issues that perpetuated discrimination and prejudice. They actively encouraged policies that promoted inclusivity and equality, both locally and nationally. Saryn campaigned for LGBTQ-inclusive curricula in schools, employment protections for LGBTQ individuals, and accessible healthcare services. By targeting the structural barriers that marginalized the LGBTQ community, Saryn aimed to create a society where acceptance and equality were the norm.

In their journey, Saryn encountered resistance, from both within and outside the LGBTQ community. Some individuals questioned their methods or disagreed with their strategies. However, Saryn remained steadfast in their commitment to dialogue and understanding. They approached their adversaries with empathy and respect, seeking to find common ground and bridge the gap in perspectives.

It is worth noting that building bridges and healing divisions is an ongoing process, one that cannot be accomplished overnight. Saryn recognized that it required patience, persistence, and a willingness to listen. They acknowledged that there would be disagreements and setbacks, but remained focused on the ultimate goal of achieving LGBTQ freedom and equality for all.

Unconventional Example:

Imagine a small conservative town in Zerana where LGBTQ acceptance is limited. Saryn decided to organize a community event called "Love Fest," aimed at bringing together individuals from different backgrounds to foster understanding and compassion. The event featured live music, art exhibits, and guest speakers who shared personal stories of LGBTQ individuals. Attendees were encouraged to engage in open dialogues and ask respectful questions.

To create a welcoming atmosphere, Saryn enlisted the support of local religious leaders, politicians, and business owners who were initially hesitant to participate. Through face-to-face meetings and one-on-one conversations, Saryn addressed their concerns and emphasized the importance of building bridges within the community.

The Love Fest event turned out to be a resounding success, attracting a diverse crowd and sparking conversations that extended beyond the event itself. It led to the formation of support groups, LGBTQ awareness campaigns, and collaborations between unlikely allies. Over time, the town saw a significant shift in attitudes, with increased acceptance and understanding of the LGBTQ community.

In this unconventional example, Saryn's approach exemplifies the power of community-based initiatives in building bridges and healing divisions. By creating a safe space for dialogue and collaboration, they facilitated transformative change that reverberated beyond the event itself.

Exercise:

Think about a community or social group where divisions exist, hindering progress and understanding. Develop a plan similar to Saryn's "Love Fest" event to foster unity and build bridges within that community. Consider the key stakeholders, potential challenges, and strategies for encouraging dialogue and collaboration. Write a brief proposal outlining your plan.

Subsection: The Toll of Fighting for Change

The journey of fighting for change is one fraught with challenges and sacrifices, and Saryn Brell's story is no exception. In this subsection, we delve into the toll that activism takes on individuals, exploring the personal and emotional sacrifices that Saryn endures in their quest for LGBTQ rights in Zerana.

The Emotional Rollercoaster

Fighting for change can be an emotional rollercoaster, with high moments of hope and progress, and low moments of frustration and despair. Saryn's journey is filled with both triumphs and tribulations, and navigating these emotional highs and lows takes a toll on their mental and emotional well-being.

At times, Saryn feels the weight of the community's hopes and expectations on their shoulders. The constant demand for progress and equality can become overwhelming, leading to emotional exhaustion and burnout. Despite these challenges, Saryn pushes forward, driven by their unwavering commitment to the cause.

Personal Relationships at Stake

Activism often demands significant personal sacrifices, and Saryn's fight for change is no different. The toll on their personal relationships is a frequently overlooked aspect of their journey. Saryn's loved ones often become collateral damage in the battle for LGBTQ rights.

Saryn's dedication to the cause leaves little time and energy for their personal life. They struggle to find a balance between their activism and nurturing meaningful connections with friends and family. Personal sacrifices, such as missed birthdays and important milestones, become all too common. Saryn's relationships are strained as their loved ones try to understand and support their relentless commitment to the cause.

Dealing with Resistance and Backlash

Fighting for change means encountering resistance and facing backlash from those who oppose LGBTQ rights. Saryn is no stranger to personal attacks, threats, and online harassment. The toll of not only receiving this hate but also navigating its emotional impact cannot be understated.

The constant barrage of negativity takes a toll on Saryn's mental health. They find themselves grappling with self-doubt, anxiety, and fear for their personal safety. Despite these challenges, Saryn stands strong, bolstered by the unwavering support of their allies and the deep conviction in their beliefs.

Self-Care in the Midst of Struggle

Amidst the chaos and demands of activism, it is essential for Saryn to prioritize self-care. They discover the importance of carving out time for themselves, engaging in activities that bring them joy and rejuvenation. Whether it's finding solace in nature, practicing mindfulness, or spending time with loved ones, self-care becomes an integral part of their resilience.

Finding community and allies who understand the toll of their fight is key for Saryn's well-being. They surround themselves with individuals who act as a support network, offering emotional and practical support, and allowing Saryn to recharge and replenish their energy.

The Importance of Boundaries

Navigating the toll of fighting for change also requires setting personal boundaries. Saryn learns that they cannot be everything for everyone, and that saying no and setting limits is crucial for their mental and emotional well-being.

Setting boundaries allows Saryn to protect themselves from further exhaustion and burnout. It enables them to focus their energy on the most impactful aspects of their activism, while also preserving their personal space and mental health.

A Call to Normalize Vulnerability

In conclusion, the toll of fighting for change is a multifaceted and deeply personal experience. Saryn's story highlights the emotional highs and lows, the sacrifices made, and the need for self-care and boundaries. Their journey serves as a reminder that vulnerability should be normalized within the activism community, and that acknowledging and addressing these tolls is essential for sustaining the fight for equality.

As readers, we are called to recognize the toll that activism takes on individuals and to support those who fight for change. By honoring their struggles and celebrating their victories, we can build a stronger and more inclusive society for all.

Section 5: A Movement is Born

Subsection: Saryn's National Platform Grows

As Saryn Brell continued to advocate for LGBTQ rights and freedom in Zerana, their influence and impact began to extend beyond the borders of their home city. Saryn's compelling message of equality and acceptance resonated with people from all walks of life, sparking a movement that would spread throughout the country.

1. One of the key aspects of Saryn's national platform was their focus on education and awareness. They recognized that in order to bring about lasting change, it was crucial to start at the root of society – the younger generations. Saryn tirelessly traveled to schools and universities across the nation, delivering passionate speeches and engaging in open discussions with students. They emphasized the importance of inclusive curriculum and advocated for comprehensive sex education that encompassed diverse sexual orientations and gender identities.

> **Problem**
>
> How can schools create a safe and inclusive environment for LGBTQ students?

SECTION 5: A MOVEMENT IS BORN

Creating safe and inclusive environments in schools can involve several strategies:

- Implementing comprehensive anti-discrimination policies that explicitly include sexual orientation and gender identity.
- Providing LGBTQ-inclusive curriculum that educates students about the history, contributions, and challenges of LGBTQ individuals.
- Training teachers and staff on LGBTQ issues, including how to address bullying, harassment, and language that perpetuates stereotypes.
- Establishing Gay-Straight Alliances (GSAs) or similar support groups that provide a space for LGBTQ students and their allies to connect and seek support.
- Encouraging open dialogue and discussions about LGBTQ issues, fostering acceptance and understanding among students.

2. Saryn's advocacy also extended to working with politicians and lawmakers to push for LGBTQ-inclusive legislation. They leveraged their growing influence to lobby for laws that protected LGBTQ individuals from discrimination in various sectors, including employment, housing, and healthcare. Saryn's persuasive arguments and personal stories of resilience and perseverance had a profound impact on policymakers, leading to the introduction and passage of groundbreaking legislation in support of LGBTQ rights.

> **Problem**
>
> How can individuals effectively advocate for LGBTQ rights through political channels?

Effective advocacy for LGBTQ rights through political channels can involve the following strategies:

- Educate yourself: Stay informed about LGBTQ issues, legislation, and policies.
- Build coalitions: Collaborate with like-minded organizations and individuals to amplify your voice and influence.
- Communicate with policymakers: Reach out to lawmakers through emails, letters, or phone calls to express your concerns and highlight the need for LGBTQ-inclusive legislation.

- Share personal stories: Personal stories have a powerful impact on policymakers and can help them understand the real-life experiences of LGBTQ individuals.

- Attend public hearings and events: Show up at public hearings and events related to LGBTQ rights to demonstrate support and engage directly with policymakers.

- Mobilize grassroots action: Organize rallies, protests, or campaigns to raise awareness and apply pressure on politicians to prioritize LGBTQ rights.

3. Saryn's national platform also involved collaborating with other LGBTQ activists and organizations across the country. Recognizing the strength in unity, Saryn worked tirelessly to build and strengthen alliances with individuals and groups who shared their passion for equality. Together, they organized national conferences, workshops, and campaigns, creating a network of support that bolstered the LGBTQ movement and amplified their message.

> **Problem**
>
> How can collaborations between different LGBTQ organizations enhance the fight for equality?

Collaborations between different LGBTQ organizations can enhance the fight for equality in several ways:

- Shared resources: Collaboration allows organizations to pool their resources, including funding, expertise, and manpower, to better address the challenges faced by the LGBTQ community.

- Amplified impact: By working together, organizations can amplify their messages and initiatives, reaching a wider audience and increasing the chances of creating significant change.

- Knowledge-sharing and learning: Collaboration provides a space for organizations to share knowledge, experiences, and best practices, leading to more effective strategies and interventions.

- Intersectionality: Collaborating with organizations that work on issues intersecting with LGBTQ rights, such as racial justice or disability rights, helps create a more inclusive and holistic approach to advocacy.

SECTION 5: A MOVEMENT IS BORN

4. Building on the success of their regional activism, Saryn began to use media appearances as a platform to advocate for LGBTQ rights on a national scale. They appeared on television talk shows, participated in radio interviews, and wrote op-eds for major newspapers, captivating the nation with their charisma and unwavering commitment. Saryn's ability to eloquently articulate the struggles faced by LGBTQ individuals and their vision for a more inclusive society inspired countless people and brought attention to the ongoing fight for equality.

> **Problem**
>
> How can media and public appearances be utilized to change public perceptions of LGBTQ individuals?

Utilizing media and public appearances to change public perceptions of LGBTQ individuals can involve the following strategies:

- Visibility and representation: Being visible and sharing personal stories allows the public to see the diverse range of LGBTQ individuals, challenging stereotypes and humanizing the community.

- Framing the narrative: Using media platforms to tell compelling stories that focus on commonalities and shared values helps bridge the gap between LGBTQ individuals and the wider public, fostering empathy and understanding.

- Education and awareness: Utilize media appearances to educate the public about LGBTQ issues, debunk myths and misconceptions, and highlight the need for inclusive policies and practices.

- Engage in inclusive dialogue: Participate in interviews and discussions that include a range of perspectives, promoting respectful and informative conversations that challenge biases and encourage critical thinking.

5. As Saryn's national platform grew, so did the impact of their speeches and advocacy efforts. Their words motivated and activated individuals across the country, inspiring many to join the fight for LGBTQ rights. Saryn's passionate and convincing arguments, coupled with their ability to connect with diverse audiences, transformed them into a powerful catalyst for change.

> **Problem**
> How can public speaking skills be honed to effectively advocate for LGBTQ rights and inspire change?

Hone public speaking skills to effectively advocate for LGBTQ rights and inspire change by focusing on the following areas:

- Content preparation: Thoroughly research and understand the topics you will be addressing, ensuring your arguments are well-informed and supported by evidence.

- Authenticity and personal connection: Share personal stories and experiences to foster a genuine connection with the audience, making your message relatable and emotionally impactful.

- Clear and compelling communication: Develop effective speaking skills, such as using engaging storytelling techniques, employing persuasive language, and utilizing vocal variety to keep the audience engaged and invested in your message.

- Nonverbal communication: Pay attention to your body language, facial expressions, and overall presence on stage, as they can greatly impact your audience's perception and engagement.

- Audience customization: Tailor your speeches to the specific needs and interests of different audiences, ensuring your message resonates with their experiences and concerns.

Saryn's national platform served as a powerful vehicle for change, as it brought attention to the struggles faced by the LGBTQ community, promoted understanding and acceptance, and pushed for tangible legal protections. But as Saryn's platform continued to grow, so did the challenges they faced. The next section explores the obstacles and setbacks encountered by Saryn on their journey to effecting lasting change.

Subsection: Collaborating with Other LGBTQ Activists

In the fight for LGBTQ rights, collaboration and solidarity play a crucial role. Saryn Brell understood the power of working together with other activists to amplify their collective voice and effect real change. Through partnerships, alliances, and coalitions, Saryn was able to build a strong network of LGBTQ activists who shared the same goal of achieving equality and freedom in Zerana.

One of the most successful collaborations was with the Zerana LGBTQ Coalition, a grassroots organization dedicated to advancing LGBTQ rights. Saryn recognized that by joining forces with this organization, they could tap into a diverse range of skills, experiences, and resources. Together, they worked tirelessly to dismantle systemic oppression, challenge discriminatory laws, and raise public awareness.

However, collaboration does not come without challenges. Coordinating efforts, aligning strategies, and managing different personalities can be complex. It requires effective communication, compromise, and a shared vision. Saryn understood the importance of creating an inclusive and supportive environment, where all voices were heard and valued. They believed in the power of unity and ensured that all members of the coalition felt empowered to contribute their unique perspectives and ideas.

To foster collaboration, Saryn implemented several strategies. Regular meetings were scheduled to discuss ongoing projects, share updates, and brainstorm new initiatives. These gatherings became not just a platform for exchanging ideas, but also an opportunity for activists to build connections and find common ground. Saryn encouraged open dialogue and constructive criticism, recognizing that diverse viewpoints can lead to more innovative solutions.

To address the specific challenges faced by LGBTQ activists, Saryn organized workshops and training sessions focused on building allyship and understanding intersectionality. They believed that it was essential to forge alliances with other social justice movements, recognizing that oppression is interconnected. By collaborating with activists fighting for racial justice, gender equality, and disability rights, Saryn sought to create a more inclusive and intersectional movement.

Collaboration extended beyond local activism, as Saryn actively sought opportunities to collaborate with LGBTQ activists on a national and international level. They attended conferences, participated in panel discussions, and engaged in online networks to connect with like-minded individuals from around the world. Through these connections, they learned from the successes and challenges of others, and brought those learnings back to Zerana.

Saryn's collaboration with other LGBTQ activists extended to creative endeavors as well. They teamed up with artists, writers, and performers to create impactful and thought-provoking works that challenged societal norms and stereotypes. Through art exhibitions, theatrical performances, and poetry slams, Saryn and their collaborators were able to reach a wider audience and spark important conversations about LGBTQ rights.

In the spirit of collaboration, Saryn also recognized the value of working with allies who were not part of the LGBTQ community. They actively sought support from politicians, celebrities, and influential figures who could amplify their message and advocate for change. Saryn understood that building bridges and finding common ground was crucial in achieving their goals.

However, collaboration was not always smooth sailing. Activism is not immune to disagreements and conflicts. Saryn encountered challenges within the LGBTQ community itself, with differing opinions on strategies, priorities, and approaches. They navigated these challenges by fostering an environment of respect and understanding, encouraging dialogue, and finding common ground.

Overall, Saryn Brell's ability to collaborate with other LGBTQ activists was a key factor in their success. By recognizing that collective action is more powerful than individual efforts, Saryn fostered a united movement that made significant strides towards LGBTQ equality in Zerana. Their legacy serves as a reminder that collaboration is essential in effecting meaningful change, and that by working together, we can create a more inclusive and just world for all.

Subsection: The Impact of Saryn's Speeches and Media Appearances

Saryn Brell's journey as an LGBTQ activist in Zerana was not characterized solely by their remarkable achievements in policy changes and legal battles. Equally significant was the profound impact of Saryn's speeches and media appearances, which helped shape public opinion, raise awareness, and mobilize support for the LGBTQ community.

Redefining the Narrative: Saryn's speeches served as a turning point in the conversation around LGBTQ rights, challenging mainstream societal norms and prejudices. With their eloquence and conviction, Saryn presented a compelling argument for equality, dismantling misconceptions and debunking harmful stereotypes about the LGBTQ community. Through their words, they humanized the experiences of LGBTQ individuals, fostering empathy and shifting public opinion.

Visibility and Representation: Saryn's media appearances played a crucial role in creating visibility for the LGBTQ community. By leveraging their platform, Saryn shattered the glass ceiling that had previously limited LGBTQ representation in the media. Their presence on talk shows, news programs, and interviews allowed them to highlight the diverse experiences of LGBTQ individuals, providing a counter-narrative to the prevailing stereotypes. This increased visibility helped pave the way for greater acceptance and understanding.

Inspiring Others to Speak Up: Saryn's compelling speeches and media appearances inspired countless individuals to find their own voice and join the fight for LGBTQ rights. Through their powerful storytelling and personal anecdotes, Saryn showed others that their stories and experiences mattered. They encouraged individuals from all walks of life to step out of their comfort zones and share their truths, fostering a sense of empowerment within the LGBTQ community.

Changing Hearts and Minds: Saryn's ability to articulate the struggles and triumphs of the LGBTQ community resonated with people across the nation, challenging deeply ingrained biases and prejudices. Their speeches and media appearances provided a platform for open dialogue, allowing individuals to confront their own prejudices and rethink their perspectives. By humanizing the LGBTQ experience, Saryn fostered empathy and compassion, leading to a gradual shift in societal attitudes towards greater acceptance of LGBTQ rights.

Initiating Policy Change: Saryn's speeches often went beyond inspiring and educating; they also played a pivotal role in influencing policy change. Their ability to communicate the urgency of LGBTQ rights to policymakers and the public helped push forward legislation that protected LGBTQ individuals from discrimination and advanced equality. Saryn's words held the power to sway public opinion, leading to increased public support for pro-LGBTQ policies and measures.

Uniting Communities: Saryn's speeches and media appearances served as a catalyst for community engagement and mobilization. By sharing their own experiences and advocating for equality, they brought people together, fostering a sense of unity and solidarity among LGBTQ individuals and their allies. Saryn's words inspired individuals to take action, sparking grassroots movements and local initiatives aimed at creating safe spaces and fostering inclusivity.

The Ripple Effect: The impact of Saryn's speeches and media appearances extended far beyond Zerana. Their advocacy reverberated on a national and even international scale, inspiring activists and policymakers worldwide to push for LGBTQ equality. Saryn's journey and messages resonated across borders, forming connections and alliances that further strengthened the global fight for LGBTQ rights.

Caveat: The Limitations of Speeches and Media: While Saryn's speeches and media appearances were undeniably powerful tools for change, it is important to acknowledge their limitations. Words alone cannot dismantle deeply rooted systems of oppression. Saryn's impact went hand in hand with grassroots organizing, coalition-building, and sustained activism. It is crucial to recognize that speeches and media appearances are just one piece of the puzzle in creating genuine and lasting change.

In conclusion, Saryn Brell's speeches and media appearances played a pivotal role in shaping the landscape of LGBTQ rights in Zerana and beyond. Through their eloquence, visibility, and passion, Saryn redefined the narrative around LGBTQ issues, inspiring others to join the fight for equality. Their words not only changed hearts and minds but also influenced policy, united communities, and left a lasting legacy for future activists. Saryn's journey proves the transformative power of speech and media in advancing social justice causes, reminding us all of the importance of using our voices to advocate for change.

Subsection: Taking the Fight to the International Stage

Once Saryn had established themselves as a prominent LGBTQ activist in Zerana, it was only a matter of time before their influence spread beyond the borders of their home country. The fight for LGBTQ rights knows no boundaries, and Saryn was determined to take their advocacy to the international stage.

Understanding Global LGBTQ Rights

Before embarking on their international journey, Saryn had to familiarize themselves with the state of LGBTQ rights worldwide. They studied the laws, policies, and cultural attitudes towards the LGBTQ community in different countries. This research allowed them to identify countries where LGBTQ individuals faced severe discrimination and persecution, as well as countries that had made progress in advancing LGBTQ rights.

Saryn also educated themselves on international human rights frameworks that protected LGBTQ rights, such as the United Nations Universal Declaration of Human Rights and the International Covenant on Civil and Political Rights. This knowledge provided them with a solid foundation and the tools necessary to challenge oppressive systems on a global scale.

Building Alliances and Collaborating

Recognizing the importance of collaboration and collective action, Saryn reached out to other LGBTQ activists and organizations around the world. They attended international conferences and participated in panel discussions, networking with activists from diverse backgrounds.

By forging alliances and working together, Saryn and their international counterparts were able to coordinate efforts and share resources and strategies. They also learned from each other's experiences and adapted successful tactics to suit local contexts.

Addressing Global LGBTQ Issues

Saryn made it their mission to address global LGBTQ issues and promote equality for all, regardless of sexual orientation, gender identity, or gender expression. They focused on several key areas:

1. **Ending Criminalization:** Saryn advocated for the decriminalization of same-sex relationships and the repeal of laws that targeted LGBTQ individuals. They worked with local activists and lawmakers to push for legal reforms that protected LGBTQ rights.

2. **Combating Violence and Discrimination:** Saryn raised awareness about the violence and discrimination faced by LGBTQ individuals globally. They highlighted specific instances of violence and discrimination, using storytelling and personal narratives to humanize the experiences of marginalized communities.

3. **Supporting LGBTQ Asylum Seekers:** Saryn recognized the unique challenges faced by LGBTQ individuals seeking asylum due to persecution in their home countries. They collaborated with organizations providing support and legal aid to LGBTQ asylum seekers, ensuring that their voices were heard and their rights protected.

4. **Advocating for Recognition and Inclusion:** Saryn campaigned for the recognition and inclusion of LGBTQ individuals in all aspects of society, including healthcare, education, employment, and family law. They called on governments to enact legislation that protected LGBTQ rights and provided equal opportunities for all.

5. **Educating and Empowering:** Saryn conducted workshops and awareness campaigns to educate communities about LGBTQ issues and to foster empathy and understanding. They aimed to dispel myths and stereotypes surrounding LGBTQ individuals, promoting acceptance and inclusion.

Engaging with International Bodies and Institutions

To have a broader impact, Saryn engaged with international bodies and institutions that had the power to influence policy and promote LGBTQ rights. They attended meetings at the United Nations and regional human rights bodies, where they advocated for the inclusion of LGBTQ rights in their agendas.

Saryn also leveraged their platform to hold governments accountable and shine a spotlight on countries with poor LGBTQ rights records. They used their social media presence to amplify marginalized voices and draw attention to human rights violations.

Celebrating Progress and Inspiring Change

Despite the challenges and setbacks, Saryn celebrated the progress made in advancing LGBTQ rights globally. They highlighted success stories and showcased countries that had taken significant steps towards equality. By sharing these accomplishments, Saryn inspired hope and encouraged others to continue the fight for LGBTQ rights.

Through their international advocacy work, Saryn aimed to create a ripple effect, inspiring activists in other countries to push for change and challenging oppressive systems that denied LGBTQ individuals their rights and freedoms.

An Unconventional Approach

In their campaign for global LGBTQ rights, Saryn employed an unconventional approach that caught the attention of both supporters and critics. They utilized the power of social media, using engaging and relatable content to appeal to a wider audience. They created videos, memes, and infographics that blended humor and activism, making complex issues accessible to a broader audience.

Saryn also embraced pop culture and entertainment to spread their message. They collaborated with musicians, artists, and popular influencers, engaging their followers in conversations about LGBTQ rights. The combination of entertainment and activism helped break down barriers and challenged societal norms.

Exercises

1. Research the current status of LGBTQ rights in a country of your choice. Identify the challenges faced by the LGBTQ community in that country and explore any progress or setbacks in LGBTQ rights.

2. Imagine you are an LGBTQ activist planning an international conference. Design a comprehensive agenda that addresses key global LGBTQ issues and allows for open discussions with activists from different regions.

3. Create a social media campaign to raise awareness about LGBTQ rights globally. Consider the use of storytelling, personal narratives, and engaging visuals to convey your message effectively.

SECTION 5: A MOVEMENT IS BORN

Resources

Books

- "Global Allies: Comparing LGBTQ Movements from Around the World" by Ryan R. Thoreson
- "This Book is Gay" by Juno Dawson
- "Transgender History: The Roots of Today's Revolution" by Susan Stryker
- "Queer Brown Voices: Personal Narratives of Latina/o LGBT Activism" edited by Uriel Quesada, Letitia Gomez, and Salvador Vidal-Ortiz

Films and Documentaries

- "Paris is Burning" (1990) directed by Jennie Livingston
- "How to Survive a Plague" (2012) directed by David France
- "The Death and Life of Marsha P. Johnson" (2017) directed by David France
- "Moonlight" (2016) directed by Barry Jenkins

Websites

- Human Rights Campaign: https://www.hrc.org/
- International Lesbian, Gay, Bisexual, Trans and Intersex Association: https://ilga.org/
- OutRight Action International: https://outrightinternational.org/
- United Nations Free & Equal Campaign: https://www.unfe.org/

Podcasts

- "Making Gay History" hosted by Eric Marcus
- "Queery with Cameron Esposito"
- "LGBTQ&A" with Jeffrey Masters

Remember, the fight for global LGBTQ rights is ongoing, and every action counts. Embrace your role as an advocate for equality and never be afraid to speak up for what is right. Together, we can create a world where everyone is free to be their authentic selves, regardless of their sexual orientation or gender identity.

Subsection: Building a Legacy that Will Last

Building a lasting legacy is a pivotal aspect of any activist's journey, and Saryn Brell understood the importance of leaving a significant impact on the LGBTQ community in Zerana and beyond. This subsection explores the strategies and actions taken by Saryn to ensure that their advocacy work would continue to resonate long after they had stepped away from the limelight.

Creating Sustainable Change

One of the first steps in building a lasting legacy is to focus on creating sustainable change. Saryn recognized that real progress could not be achieved through temporary measures or quick fixes. Instead, they worked tirelessly to implement long-term policies and initiatives that would continue to protect and empower the LGBTQ community for years to come.

For instance, Saryn played a crucial role in advocating for comprehensive LGBTQ-inclusive legislation in Zerana. This legislation not only focused on legalizing same-sex marriage but also encompassed protections against discrimination in housing, employment, and public accommodations. By laying a strong foundation of legal protections, Saryn ensured that the LGBTQ community could navigate their lives with dignity and equality, even in the face of opposition.

Education and Awareness

Another vital aspect of building a lasting legacy is to focus on education and awareness. Saryn firmly believed that change starts with knowledge and understanding. They dedicated considerable efforts to educate the public about LGBTQ issues, combating stereotypes, and promoting empathy and inclusion.

Saryn's use of speeches and media appearances proved instrumental in spreading their message to a wide audience. Their ability to connect with people on a personal level and share their own experiences humanized the struggle for LGBTQ rights. Saryn's speeches captured hearts and minds, inspiring individuals from all walks of life to embrace diversity and strive for equality.

Furthermore, Saryn was a passionate advocate for LGBTQ-inclusive education in schools. They recognized the importance of creating safe and supportive environments for LGBTQ students, where they could learn, grow, and express their authentic selves without fear of discrimination or harassment. By advocating for LGBTQ-inclusive curricula and resources, Saryn laid the groundwork for a more inclusive education system and a more accepting society.

Empowering the Next Generation

Building a legacy involves empowering the next generation of activists. Saryn understood that their work would have a lasting impact only if it inspired others to continue the fight for equality and justice.

To achieve this, Saryn actively mentored and supported young activists, providing guidance and resources to help them navigate the complexities of advocacy work. They established scholarship programs and internships, enabling LGBTQ youth to develop their skills and contribute to the movement. By nurturing the talents and passions of young activists, Saryn ensured that their legacy would be carried forward with strength and resilience.

Moreover, Saryn emphasized the importance of intersectionality in activism. They recognized that fighting for LGBTQ rights goes hand in hand with fighting against other forms of discrimination and oppression. Saryn actively collaborated with activists from various social justice movements, bridging gaps and creating solidarity across different communities. This approach not only strengthened the LGBTQ movement but also served as a powerful example of inclusivity and unity.

Documenting and Preserving History

Preserving history is crucial for understanding the progress made by the LGBTQ community and its ongoing struggles. Saryn recognized this and took steps to document their journey and the broader LGBTQ movement in Zerana.

They worked closely with archivists and historians to ensure that the stories and experiences of LGBTQ activists were recorded and preserved for future generations. Saryn's personal archives, including diaries, correspondence, and photographs, provided valuable insights into the challenges faced by LGBTQ individuals in Zerana and the milestones achieved through collective efforts.

Furthermore, Saryn encouraged others to share their stories and document their activism. They believed that every individual's voice and experience added depth and richness to the collective narrative. By leaving a legacy of documented history, Saryn enabled future generations to learn from the past and continue the fight for equality.

Ensuring Organizational Continuity

To ensure a lasting legacy, Saryn recognized the need for strong and sustainable organizational structures. They understood that true change could not rely solely on individual efforts but required the collective power of organized movements.

To this end, Saryn focused on building effective LGBTQ organizations and networks that would continue the work even after their own active involvement.

They fostered collaboration among LGBTQ activists, created mentoring programs, and established clear leadership pathways to ensure smooth transitions and ongoing support for future advocates.

Saryn also prioritized diversifying leadership within LGBTQ organizations, recognizing the importance of representation and inclusivity. They actively encouraged individuals from marginalized communities within the LGBTQ spectrum to take on leadership roles and shape the direction of the movement. This approach aimed to prevent a single narrative or perspective from dominating the advocacy landscape and ensured that the movement remained dynamic and responsive to the diverse needs of the LGBTQ community.

Thinking Boldly and Unconventionally

To truly build a legacy that will last, innovation and creativity are vital. Saryn Brell was not afraid to challenge the status quo and think outside the box. They understood that unconventional approaches could yield extraordinary results.

For example, Saryn utilized social media and digital platforms to amplify their message and engage with a broader audience. Their strong online presence, coupled with strategic use of hashtags and viral campaigns, significantly increased the visibility and impact of their advocacy work.

Saryn also actively leveraged popular culture to promote LGBTQ visibility and acceptance. They collaborated with artists, filmmakers, and writers to ensure diverse and authentic LGBTQ representation in mainstream media. By harnessing the power of storytelling and art, Saryn helped reshape societal perceptions and break down barriers to acceptance.

Conclusion

Building a legacy that will last requires a multifaceted approach, encompassing sustainable change, education, empowerment, documentation, and innovation. Saryn Brell's journey as an LGBTQ activist demonstrates the power of these strategies and their potential to leave a profound impact on society.

By focusing on the long-term, nurturing the next generation, preserving history, and thinking boldly, Saryn laid the groundwork for a more inclusive and accepting world. Their legacy inspires and guides countless individuals in the ongoing fight for LGBTQ rights, and their transformative impact will reverberate for generations to come.

Subsection: The Weight of Being a Symbol for an Entire Community

Being a symbol for an entire community is undoubtedly an immense responsibility. Saryn Brell, as a prominent LGBTQ activist, understood the weight that came with being a symbol for the LGBTQ community in Zerana and beyond. In this section, we will delve into the challenges faced by Saryn in this role and explore the impact such representation can have on an individual.

First and foremost, Saryn had to grapple with the pressure of being a role model. As a symbol for the LGBTQ community, their actions and words were closely scrutinized. The world looked to Saryn for guidance, inspiration, and validation. This put them in a position where every decision mattered, both personally and politically. Saryn had to navigate the complexities of representing a diverse community while ensuring their own authenticity and staying true to their values.

Additionally, being a symbol meant that Saryn's personal life became public property. Every aspect of their life was analyzed, from their relationships to their appearance. This invasion of privacy took a toll on Saryn's mental and emotional well-being. They had to constantly balance the need for transparency with the need for personal boundaries, all while remaining accountable to the community they represented.

Another challenge that Saryn faced was the burden of expectation. The LGBTQ community looked to Saryn as a beacon of hope and progress. Their successes were celebrated, but their failures were magnified. Saryn had to navigate the delicate balance of setting achievable goals for the community while also managing the disappointment and backlash that came with setbacks or compromises. It was a constant challenge to meet the ever-evolving expectations of a diverse community with varied needs and desires.

Moreover, Saryn had to face the inevitable loneliness that comes with being a symbol. While they were surrounded by supporters, allies, and admirers, there were times when Saryn felt isolated. They carried the weight of the community's struggles on their shoulders, often sacrificing personal relationships and moments of respite to fight for equality. Saryn's own needs sometimes took a backseat to the demands of their role, making them feel detached and alone, even in a room full of people.

However, being a symbol for an entire community also brought about profound moments of connection and pride for Saryn. They became a unifying force, bringing people together and fostering a sense of belonging. Saryn witnessed firsthand the impact their words and actions had on the lives of LGBTQ individuals, inspiring a new generation of activists and amplifying marginalized voices. This sense of purpose and the knowledge that their work was making a difference gave Saryn the strength to persevere through the challenging times.

In conclusion, the weight of being a symbol for an entire community is a complex and multifaceted experience. Saryn Brell, in their role as an LGBTQ activist, faced numerous challenges, including the pressure of being a role model, the invasion of privacy, the burden of expectation, and the loneliness that comes with such a responsibility. However, amidst the challenges, Saryn also found moments of connection, pride, and purpose. Their journey serves as a reminder of the power and impact that symbols can have on communities seeking equality and justice.

Chapter 2: Triumphs, Tribulations, and Tequilas

Chapter 2: Triumphs, Tribulations, and Tequilas

Chapter 2: Triumphs, Tribulations, and Tequilas

Chapter 2 of "Saryn Brell: A Voice for LGBTQ Freedom in Zerana – Unauthorized" takes us on a rollercoaster ride through Saryn's life, highlighting their triumphs, tribulations, and a few tequila-fueled escapades along the way. In this chapter, we delve deep into the pivotal moments that shaped Saryn's activism and advocacy for LGBTQ rights in Zerana and beyond.

2.1 Section 1: From Small Wins to Big Victories

Saryn's journey towards becoming a prominent LGBTQ activist in Zerana was not without its share of obstacles. This section celebrates the small wins and chronicles the rise of Saryn's influence in the fight for equality.

Subsection: Saryn's Role in Legalizing Same-Sex Marriage in Zerana

In this subsection, we explore Saryn's pivotal role in the landmark legalization of same-sex marriage in Zerana. We dive into the legal battles, the tireless advocacy, and the emotional stories that propelled this historic victory. From lobbying lawmakers to organizing protests and engaging with the media, Saryn's tenacity and unwavering dedication to this cause fueled the transformation of Zerana's legal landscape.

By highlighting Saryn's personal journey and emphasizing the real-life stories of LGBTQ couples who fought for their love, we bring the humanity and deeply personal aspect of this triumph to the forefront. Readers will gain a deeper understanding of the impact of legalizing same-sex marriage and the long-lasting effects it has on individuals and society as a whole.

Subsection: The Fight for Comprehensive LGBTQ-Inclusive Legislation

Moving beyond the legal battle for marriage equality, Saryn's advocacy extends to fighting for comprehensive LGBTQ-inclusive legislation. In this subsection, we delve into the complexities of navigating the political landscape, engaging with lawmakers, and building coalitions with progressive allies.

Using real-world examples of discriminatory policies and their devastating effects on LGBTQ individuals, we shed light on the urgent need for legislation that protects the rights and well-being of every member of the LGBTQ community. From employment protections to healthcare access, Saryn's tireless efforts and strategic collaborations paved the way for groundbreaking legislation that went far beyond mere symbolism.

Subsection: Eradicating Conversion Therapy and other Harmful Practices

The battle against conversion therapy and other harmful practices aimed at altering sexual orientation and gender identity is at the heart of this subsection. By delving into the personal stories of survivors who have endured the traumas inflicted by these practices, we humanize the issue and bring to light the urgent necessity to eradicate them once and for all.

Saryn's relentless pursuit of education, evidence-based research, and collaboration with mental health professionals played a pivotal role in raising awareness about the detrimental consequences of conversion therapy. This subsection exposes the deeply-rooted prejudices and systemic barriers that activists like Saryn faced while advocating for legislation to ban these practices, and how they overcame them with perseverance and unwavering determination.

Subsection: Expanding Protections for Transgender Individuals

In this subsection, we shine a spotlight on Saryn's efforts to expand legal protections for transgender individuals in Zerana. From pushing for inclusive healthcare policies to advocating for comprehensive transgender rights legislation, Saryn's work drove meaningful change and laid the foundation for a more inclusive society.

Using powerful personal profiles of transgender individuals whose lives have been impacted by discrimination, we show the transformative power of Saryn's advocacy. Their work goes beyond policy-making, focusing on changing public

CHAPTER 2: TRIUMPHS, TRIBULATIONS, AND TEQUILAS

perceptions and ensuring that the transgender community is seen, heard, and embraced for who they are.

Subsection: Celebrating Milestones and Reflecting on Progress

This subsection allows us to take a step back and reflect on the significant milestones and progress achieved through Saryn's tireless activism. By highlighting the groundbreaking legislation, policy changes, and societal shifts that have occurred, we celebrate the victories won and acknowledge the collective effort necessary to create lasting change.

To further engage readers, we include interactive elements such as profiles of individuals who have been positively impacted by Saryn's advocacy. Their stories serve as reminders of the incredible ripple effect that dedication and passion can have on a community. Through their triumphs, we learn invaluable lessons about resilience, collaboration, and the power of collective action.

Subsection: The Constant Battle for Equality

In this subsection, we address the ongoing challenges and setbacks faced by Saryn and the LGBTQ community in the fight for equality. We discuss the backlash from conservative groups, legal challenges to progressive policies, and the need for continued vigilance to protect the hard-won rights.

By exploring the nuances of these challenges and providing examples of how Saryn and other activists navigate these obstacles, we illuminate the intertwined nature of progress and regression in the ongoing pursuit of LGBTQ rights. Through their resilience, determination, and unwavering commitment, Saryn inspires readers to persevere in their own personal struggles and fight for a more inclusive society.

Note: In the spirit of John Krasinski's entertaining writing style, this section includes a lighter touch on an otherwise serious topic. The presence of tequila references adds a playful element that reflects the unconventional style adopted for this unauthorized biography. It is essential to strike a balance between humor and sensitivity when discussing delicate subject matters, so the tone remains respectful and cognizant of the significance of the topics being explored.

Section 1: From Small Wins to Big Victories

Subsection: Saryn's Role in Legalizing Same-Sex Marriage in Zerana

In this section, we will explore Saryn Brell's influential role in the fight for legalizing same-sex marriage in Zerana. Saryn's dedication to equality and justice paved the way for significant progress in LGBTQ rights, and their efforts in this area were particularly groundbreaking.

The Historical Context

To understand the significance of Saryn's role in legalizing same-sex marriage, we must first consider the historical context in Zerana. Like many countries, Zerana had a history of discrimination against the LGBTQ community. Same-sex relationships were stigmatized, and LGBTQ individuals faced pervasive societal prejudice and legal barriers to their rights.

However, the late 20th and early 21st centuries witnessed a global shift in attitudes towards LGBTQ rights. Zerana was no exception, as a growing number of citizens and activists began challenging the discriminatory laws and advocating for change.

Challenging Homophobia and Discrimination

Saryn Brell emerged as a prominent LGBTQ activist in Zerana, unafraid to confront homophobia and discrimination head-on. Their relentless efforts helped raise awareness about the unequal treatment of LGBTQ individuals and gather support for legal reforms.

Saryn organized rallies, public speeches, and media appearances to shed light on the emotional and personal toll faced by same-sex couples who were denied the right to marry. They shared powerful stories of commitment, love, and the importance of legal recognition for same-sex relationships.

Building a Coalition

Equally crucial to Saryn's success was their ability to build a diverse coalition of supporters. They actively engaged with community organizations, LGBTQ advocacy groups, and allies from religious, political, and cultural backgrounds. Saryn understood the importance of unity in the face of opposition and worked tirelessly to bridge gaps between different communities.

By fostering dialogue and collaboration, Saryn ensured that the fight for same-sex marriage in Zerana extended beyond LGBTQ circles. They emphasized that it was not just an LGBTQ issue, but a matter of equal rights for all citizens.

Strategic Legal Advocacy

Saryn, with their background in political science, combined their activist efforts with strategic legal advocacy. They played a vital role in working with legal experts to develop robust arguments in favor of same-sex marriage.

Saryn and their legal team meticulously reviewed national and international laws, constitutions, and human rights treaties to strengthen their case. They highlighted the fundamental principles of equality, freedom of expression, and the right to marry as protected by the Constitution of Zerana.

Public Education and Awareness

One of Saryn's greatest achievements was their commitment to public education and awareness. They recognized that changing public opinion was essential for the success of legalizing same-sex marriage.

Saryn tirelessly toured schools, universities, and community centers across the country, delivering educational workshops on LGBTQ history, rights, and the importance of marriage equality. They engaged in open, honest, and respectful conversations, debunking misconceptions and dispelling stereotypes surrounding same-sex relationships.

Landmark Legal Battles

Saryn's dedication ultimately led them to be a key figure in several landmark legal battles. Alongside a team of dedicated lawyers, they challenged existing laws that denied same-sex couples the right to marry.

In the landmark case of *Brell v. Zerana*, Saryn's legal team argued that the prohibition of same-sex marriage violated the constitutional rights to equality and freedom of expression. They highlighted the importance of recognizing the commitments and love shared by same-sex couples and the psychological and emotional harm caused by denying them equal rights.

The Influence of Saryn's Activism

Saryn's activism and legal advocacy had a profound influence on public opinion and the judiciary in Zerana. Their unwavering commitment to equality and justice mobilized citizens across the country and created a national conversation on LGBTQ rights.

Their efforts led to a groundswell of support for legalizing same-sex marriage, resulting in public demonstrations, grassroots campaigns, and increased visibility for the LGBTQ community. Public opinion polls showed a steady increase in support for marriage equality, with a clear majority of Zerana citizens favoring legal reform.

The Landmark Decision

Finally, in a historic ruling, the Supreme Court of Zerana declared the prohibition of same-sex marriage unconstitutional in the case of *Brell v. Zerana*. The court recognized the importance of marriage as a fundamental right and acknowledged that denying same-sex couples the right to marry was a violation of their constitutional rights.

Saryn's role in this watershed moment cannot be overstated. Their activism and tireless advocacy contributed to the legal arguments that ultimately convinced the court to strike down the discriminatory laws.

Legacy and Continuing Challenges

Although the legalization of same-sex marriage was a monumental achievement, Saryn recognized that the fight for LGBTQ rights was far from over. They remained committed to addressing the remaining challenges faced by the LGBTQ community, including ensuring comprehensive anti-discrimination protection and fostering inclusivity in all aspects of society.

Saryn's legacy continues to inspire current and future activists to fight for equality, justice, and dignity for all LGBTQ individuals. Their role in legalizing same-sex marriage in Zerana serves as a testament to the power of activism, collaboration, and unwavering determination in the face of adversity.

Further Reading

If you're interested in learning more about the legal battles and activism surrounding same-sex marriage in Zerana, the following resources may be of interest:

- *Beyond Equality: The Fight for Same-Sex Marriage in Zerana* by Elena Thompson
- *Love and Justice: A Journey towards Marriage Equality in Zerana* by Liam Sanchez

- *Courageous Hearts: Stories of LGBTQ Activism in Zerana* edited by Maria Rodriguez

- *Marriage Equality and the Law: A Comparative Analysis of Zerana and Global Perspectives* by Jonathan Davis

These books offer comprehensive insights into the legal, social, and personal aspects of the fight for same-sex marriage and LGBTQ rights in Zerana.

Exercise: Reflecting on LGBTQ Rights

Think about your own country or community. Reflect on the progress made towards LGBTQ rights in recent years. Identify areas where there is still work to be done and brainstorm ways to contribute to the ongoing fight for equality and justice. Share your thoughts with friends, family, or in LGBTQ support groups to encourage dialogue and collaboration. Remember, change starts with individual actions and collective efforts.

Subsection: The Fight for Comprehensive LGBTQ-Inclusive Legislation

In this subsection, we delve into Saryn Brell's pivotal role in advocating for comprehensive LGBTQ-inclusive legislation in Zerana. Saryn's tireless efforts and unwavering determination have been instrumental in driving significant change and progress for the LGBTQ community. Through grassroots organizing, strategic lobbying, and coalition-building, Saryn has helped lay the foundation for a more inclusive and equal society.

The Current State of LGBTQ Rights in Zerana

To understand the significance of Saryn's fight for comprehensive LGBTQ-inclusive legislation, we must first examine the prevailing challenges faced by the LGBTQ community in Zerana. Despite some progress in recent years, LGBTQ individuals continue to experience discrimination, prejudice, and inequality in various aspects of their lives.

One of the major barriers to equality is the absence of comprehensive legislation that protects LGBTQ rights in areas such as employment, housing, healthcare, education, and public accommodations. Without explicit legal protections, LGBTQ individuals are vulnerable to discrimination, harassment, and unequal treatment.

Additionally, transgender individuals often face obstacles in obtaining legal recognition of their gender identity, accessing healthcare services, and navigating societal acceptance. The lack of legal protections and societal support further exacerbates the marginalization and discrimination faced by transgender individuals.

Advocating for LGBTQ-Inclusive Legislation

Saryn recognized the urgent need to address these disparities and fought tirelessly to secure comprehensive LGBTQ-inclusive legislation in Zerana. Their advocacy efforts centered on five key areas:

1. **Employment and Non-Discrimination Policies** Saryn sought to enact legislation that prohibits discrimination based on sexual orientation and gender identity in the workplace. They worked in close collaboration with LGBTQ organizations, labor unions, and progressive lawmakers to introduce and champion the passage of the Employment Non-Discrimination Act (ENDA).

    The ENDA aimed to protect LGBTQ individuals from being fired, denied a job, or facing adverse employment actions solely due to their sexual orientation or gender identity. Saryn rallied support by highlighting success stories of LGBTQ individuals who were unjustly discriminated against, raising awareness of the need for comprehensive employment protections.

2. **Housing and Public Accommodations** Recognizing that safe and inclusive housing is a fundamental right, Saryn focused their advocacy on legislation to protect LGBTQ individuals from housing discrimination. They collaborated with grassroots organizations, community leaders, and housing advocates to introduce the Fair Housing and Public Accommodations Act (FHPAA).

    The FHPAA aimed to prohibit landlords and housing providers from denying housing or imposing unfair terms and conditions based on a person's sexual orientation or gender identity. Saryn highlighted heartbreaking stories of LGBTQ individuals who were denied housing or faced eviction simply because of who they are, galvanizing public support for the legislation.

3. **Healthcare and Insurance Coverage** Saryn recognized the critical need for LGBTQ-inclusive healthcare policies and insurance coverage. They worked closely with healthcare professionals, LGBTQ health advocacy groups, and progressive lawmakers to propose the Comprehensive LGBTQ Healthcare Act (CLHA).

The CLHA sought to ensure that LGBTQ individuals have access to inclusive and culturally competent healthcare services without fear of discrimination or bias. Saryn emphasized the importance of healthcare providers receiving LGBTQ cultural competency training to provide quality care to the community. They also highlighted the significant health disparities faced by LGBTQ individuals, including mental health challenges and the need for gender-affirming healthcare.

4. LGBTQ-Inclusive Education Understanding that education plays a vital role in creating an inclusive society, Saryn advocated for LGBTQ-inclusive curriculum in schools. They collaborated with educators, LGBTQ youth organizations, and progressive policymakers to introduce the LGBTQ-Inclusive Education Act (LIEA).

The LIEA aimed to mandate that schools teach LGBTQ-inclusive history, literature, and health education, fostering a more inclusive learning environment for all students. Saryn stressed the importance of promoting acceptance, tolerance, and understanding among students and combating the harmful effects of bullying and discrimination.

5. Transgender Rights and Legal Recognition Saryn championed legislation that protects the rights of transgender individuals and ensures their legal recognition. They worked alongside transgender activists, legal experts, and supportive lawmakers to propose the Transgender Equality Act (TEA).

The TEA aimed to streamline the legal gender recognition process, prohibit discrimination against transgender individuals in various sectors, and ensure access to gender-affirming healthcare and social services. Saryn shared personal stories of transgender individuals who faced immense hurdles in having their identity recognized, underscoring the urgency for legal reforms.

Overcoming Challenges and Securing Victories

The fight for comprehensive LGBTQ-inclusive legislation was not without hurdles. Saryn faced opposition from conservative lawmakers, religious organizations, and individuals with deep-rooted biases. They encountered resistance from those who believed that LGBTQ rights were contrary to their religious or traditional values.

To overcome these challenges, Saryn employed a multi-faceted approach. They organized grassroots campaigns, mobilized LGBTQ communities, formed broad-based coalitions with allied organizations, and engaged in strategic lobbying efforts. Saryn leveraged public opinion through media appearances, community events, and powerful speeches that humanized the LGBTQ experience and debunked harmful stereotypes.

Moreover, Saryn engaged in dialogue with opponents, seeking to address their concerns and foster understanding. They facilitated discussions, organized town halls, and encouraged open-mindedness among adversaries. By emphasizing the shared values of equality, justice, and dignity, Saryn aimed to bridge ideological divides and build support for LGBTQ-inclusive legislation.

Through their unwavering dedication, Saryn achieved significant victories in the fight for comprehensive LGBTQ-inclusive legislation. Their efforts resulted in the passage of ENDA, FHPAA, CLHA, LIEA, and TEA, providing crucial legal protections and promoting inclusivity throughout Zerana.

The Legacy of Saryn's Advocacy

Saryn's fight for comprehensive LGBTQ-inclusive legislation created a lasting legacy that transcends borders. Their successes in Zerana inspired activists in other countries to push for similar reforms, sparking a global movement for LGBTQ rights.

The legislative victories achieved under Saryn's leadership have had a profound impact on the lives of LGBTQ individuals in Zerana. These laws have ensured equal opportunities, protected against discrimination, and fostered an inclusive society that respects and celebrates diversity.

However, Saryn's fight is not over. The ongoing struggle for LGBTQ rights requires continued activism, education, and awareness. Saryn's legacy serves as a reminder that change is possible, but it requires persistence, resilience, and a collective commitment from individuals and communities.

Further Resources and Concluding Thoughts

For readers eager to learn more about LGBTQ rights and advocacy, the following resources provide a deeper understanding of the issues discussed in this subsection:

1. *Transgender Rights: Exploring Issues and Debates* by Paisley Currah, Richard M. Juang, and Shannon Price Minter

2. *Sexual Orientation Politics: Identity, Citizenship, and Inclusion* edited by Jaime M. Grant, Lisa M. Hope, and M. V. Lee Badgett

3. *This Book is Gay* by Juno Dawson

4. *The LGBTQ Rights Movement: From Stonewall to Today* by Ellen Rodger

SECTION 1: FROM SMALL WINS TO BIG VICTORIES

In conclusion, Saryn Brell's fight for comprehensive LGBTQ-inclusive legislation in Zerana has been a transformative force in the ongoing struggle for equality and social justice. Through their visionary leadership, strategic advocacy, and unwavering determination, Saryn has set the stage for a more inclusive and equal society. However, the fight for LGBTQ rights continues, and it requires the collective efforts of individuals, communities, and policymakers to build upon Saryn's legacy and ensure a future of equality for all.

Subsection: Eradicating Conversion Therapy and other Harmful Practices

In this subsection, we delve into the important work of Saryn Brell in eradicating conversion therapy and other harmful practices targeting the LGBTQ community. Conversion therapy, also known as reparative therapy or ex-gay therapy, refers to efforts to change a person's sexual orientation or gender identity. It has been widely discredited and condemned by major medical and mental health associations worldwide due to its harmful and ineffective nature.

Understanding Conversion Therapy

Conversion therapy encompasses a range of practices, including talk therapy, religious interventions, aversion therapy, and even physical treatments like electric shocks. These practices are rooted in the false belief that being LGBTQ is a mental disorder or a sin that can and should be cured.

The consequences of conversion therapy can be devastating, leading to increased rates of depression, anxiety, self-harm, and suicide among LGBTQ individuals who have undergone such treatments. It is crucial to raise awareness about the harm caused by these practices and advocate for their complete abolition.

The Legal Battle

Saryn Brell recognized the urgency of fighting against conversion therapy and became a leading voice in the legal battle to ban these practices. They worked tirelessly to advocate for legislation that protects LGBTQ individuals from being subjected to conversion therapy, both as minors and adults.

In this fight, Saryn faced significant opposition from conservative religious groups and individuals who argue for the right to practice conversion therapy based on religious freedom. They also encountered resistance from some politicians who questioned the validity of conversion therapy survivors' testimonies and the science behind banning such practices.

Supporting Survivors and Advocating for Change

One of Saryn's key strategies in eradicating conversion therapy was to center and amplify the voices and experiences of survivors. They provided a platform for survivors to share their stories, creating a network of support and empowerment. By sharing these stories, Saryn aimed to humanize the issue and raise public awareness about the significant harm caused by conversion therapy.

Additionally, Saryn collaborated with mental health professionals, LGBTQ organizations, and allies to educate the public about the dangers of conversion therapy. They organized workshops, panel discussions, and training programs to equip mental health providers with the necessary knowledge and tools to support LGBTQ individuals without resorting to harmful and discriminatory practices.

Legislative Success and Ongoing Challenges

Through Saryn's tenacity and advocacy, they were instrumental in achieving legislative victories against conversion therapy. They championed the passing of comprehensive bans on conversion therapy in Zerana and collaborated with other activists to push for similar legislation in other parts of the country and internationally.

However, the fight to eradicate conversion therapy is far from over. Challenges persist, including implementing and enforcing the legislation, reaching remote or conservative areas where conversion therapy may still be practiced, and challenging the beliefs and attitudes that underpin these harmful practices.

Promoting Affirmative and Inclusive Mental Health Care

Alongside the efforts to ban conversion therapy, Saryn focused on promoting affirmative and inclusive mental health care for LGBTQ individuals. They highlighted the importance of mental health professionals using LGBTQ-affirming approaches that respect and affirm individuals' sexual orientations and gender identities.

Saryn collaborated with mental health organizations to develop guidelines and training programs that help mental health providers better understand the unique experiences and challenges faced by LGBTQ individuals. These initiatives aimed to create safe and inclusive spaces where LGBTQ individuals can seek support without fear of prejudice or discrimination.

Educating the Public and Challenging Stigma

To combat the stigma surrounding LGBTQ identities and counter the misinformation perpetuated by proponents of conversion therapy, Saryn embarked on a relentless public education campaign. They utilized various platforms, including social media, public speaking engagements, and media interviews, to dispel myths, challenge stereotypes, and promote acceptance and understanding.

Saryn's approach was captivating and thought-provoking, combining personal anecdotes, scientific research, and a touch of humor to engage a wide audience. By humanizing the LGBTQ experience, they were able to generate empathy and encourage others to challenge their preconceived notions and biases.

Conclusion

Saryn Brell's advocacy against conversion therapy and harmful practices has paved the way for significant achievements in LGBTQ rights. Their work to raise awareness, support survivors, and advocate for legislation has brought us closer to a future in which all individuals can live authentically without fear of being subjected to harmful and discriminatory practices.

As we reflect on Saryn's journey, it is essential to remember the resilience and strength they displayed throughout their activism. Their efforts serve as an inspiration, a reminder that change is possible, and that the fight for equality and dignity continues. By joining forces and challenging harmful beliefs and practices, we can help create a world where everyone is free to be their authentic selves.

Subsection: Expanding Protections for Transgender Individuals

In recent years, there has been a growing recognition of the unique challenges faced by transgender individuals in society. From access to healthcare and employment to discrimination and violence, transgender people have historically been marginalized and overlooked. In this subsection, we explore the efforts made to expand protections and rights for transgender individuals in Zerana.

The Current Climate

Before we dive into the progress made, it is essential to understand the existing climate for transgender individuals in Zerana. Many transgender people face discrimination in various aspects of their lives, including healthcare, housing, employment, and public accommodations. The lack of legal protections often leaves them vulnerable to discrimination, violence, and social exclusion.

Legal Protections

Efforts to expand legal protections for transgender individuals have gained momentum in recent years. In Zerana, landmark legislation has been introduced to address the discrimination faced by transgender people. The Transgender Rights Act, passed in 20XX, provides comprehensive legal protections for gender identity and expression.

Under this act, it is illegal to discriminate against transgender individuals in employment, housing, public accommodations, education, and healthcare. It ensures that transgender people can access essential services without fear of harassment or discrimination. Additionally, the act allows transgender individuals to change their legal gender marker on identification documents, ensuring their recognition and respect.

Healthcare Access

Access to inclusive and affirming healthcare is crucial for the wellbeing of transgender individuals. Recognizing this, Zerana has taken significant steps to improve healthcare access for transgender people. Insurance companies are now required to cover gender-affirming treatments, including hormone therapy and gender confirmation surgeries. Furthermore, medical professionals are receiving comprehensive training to better understand the specific healthcare needs of transgender patients.

Education and Public Awareness

Creating a more inclusive society begins with education and public awareness. Zerana has implemented education programs to promote understanding and acceptance of transgender individuals in schools and universities. These programs aim to counteract misinformation and reduce stigma surrounding transgender identities.

Public awareness campaigns have also played a crucial role in changing societal perceptions. Through media campaigns, workshops, and community events, Zerana is fostering empathy, understanding, and support for transgender individuals. By highlighting the challenges they face and their contributions to society, these campaigns have been pivotal in creating a more accepting environment.

Supportive Organizations

Supportive organizations and advocacy groups have been instrumental in advancing transgender rights in Zerana. These organizations provide resources, support, and legal assistance for transgender individuals facing discrimination. They also work closely with policymakers to push for legislation that protects the rights of transgender individuals. Through grassroots efforts and public engagement, these organizations have amplified the voices of transgender people and helped secure significant victories for their rights.

Championing Equality

While progress has been made in expanding protections for transgender individuals, there is still much work to be done. Advocates are continuing to fight for comprehensive legislation that addresses the specific needs of transgender people in areas such as employment, housing, and healthcare. Additionally, efforts are being made to challenge societal attitudes and dismantle the systemic barriers that transgender individuals face.

It is essential for individuals and communities to support the rights of transgender people actively. Allies can do so by educating themselves, challenging transphobic beliefs, and advocating for inclusive policies and practices in all areas of life. By championing equality and amplifying the voices of transgender individuals, we can work towards a more just and inclusive society for everyone.

Conclusion

The expansion of protections for transgender individuals in Zerana is a testament to the power of activism, advocacy, and legislative change. Through the Transgender Rights Act and other initiatives, significant progress has been made in ensuring equal rights and opportunities for transgender people. However, there is still much to be done to address the systemic challenges they face. By continuing to push for change, educating ourselves and others, and supporting transgender individuals, we can create a more inclusive and just society for everyone.

Subsection: Celebrating Milestones and Reflecting on Progress

In this subsection, we will explore the milestones achieved and progress made in LGBTQ rights as we celebrate Saryn Brell's incredible journey as an LGBTQ activist. We will reflect on the challenges faced, the victories won, and the ongoing fight for equality.

Background: The LGBTQ rights movement has made significant strides over the years, with milestones such as the decriminalization of same-sex relationships, the recognition of same-sex marriages, and the increased visibility and acceptance of transgender individuals. However, there is still much work to be done to achieve full equality and eradicate discrimination.

Principles: The principles guiding the LGBTQ rights movement include equality, inclusivity, and the recognition of fundamental human rights for all individuals, regardless of their sexual orientation or gender identity. Activists like Saryn Brell have played a crucial role in raising awareness, challenging societal norms, and pushing for legal and social change.

Progress Made: Over the years, there have been several significant milestones in the fight for LGBTQ equality. For example:

1. **Legalizing Same-Sex Marriage:** One of the most significant victories in LGBTQ rights has been the legalization of same-sex marriage. Saryn Brell and other activists tirelessly worked to challenge discriminatory laws and fought for marriage equality. Their efforts led to landmark court decisions and legislative changes, which recognized the right of same-sex couples to marry and receive the same legal benefits and protections as heterosexual couples.

2. **Inclusive Legislation:** Another milestone in LGBTQ rights is the enactment of inclusive legislation. Activists like Saryn have advocated for comprehensive laws that protect LGBTQ individuals from discrimination in housing, employment, public accommodations, and other areas. These laws aim to create a more inclusive society and ensure equal opportunities for everyone, regardless of their sexual orientation or gender identity.

3. **Combatting Harmful Practices:** Advocacy efforts have also focused on eradicating harmful practices targeting LGBTQ individuals, such as conversion therapy. Saryn and fellow activists have worked relentlessly to raise awareness about the damaging effects of conversion therapy and push for its ban. Through their efforts, more jurisdictions have taken steps to outlaw this practice and protect LGBTQ youth from the harm it causes.

Challenges and Solutions: Despite significant progress, the fight for LGBTQ equality continues to face challenges. Some of the challenges include:

- **Resistance and Opposition:** LGBTQ activists often face resistance from individuals and groups that hold discriminatory views or are resistant to

SECTION 1: FROM SMALL WINS TO BIG VICTORIES

change. These opponents may use religion, tradition, or cultural beliefs to justify their discriminatory actions. In the face of such challenges, activists like Saryn Brell have employed various strategies to challenge misconceptions, promote understanding, and highlight the importance of equality and inclusivity.

- **Legislative Barriers:** Achieving full LGBTQ equality requires overcoming legislative barriers that impede progress. While some jurisdictions have made significant strides through inclusive legislation, others still have laws that discriminate against LGBTQ individuals. Lobbying, grassroots organizing, and public education are tools activists use to challenge discriminatory laws and promote legislative change.

- **Intersectionality and Inclusivity:** The LGBTQ rights movement has increasingly embraced the principles of intersectionality, recognizing that discrimination against individuals varies based on factors such as race, ethnicity, socioeconomic status, and disability. Activists like Saryn Brell have made it a point to ensure that the fight for LGBTQ rights includes and addresses the unique challenges faced by marginalized communities within the LGBTQ umbrella. This approach allows for a more comprehensive understanding of the struggles faced by LGBTQ individuals and fosters a more inclusive movement.

Examples and Resources: To better understand the milestones achieved and progress made in LGBTQ rights, we can look at specific examples and resources:

- **Stonewall Riots:** The Stonewall Riots in 1969 marked a turning point in the LGBTQ rights movement, leading to increased visibility and activism. Books like "Stonewall: The Riots That Sparked the Gay Revolution" by David Carter provide a comprehensive account of this milestone event.

- **Human Rights Campaign (HRC):** The HRC is a prominent LGBTQ advocacy organization that provides resources and information on LGBTQ rights. Their publications, reports, and website offer valuable insights into the milestones and progress of the LGBTQ rights movement.

- **Legal Cases and Court Decisions:** Landmark legal cases and court decisions have played a significant role in advancing LGBTQ rights. Examples include Obergefell v. Hodges (2015), which legalized same-sex marriage in the United States, and R. v. Morgentaler (1988), which decriminalized abortion in Canada. Exploring these cases and their impact can shed light on the milestones achieved in LGBTQ rights.

Unconventional Approach: One unconventional yet powerful approach to celebrating milestones and reflecting on progress is through storytelling. Sharing personal narratives, experiences, and struggles not only humanizes the LGBTQ rights movement but also helps build empathy and understanding among individuals who may not be familiar with the challenges faced by the LGBTQ community.

By highlighting the stories of LGBTQ individuals and their allies, we can create a deeper connection, challenge stereotypes, and inspire others to join the fight for equality. Documentaries, memoirs, and other forms of media that capture personal stories can be powerful tools in this process.

Conclusion: Celebrating milestones and reflecting on progress is an integral part of the LGBTQ rights movement. In this subsection, we explored achievements such as the legalization of same-sex marriage, the enactment of inclusive legislation, and the fight against harmful practices. We also discussed the challenges faced and provided examples and resources for further exploration. As we continue Saryn Brell's inspiring journey, it is important to recognize how far we have come while remaining committed to achieving full equality for all LGBTQ individuals.

Subsection: The Constant Battle for Equality

In this section, we will delve into the ongoing challenges faced by Saryn Brell and the LGBTQ community in their fight for equality. We will explore the persistent barriers they have encountered and the strategies employed to overcome them. Through this exploration, we aim to highlight the importance of resilience, determination, and collective action in the pursuit of social change.

The Struggle for Legal Protection

One of the primary obstacles in the battle for LGBTQ rights has been the lack of comprehensive legal protection. Discrimination in employment, housing, and public accommodations has been a pervasive issue, leading to societal marginalization and inequality. Saryn Brell, along with other activists, recognized the urgency of enacting legislation to safeguard the rights of LGBTQ individuals.

One key milestone in this ongoing struggle was Saryn's instrumental role in legalizing same-sex marriage in Zerana. Through lobbying efforts, grassroots campaigns, and strategic alliances, Saryn and their allies advocated for equal rights and challenged the prevailing conservative ideologies. This achievement was a testament to the power of persistence and collective action in the face of staunch opposition.

However, the battle for comprehensive LGBTQ-inclusive legislation did not stop with marriage equality. Saryn and their supporters continued to push for laws that would protect LGBTQ individuals from discrimination in all spheres of life. They actively worked towards the eradication of conversion therapy and other harmful practices that perpetuated discrimination and stigma.

Addressing Societal Prejudice and Bias

While legal advancements were critical in the fight for LGBTQ equality, tackling societal prejudice and bias posed an ongoing challenge. Saryn and their allies had to confront deeply entrenched stereotypes and homophobia that perpetuated discrimination and inequality at an interpersonal level.

Through public speaking engagements, educational workshops, and media appearances, Saryn advocated for the destigmatization of LGBTQ identities and promoted acceptance and understanding. They shared personal stories, debunked stereotypes, and offered a counter-narrative to challenge the prevailing biases.

One of the unconventional, yet effective, strategies employed by Saryn was the use of humor and wit to disarm prejudice. Through their engaging and often hilarious speeches, Saryn showcased the absurdity of heteronormative assumptions and encouraged people to question their own biases. This approach not only entertained audiences but also facilitated open dialogue and fostered empathy.

Combatting Online Harassment and Trolling

The advent of social media brought about new challenges in the battle for equality, with online harassment and trolling becoming pervasive issues. Saryn, like many LGBTQ activists, became the target of hate speech, threats, and misinformation campaigns on various digital platforms.

To address this issue, Saryn employed a multi-faceted approach. They collaborated with online platforms to implement stricter policies against hate speech and harassment, ensuring a safer space for LGBTQ individuals. They also worked with cybersecurity experts to enhance personal online security measures and raise awareness about the dangers of online harassment.

Furthermore, Saryn initiated campaigns to counter online hate with messages of love and support. They encouraged their followers and allies to show solidarity by actively combating hate speech and amplifying positive narratives. This grassroots approach proved effective in creating resilient communities and fostering a sense of belonging.

The Personal Sacrifices of LGBTQ Activism

It is crucial to acknowledge the personal sacrifices made by LGBTQ activists, including Saryn Brell, in their tireless pursuit of equality. The constant battle for change takes a significant toll on their mental, emotional, and physical well-being.

Saryn, like many activists, experienced burnout and mental health struggles as a result of their relentless efforts. Balancing personal challenges, relationships, and self-care with advocacy work became an ongoing juggling act. Recognizing the importance of self-preservation, Saryn advocated for establishing support networks and fostering a culture of care within the LGBTQ community.

Saryn's story serves as a reminder that activism is a marathon, not a sprint. It requires resilience, self-awareness, and a commitment to personal well-being. By sharing their vulnerabilities and navigating these challenges openly, Saryn inspired others to prioritize self-care and seek support when needed.

Fostering Unity and Collaboration

The fight for LGBTQ equality cannot be won by a single individual or organization. It requires collaboration, coalition-building, and partnership with diverse stakeholders. Saryn understood the importance of fostering unity within the LGBTQ community and reaching out to potential allies.

They actively built bridges with politicians, celebrities, and religious leaders who shared their vision of equality. Saryn recognized the value of finding common ground and working together towards a shared goal. While this approach faced criticism and resistance from some within the LGBTQ community, Saryn remained steadfast in their belief that collaboration was essential for effecting lasting change.

Through collective action, LGBTQ activists like Saryn have been able to amplify their voices, mobilize on a larger scale, and challenge discriminatory policies and practices effectively.

Conclusion

The constant battle for equality faced by Saryn Brell and other LGBTQ activists underscores the persistent struggle against discrimination and bias. From challenging discriminatory laws to combatting societal prejudice, activists like Saryn continue to push boundaries and create change.

Through their unwavering determination, resilience, and collaborative efforts, Saryn and their allies make progress towards a more inclusive society. Their stories of personal sacrifice, self-care, and strategic advocacy serve as inspiration for future LGBTQ activists, reminding us that the fight for equality is an ongoing endeavor that requires unity, resilience, and a commitment to social change.

Section 2: Speaking Truth to Power

Subsection: Confronting Political Opposition and Bigotry

In this subsection, we delve into one of the most challenging aspects of Saryn's activism journey – confronting political opposition and bigotry. Throughout her career, Saryn faced resistance from individuals, groups, and even entire political systems that were resistant to LGBTQ rights and equality. This subsection explores the strategies she employed, the obstacles she encountered, and the impact of her tireless efforts to combat bigotry.

Challenges and Obstacles

Confronting political opposition and bigotry is no easy task. Saryn encountered a myriad of challenges throughout her activism journey, testing her resolve and determination. Some of the key obstacles she faced include:

- **Legal Roadblocks:** Existing laws and policies that discriminated against the LGBTQ community posed major hurdles. Saryn had to navigate through a complex legal landscape, identifying discriminatory statutes and advocating for their amendment or removal.

- **Stigma and Prejudice:** The deeply ingrained societal stigma and prejudice towards the LGBTQ community presented a significant barrier. Saryn had to confront and challenge the prevailing attitudes, debunking stereotypes and promoting greater understanding and acceptance.

- **Opposition from Religious Organizations:** Religious organizations, with their strong influence on public opinion and policymaking, often stood in direct opposition to LGBTQ rights. Saryn faced hostility from these institutions, requiring her to engage in constructive dialogue and bridge the gap between religious beliefs and LGBTQ rights.

Strategies and Actions

To tackle political opposition and bigotry, Saryn employed a range of strategies and took decisive actions. Let's explore some of the key approaches she adopted:

- **Education and Awareness:** Saryn understood the power of knowledge and education in dismantling bigotry. She spearheaded awareness campaigns, conducting workshops, and organizing panel discussions to foster understanding and empathy among politicians, community leaders, and the general public.

- **Coalition Building:** Recognizing the strength in unity, Saryn actively sought partnerships with like-minded organizations and individuals to amplify their collective voices. By forging strategic alliances, she created a broader coalition that could exert more significant pressure on politicians and policymakers.

- **Political Lobbying:** Saryn recognized the importance of engaging directly with political leaders to influence policy change. Through targeted lobbying efforts, she sought to highlight the urgency of LGBTQ rights, presenting evidence-based arguments and personal stories to sway decision-makers.

- **Nonviolent Resistance:** Inspired by the teachings of civil rights activists before her, Saryn embraced nonviolent resistance as a powerful tool to confront political opposition. Peaceful protests, sit-ins, and demonstrations became an integral part of her activism, garnering media attention and raising public awareness.

Real-World Examples

To illustrate the effectiveness of Saryn's strategies, let's examine a couple of real-world examples where she successfully confronted political opposition and bigotry:

- **Campaign for LGBTQ-Inclusive Curricula:** Saryn spearheaded a campaign to introduce LGBTQ-inclusive curricula in schools. She worked closely with educators, parents, and LGBTQ organizations to develop comprehensive educational materials that promoted acceptance and inclusion. Through persistent lobbying and constructive dialogue with policymakers, she managed to secure approval for the inclusion of LGBTQ history and contributions in the school curriculum, challenging the political opposition head-on.

- **Advocacy for Conversion Therapy Bans:** Saryn recognized the harm inflicted by conversion therapy and made it a priority to advocate for its ban. She organized rallies, brought forward survivors' stories, and conducted research studies highlighting the negative effects of this harmful practice. Her relentless efforts paid off when she successfully lobbied for the passage of legislation that banned conversion therapy in Zerana, further diminishing the scope for bigotry within the political system.

Caveats and Unconventional Approaches

Confronting political opposition and bigotry requires resilience and adaptability. Saryn understood that conventional approaches might not always yield the desired results. Here are two unconventional approaches she incorporated into her activism:

- **Personal Storytelling:** Saryn encouraged fellow activists and LGBTQ individuals to share their personal stories, humanizing the struggles faced by the community. By fostering empathy through storytelling, she effectively challenged stereotypes and changed hearts and minds.

- **Using Humor as a Weapon:** Saryn employed humor as a powerful tool to disarm opponents and challenge their prejudices. She utilized satire, comedy sketches, and memes to expose the absurdity behind discriminatory beliefs, often leading to reflection and introspection among those who held bigoted views.

Conclusion

Confronting political opposition and bigotry is an ongoing battle in the fight for LGBTQ rights. Saryn Brell's unwavering commitment to challenging the status quo and combating prejudice played a pivotal role in reshaping public opinion and influencing policy change. Her strategies, actions, and unconventional approaches provide valuable lessons for activists everywhere, highlighting the importance of perseverance, coalition-building, education, and the power of personal storytelling. As we continue this unauthorized biography, we explore the triumphs and tribulations that await Saryn in her relentless pursuit of equality and justice.

Subsection: Standing Up to Religious Organizations and Conservative Ideologies

In Saryn Brell's journey as an LGBTQ activist, one of the most challenging aspects has been confronting religious organizations and conservative ideologies. These powerful entities often perpetuate discrimination and hold deeply ingrained beliefs that hinder the progress of LGBTQ rights. In this subsection, we will explore the strategies employed by Saryn to challenge these institutions and promote inclusivity.

Religious organizations, with their dogmas and longstanding traditions, have traditionally been resistant to change. Many religious doctrines view homosexuality as a sin or consider it to be against the natural order. As an activist, Saryn encountered numerous religious organizations that opposed LGBTQ rights, and sought to address the misconceptions and prejudices perpetuated by these institutions.

To tackle this issue, Saryn became an advocate for open dialogue and engagement with religious leaders and believers. Recognizing the importance of religious freedom, they emphasized that acceptance of LGBTQ individuals does not require abandoning religious beliefs. Saryn's approach involved respectfully challenging religious interpretations and highlighting the importance of love, compassion, and acceptance within religious teachings.

One of the strategies Saryn employed was organizing interfaith dialogues and panel discussions. These events provided a platform for religious leaders, LGBTQ individuals, and advocates to discuss their perspectives openly. By fostering understanding and challenging stereotypes, Saryn aimed to bridge the gap between religion and LGBTQ rights. These discussions often addressed biblical interpretations, historical context, and the evolving nature of religious beliefs.

Additionally, Saryn leveraged their own personal story to connect with religious communities. By sharing their experiences, struggles, and the journey to self-acceptance, they aimed to humanize LGBTQ individuals and challenge stereotypes. Through storytelling and vulnerability, Saryn highlighted the fact that sexual orientation and gender identity are not choices, but inherent qualities.

It's important to note that Saryn's approach was not without its criticisms and challenges. They faced staunch opposition from conservative ideologies that viewed LGBTQ rights as an attack on traditional values. Conservative leaders often framed LGBTQ activism as a threat to family structures and religious freedom. However, Saryn remained steadfast in their commitment to inclusivity and equality.

To navigate this complex landscape, Saryn employed various strategies to counter conservative ideologies. One such approach was using data and research to debunk common myths and misconceptions. They collaborated with scholars, experts, and LGBTQ organizations to compile comprehensive resources that countered unfounded claims made by conservative groups.

Furthermore, Saryn engaged in strategic media campaigns to challenge conservative narratives. They utilized social media, interviews, and public speaking engagements to address the concerns and fears propagated by conservative ideologies. By presenting facts, sharing personal stories, and promoting empathy, Saryn aimed to shift public opinion and challenge conservative beliefs.

Saryn also recognized the importance of creating alliances with progressive religious organizations and leaders who were supportive of LGBTQ rights. By working together, they aimed to foster an environment that accepted diversity and championed equality. Saryn collaborated with these allies to organize events, initiatives, and campaigns that challenged conservative ideologies from within religious spaces.

One of the unconventional yet effective methods employed by Saryn was utilizing humor and satire to expose the inconsistencies and hypocrisies of conservative ideologies. Through engaging storytelling, clever satirical skits, and parodies, Saryn challenged the rigid beliefs and opened up conversations in a non-threatening manner. This approach allowed them to reach audiences who might have otherwise dismissed LGBTQ issues.

In conclusion, standing up to religious organizations and conservative ideologies has been a significant aspect of Saryn's activism. By engaging in respectful dialogue, debunking myths, utilizing strategic media campaigns, and building alliances with progressive religious organizations, Saryn worked to challenge prejudices and promote inclusivity. Their commitment to opening hearts and minds, and the ability to bridge the gap between different viewpoints, has contributed greatly to the progress of LGBTQ rights. Despite the challenges faced, Saryn's determination to stand up against religious organizations and conservative ideologies serves as an inspiration to activists fighting for equality worldwide.

Subsection: Debunking Stereotypes and Overcoming Prejudice

Stereotypes and prejudice against the LGBTQ community have been deeply ingrained in society for centuries. In this subsection, we will explore the importance of debunking these stereotypes and discuss strategies to overcome prejudice.

Challenging Stereotypes

Stereotypes are oversimplified generalizations about a particular group of people, often based on assumptions or limited understanding. They can be harmful as they perpetuate negative biases and reinforce discrimination. It is crucial to challenge these stereotypes in order to create a more inclusive and accepting society.

One common stereotype surrounding LGBTQ individuals is that they are promiscuous or sexually deviant. This harmful portrayal not only dehumanizes LGBTQ people but also ignores the diversity within the community. To debunk this stereotype, it is important to highlight LGBTQ individuals who have healthy and committed relationships, just like anyone else. Including these positive examples in public discourse and media representation can help dispel the misconception.

Another stereotype often associated with the LGBTQ community is the idea that being LGBTQ is a choice or a phase. This misconception disregards the experiences and struggles of LGBTQ individuals. To challenge this stereotype, we can share personal stories and experiences of individuals who have known their sexual orientation or gender identity from a young age. By creating empathy and understanding, we can break down the notion that being LGBTQ is a choice.

Educating and Empowering

Educating society about the realities of LGBTQ lives is crucial in overcoming prejudice. This education can take many forms, from schools implementing LGBTQ-inclusive curricula to community workshops and awareness campaigns. By providing accurate information, we can combat ignorance and challenge harmful stereotypes.

Empowering LGBTQ individuals to share their personal stories can also be an effective tool in combating prejudice. When people hear firsthand accounts of discrimination and the impact it has on individuals' lives, it helps break down barriers and fosters empathy. Creating safe spaces for LGBTQ individuals to share their experiences can contribute to reducing prejudice.

Promoting Intersectionality

Intersectionality recognizes that individuals can experience multiple forms of oppression simultaneously. It is important to highlight the diverse experiences within the LGBTQ community, including those of LGBTQ people of color, transgender individuals, and individuals with disabilities, among others.

By acknowledging and addressing the unique challenges faced by different groups within the LGBTQ community, we can work towards creating an inclusive movement that leaves no one behind. This means amplifying the voices of those who are marginalized within the community and ensuring that their experiences are heard and validated.

Fostering Personal Connections

Overcoming prejudice often requires individuals to challenge their preconceived notions and engage in meaningful dialogue. By fostering personal connections between people from different backgrounds, we can bridge the gap of understanding and break down stereotypes.

Encouraging LGBTQ individuals and allies to share their stories and engage in conversations with individuals who may hold prejudiced views can be a powerful tool for change. This can be facilitated through support groups, community events, or even online forums. The ultimate goal is to create a safe space for open and honest communication, leading to increased understanding and empathy.

Real-World Example

To illustrate the impact of debunking stereotypes and overcoming prejudice, let's consider the story of Alex, a transgender man. Alex had always known that his gender identity did not align with the sex assigned to him at birth. Throughout his life, he faced discrimination and prejudice from those who did not understand or accept transgender identities.

However, by openly sharing his story and educating others about transgender experiences, Alex was able to challenge stereotypes and misconceptions. Through public speaking engagements, media interviews, and his online presence, he provided an opportunity for others to learn and grow. His bravery and willingness to engage in dialogue helped change hearts and minds and contributed to a more accepting society.

Conclusion

Debunking stereotypes and overcoming prejudice against the LGBTQ community is an ongoing battle. By challenging harmful stereotypes, educating and empowering individuals, promoting intersectionality, fostering personal connections, and sharing real-life stories, we can work towards a world that embraces diversity and celebrates LGBTQ identities. It is through these efforts that we can create a more inclusive and accepting society for all.

Subsection: Braving Online Harassment and Trolling

In today's digital age, where social media platforms and online forums dominate our communication channels, LGBTQ activists like Saryn Brell face a new set of challenges. One of the most prevalent threats they encounter is online harassment and trolling. In this subsection, we will explore the difficulties activists face in the digital world, strategies to combat online hate, and the importance of resilience and self-care.

The Rise of Online Harassment

With the exponential growth of social media platforms, online anonymity has emboldened individuals to engage in hateful and harassing behavior. For LGBTQ activists like Saryn Brell, this means being subjected to derogatory comments, threats, and even doxxing – the malicious act of exposing personal information to incite harm. Such online abuse can take a devastating toll on activists' mental health, personal lives, and overall well-being.

Recognizing Different Forms of Online Harassment

Online harassment can manifest in various forms, ranging from derogatory comments to organized campaigns of hate. Some common tactics include:

- **Trolling**: Purposefully disrupting online discussions with inflammatory remarks to incite emotional responses.

- **Bullying**: Consistently targeting individuals with personal attacks, derogatory language, and threats.

- **Doxxing**: Sharing private information, such as home addresses or phone numbers, to encourage offline harm.

- **Hate Speech**: Engaging in discriminatory, derogatory, or dehumanizing language to demean LGBTQ individuals and activists.

Strategies to Combat Online Hate

Braving online harassment and trolling requires a multi-faceted approach that focuses on self-care, cybersecurity, and community support. Here are some strategies that activists can employ:

- **Building a Support Network:** Connecting with fellow activists and LGBTQ communities provides a safe space to share experiences and seek advice, amplifying the collective strength in combating online harassment.

- **Implementing Cybersecurity Measures:** Activists should ensure their online accounts are secure by using strong, unique passwords, enabling two-factor authentication, and regularly updating privacy settings.

- **Reporting and Blocking:** Most social media platforms have reporting mechanisms to report abusive behavior. Activists should not hesitate to block or mute individuals who engage in harassment to maintain their mental health and well-being.

- **Engaging Allies:** Encouraging allies to actively participate in countering online hate can help amplify positive messages and drown out negativity. This collective effort promotes a more inclusive and supportive online environment.

Practicing Resilience and Self-Care

Being an LGBTQ activist subjected to online harassment can be emotionally draining. It is crucial for activists like Saryn Brell to prioritize self-care, mental health, and emotional well-being. Here are some self-care practices that can help navigate the challenges of online hate:

- **Setting Boundaries:** Activists should establish boundaries in terms of their online presence and engagement. This could include limiting exposure to negative comments or taking breaks from social media when necessary.

- **Seeking Professional Support:** Engaging with mental health professionals who specialize in trauma and cyberbullying can provide activists with the necessary tools and coping mechanisms to navigate the emotional impact of online harassment.

- **Engaging in Offline Activities:** Dedicate time to activities that bring joy and a sense of fulfillment outside of online activism. This can help recharge and maintain a sense of perspective.

- **Practicing Mindfulness and Meditation:** Exploring mindfulness techniques and meditation practices can foster resilience, reduce stress, and promote emotional well-being.

The Power of Positive Engagement

While it is necessary to address and combat online hate, activists should also focus on building positive online spaces. Engaging in constructive dialogue, sharing personal stories, and highlighting achievements within the LGBTQ community can help foster understanding, empathy, and acceptance. By promoting positivity, activists can counteract the harmful effects of online harassment and create meaningful change in public opinion.

Unconventional Perspective: The Mute Button

In the realm of online activism, sometimes the most effective response to online harassment is silence. Activists can employ the power of the "mute" button to disengage from harmful conversations or individuals who only seek to incite anger. By recognizing that not every battle needs to be fought, activists can conserve their emotional energy for issues that truly matter and prioritize their well-being.

In conclusion, online harassment and trolling pose significant challenges for LGBTQ activists like Saryn Brell. By recognizing different forms of harassment, implementing strategies to combat online hate, practicing self-care, and promoting positive engagement, activists can navigate the digital landscape while preserving their mental health and continuing their fight for equality.

Subsection: Saryn's Personal Sacrifices for the Cause

Saryn Brell's journey as an LGBTQ activist has been marked by numerous personal sacrifices. Their unwavering commitment to the cause has demanded significant sacrifices in various aspects of their life. In this subsection, we will explore the sacrifices Saryn has made and the challenges they have faced along the way.

One of the most significant personal sacrifices Saryn has made is in their relationships. Activism often requires immense dedication, leaving little time for personal connections. Saryn's relentless pursuit of LGBTQ rights has meant sacrificing precious moments with friends and loved ones. They have missed family gatherings, birthdays, and important milestones in the lives of those closest to them. However, Saryn recognizes the urgency and importance of their work, accepting these sacrifices as a necessary part of their mission.

Another sacrifice Saryn has endured is the constant threat to their personal safety. LGBTQ activists like Saryn often face harassment, intimidation, and even physical violence. They have been targeted by hate groups, faced death threats, and experienced online harassment. Despite these dangers, Saryn remains undeterred, knowing that their activism is a beacon of hope for countless individuals who are marginalized and oppressed.

Financial stability is yet another sacrifice that Saryn has had to make. Activism is rarely lucrative, and Saryn has faced financial hardships as a result. They have worked multiple jobs, living frugally to sustain their advocacy work. Saryn understands that financial stability is not their primary focus; rather, it is the pursuit of justice and equality for all LGBTQ individuals. Their commitment to the cause is unwavering, even in the face of financial uncertainty.

Furthermore, Saryn has sacrificed their privacy and personal space. As their activism gained prominence, Saryn became a public figure, constantly scrutinized by the media and the public. Their every move, both online and offline, is analyzed and criticized. Privacy becomes a luxury almost unattainable. Saryn's personal life is a subject of public interest, and maintaining personal boundaries has become a challenge. However, they remain steadfast in their mission, knowing that their sacrifices contribute to raising awareness and effecting change.

The sacrifices Saryn has made are not without their emotional toll. Activism can be an emotionally challenging endeavor, often leading to burnout, stress, and mental health struggles. Saryn has had to battle with emotional fatigue, experiencing moments of doubt and weariness. However, they have developed coping mechanisms and self-care practices to navigate these emotional challenges. Saryn reminds themselves of the larger purpose of their activism and seeks support from friends, allies, and mental health professionals when needed.

It is worth noting that personal sacrifices in activism are not unique to Saryn alone. Many activists find themselves making similar sacrifices along their journey for social change. The sacrifices made by Saryn and countless others demonstrate the incredible dedication and resilience required to fight for justice and equality.

As readers, we can learn from Saryn's sacrifices. Their story reminds us of the importance of staying committed to causes that require sacrifice and personal dedication. It demonstrates the power of collective action and the transformative potential of individuals who are willing to put everything on the line for what they believe in.

By recognizing the sacrifices made by activists like Saryn, we can truly appreciate the depth of their contributions to society. Their stories inspire us to be more engaged, more empathetic, and more determined in our own pursuits for a better world. Saryn's sacrifices serve as a reminder that true change often comes at a personal cost, but it is a cost worth paying for a more just and inclusive society.

Note: This subsection provides an overview of the sacrifices Saryn Brell has made as an LGBTQ activist. It highlights the personal, emotional, financial, and safety sacrifices that often come with the territory of advocacy. The subsection aims to shed light on the challenges faced by activists and inspire readers to appreciate the dedication and resilience required to create lasting change.

Subsection: The Emotional Toll of Advocacy

Advocating for LGBTQ rights can be an incredibly rewarding experience, but it also comes with its fair share of emotional challenges. In this subsection, we will explore the emotional toll that advocacy can take on activists like Saryn Brell and discuss coping mechanisms and self-care practices to protect one's mental health.

Navigating Emotional Struggles

Advocacy work can be emotionally draining, as it often involves confronting bigotry, discrimination, and hate. Activists like Saryn Brell face constant opposition and backlash from those who seek to maintain the status quo. The emotional toll of advocacy is often undervalued and overlooked, but it is crucial to address these struggles to ensure the well-being of activists.

One of the primary emotional challenges faced by LGBTQ activists is dealing with the negativity and hate directed towards them. Activists often face personal attacks, online harassment, and hate speech. It can be disheartening and emotionally exhausting to constantly fight against discrimination and bigotry.

Moreover, the weight of responsibility can take a toll on activists. Saryn, like many others, feels a deep sense of duty towards the LGBTQ community, which can lead to burnout and emotional depletion. There is a constant pressure to speak up, fight for change, and be a role model for others. This burden can be overwhelming at times.

Coping Mechanisms and Self-Care Practices

Recognizing the emotional toll of advocacy is the first step towards taking care of one's mental health. Here are some coping mechanisms and self-care practices that activists, including Saryn, have found helpful:

- **Creating boundaries:** Setting boundaries is essential for self-preservation. Activists need to establish limits on their time, energy, and emotional investment. Learning to say no and prioritizing self-care is crucial.
- **Building a support network:** Surrounding oneself with a supportive community can provide emotional validation and understanding. The LGBTQ community and allies often serve as a source of strength and encouragement for activists like Saryn.

- **Seeking therapy or counseling:** Professional therapy or counseling can provide activists with a safe space to process their emotions, navigate their challenges, and develop coping strategies. It is essential to destigmatize seeking mental health support.

- **Engaging in self-reflection:** Taking time to reflect on personal values, motivations, and goals helps activists stay connected to their purpose. Journaling, meditation, or engaging in self-reflection exercises can provide clarity and emotional grounding.

- **Practicing self-compassion:** Activists often hold themselves to high standards and may experience self-criticism. Practicing self-compassion involves treating oneself with kindness, understanding, and forgiveness. Remembering that self-care is not selfish but essential for long-term advocacy is critical.

- **Engaging in hobbies and self-care activities:** Activists need to have activities outside of their advocacy work to recharge and find joy. Engaging in hobbies, spending time with loved ones, exercising, or simply taking time for oneself can all contribute to emotional well-being.

- **Maintaining work-life balance:** Activists need to establish a healthy work-life balance to prevent burnout. It is important to prioritize rest, relaxation, and leisure activities to maintain physical and emotional well-being.

The Importance of Emotional Resilience

While acknowledging the emotional toll of advocacy is vital, it is equally important to foster emotional resilience. Emotional resilience refers to one's ability to adapt, bounce back from setbacks, and maintain a sense of well-being in the face of adversity. Developing emotional resilience allows activists to continue their advocacy work while taking care of their mental health.

Building emotional resilience involves:

- **Building a positive mindset:** Cultivating optimism and focusing on one's strengths can help activists overcome challenges and setbacks.

- **Developing effective coping strategies:** Identifying healthy and adaptive coping mechanisms, such as deep breathing exercises, mindfulness techniques, or engaging in creative outlets, can help manage stress and emotional tension.

- **Building emotional intelligence:** Emotional intelligence involves recognizing and understanding one's emotions, as well as empathizing with others. Developing emotional intelligence helps activists navigate their own emotions, handle conflicts, and build positive relationships.

- **Engaging in self-care routines:** Regular self-care practices and routines can help maintain emotional well-being. This includes getting enough sleep, eating a balanced diet, and engaging in activities that bring joy and relaxation.

- **Seeking support and connection:** Activists should lean on their support networks, attend support groups or seek mentorship from experienced activists. Connecting with others who share similar experiences can provide invaluable emotional support and guidance.

Addressing Emotional Challenges through Activism

It is essential to recognize that advocating for LGBTQ rights can also be empowering and therapeutic. Turning negative emotions into productive action can help activists regain a sense of purpose, hope, and accomplishment. Activism allows individuals to channel their emotions into advocacy work, creating real change and finding healing in the process.

Real-world Example: Saryn Brell channeled her anger and frustration about the discrimination she faced into passionate speeches, political campaigns, and community activism. By addressing her emotional challenges head-on through advocacy, Saryn not only fought for change but also found personal fulfillment and healing.

Remembering the Need for Self-Preservation

While the emotional toll of advocacy should not be ignored, it is crucial to strike a balance between activism and self-preservation. Activists like Saryn Brell must prioritize their mental health and well-being to sustain long-term change. Taking breaks, setting boundaries, and engaging in self-care practices should not be seen as a sign of weakness, but rather as a means of ensuring a sustainable and impactful advocacy journey.

Beyond the Subsection

In the next section, we will explore the importance of allies and adversaries in the fight for LGBTQ rights. We will discuss the significance of building bridges and

SECTION 2: SPEAKING TRUTH TO POWER

fostering unity, as well as the challenges of facing resistance both within and outside the LGBTQ community.

Section 3: The Dark Side of Activism

Subsection: Burnout and Mental Health Struggles

In the pursuit of advocacy and activism, Saryn Brell faced numerous challenges, including the toll it took on their mental health. This subsection explores the concept of burnout and the various mental health struggles that activists like Saryn often face.

Understanding Burnout

Burnout is a state of emotional, physical, and mental exhaustion caused by excessive and prolonged stress. It is a common experience for activists who tirelessly fight for social change. The demands of advocacy work, combined with the personal and societal pressures, can drain one's energy and erode their sense of fulfillment.

The Factors Contributing to Burnout

1. Emotional and Compassion Fatigue: Advocacy involves engaging with emotional and distressing issues, which can lead to emotional fatigue. Constant exposure to the pain and trauma experienced by marginalized communities can take a toll on an activist's emotional well-being.
    2. High Expectations and Perfectionism: Activists, including Saryn, often set high standards for themselves and feel a sense of responsibility to create meaningful change. The constant pressure to achieve progress can lead to burnout and self-doubt.
    3. Limited Resources: Activists frequently face limited resources, be it funding, support, or time. This can lead to feelings of frustration, exhaustion, and a lack of motivation.
    4. Lack of Work-Life Balance: Advocacy work often demands significant time and energy, making it challenging for activists to maintain a healthy work-life balance. This imbalance can contribute to increased stress and burnout.

Recognizing the Signs and Symptoms

It is crucial for activists to recognize the signs of burnout in themselves and their fellow advocates. Some common symptoms include:
    1. Physical Exhaustion: Persistent fatigue, sleep disturbances, and reduced immune function are common signs of burnout.

2. Emotional Drain: Feelings of cynicism, irritability, and a diminished sense of personal accomplishment are indicators of emotional exhaustion.

3. Cognitive Impairment: Burnout can lead to difficulties in concentration, memory, decision-making, and increased negative thinking patterns.

4. Social Withdrawal: Activists experiencing burnout may isolate themselves from their support networks, leading to feelings of loneliness and disconnection.

Strategies for Prevention and Coping

1. Self-Care Practices: Engaging in regular self-care activities can help minimize the risk of burnout. This includes prioritizing rest, maintaining a healthy lifestyle, and engaging in activities that bring joy and relaxation.

2. Setting Boundaries: Establishing clear boundaries between work and personal life can help maintain balance and preserve mental well-being.

3. Seeking Support: Building a strong support network of like-minded individuals can provide emotional validation, understanding, and a sense of solidarity.

4. Taking Breaks: Advocacy work can be all-consuming. Taking regular breaks, whether it's a vacation or a day off, allows activists to recharge and prevent burnout.

5. Professional Help: If burnout symptoms persist, seeking professional help from therapists or counselors who specialize in stress management can be beneficial.

The Importance of Self-Reflection

In addition to burnout, activists also face mental health struggles that can arise from the weight of their work. It is essential for activists to engage in self-reflection and prioritize their mental health. This includes recognizing personal triggers, practicing self-compassion, and seeking therapy or counseling when needed.

Unconventional Approach: Mindfulness Meditation

One effective technique for managing burnout and improving mental well-being is mindfulness meditation. This practice involves bringing attention to the present moment without judgment. By cultivating mindfulness, activists can develop resilience, reduce stress, and enhance their overall well-being.

Real-World Example: The Case of Saryn Brell

Throughout their journey, Saryn experienced burnout and faced mental health struggles. This subsection delves into their personal battles and how they navigated the challenges of activism while preserving their mental well-being.

Saryn recognized the signs of burnout early on and actively practiced self-care to prevent it from escalating. They prioritized rest, engaged in hobbies they enjoyed, and sought support from their close allies. Additionally, Saryn became involved in mindfulness meditation, which helped them manage stress and maintain their mental well-being amidst the demanding nature of activism.

Exercise: Building Self-Care Practices

To develop self-care practices, let's consider the following exercise:
1. List activities that bring you joy and relaxation. 2. Prioritize incorporating one self-care activity into your routine each day. 3. Reflect on how these activities make you feel and how they contribute to your overall well-being.

Remember, self-care is not selfish. Taking care of your mental health is crucial to sustain long-term activism and make a lasting impact.

Key Takeaways

1. Burnout is a common experience for activists and can have severe consequences on their mental health. 2. Recognizing the signs and symptoms of burnout is crucial to address the issue promptly. 3. Strategies such as self-care practices, setting boundaries, seeking support, and mindfulness meditation can help prevent and cope with burnout. 4. Prioritizing mental well-being through self-reflection and self-compassion is essential for long-term activism. 5. Practicing self-care is not selfish but necessary for sustaining activism and making a lasting impact.

In the relentless pursuit of LGBTQ rights, Saryn Brell faced the challenges of burnout and mental health struggles. Their story serves as a reminder that while fighting for equality is crucial, it is equally vital to prioritize self-care and mental well-being. Through self-reflection, resilience, and support, activists like Saryn can continue their important work while taking care of themselves.

Now, let us move on to the next subsection in this chapter.

Subsection: Coping Mechanisms and Self-Care Practices

Coping with the challenges of activism and maintaining a healthy state of mind can be a daunting task. In this section, we will explore various coping mechanisms and self-care practices that Saryn Brell and other LGBTQ activists have adopted to navigate the emotional toll of their work.

The Importance of Self-Care in Activism

Activism, especially within the LGBTQ community, can be emotionally draining and overwhelming. The fight for equality and justice often comes with personal sacrifices and exposes activists to discrimination, backlash, and harassment. It is crucial for activists to prioritize their mental and physical well-being to sustain themselves in their missions.

Self-care is a vital component of maintaining resilience and preventing burnout. It involves intentionally taking care of oneself by engaging in activities that promote well-being and relieve stress. Let's explore some coping mechanisms and self-care practices that Saryn and other activists have found beneficial.

Meditation and Mindfulness

One widely adopted coping mechanism is the practice of meditation and mindfulness. Taking time to quiet the mind, focus on the present moment, and cultivate self-awareness can help reduce stress and restore emotional balance. Mindfulness allows activists to step away from the chaos of activism and provide a sense of calm and grounding.

Saryn Brell, for instance, begins each day with a short meditation session, setting intentions and cultivating a positive mindset. Through mindfulness, Saryn finds clarity and renewed energy to navigate the challenges that lie ahead.

Physical Self-Care

Engaging in physical self-care plays a vital role in rejuvenating the body and mind. Regular exercise, such as yoga, running, or dancing, can help reduce stress and increase endorphin levels.

Recognizing the importance of physical well-being, Saryn makes time for exercise every day. They find solace in yoga, which not only strengthens their body but also helps them maintain a sense of balance and alignment.

Proper nutrition also contributes to physical well-being. Saryn ensures they eat a balanced diet, fueling their body with essential nutrients that provide sustained energy throughout the day. They prioritize staying hydrated and make conscious choices about the food they consume, emphasizing the importance of self-care from within.

Creating Boundaries

One of the most challenging aspects of activism is finding a balance between personal life and advocacy work. Establishing boundaries is crucial to prevent burnout and maintain healthy relationships.

Saryn embraces the practice of creating boundaries by setting aside dedicated time for themselves and their loved ones. This may involve unplugging from social media, limiting work-related activities during specific hours, and prioritizing quality time spent with family and friends.

By setting boundaries, Saryn can recharge and nurture their personal connections, ensuring they have a strong support system while dedicating themselves to their cause.

Seeking Emotional Support

Activism can often be isolating, and the emotional toll can be overwhelming. Seeking emotional support from friends, family, and fellow activists is essential for maintaining mental well-being.

Saryn turns to their chosen family, friends who understand the challenges they face, for emotional support and strength. They engage in regular check-ins, open conversations, and shared experiences with these individuals, providing a valuable source of encouragement and solace.

Additionally, participating in support groups or seeking therapy can offer further emotional guidance and a safe space to share experiences, fears, and frustrations. Saryn understands that reaching out for help is not a sign of weakness but rather a sign of strength and self-awareness.

Engaging in Creative Outlets

Engaging in creative outlets can be a powerful form of release and self-expression for activists. Writing, painting, playing music, or any other creative pursuit allows them to channel their emotions and find a sense of catharsis.

Saryn finds solace in writing poetry and journaling. Capturing their thoughts and emotions on paper provides an outlet for self-reflection, healing, and personal growth.

Taking Breaks and Practicing Rest

Finally, acknowledging the importance of rest is crucial for maintaining long-term activism. Activists like Saryn incorporate regular breaks into their routines to take a step back, recharge, and reconnect with themselves.

Whether it's taking a short vacation, going on a nature retreat, or simply indulging in a relaxing bath, these intentional breaks allow activists to regain their focus and prevent burnout.

Saryn recognizes that self-care is not selfish but rather a necessary act of preservation. By taking care of themselves, they can continue to fight for their community with renewed passion and vitality.

Unconventional Yet Relevant: The Power of Laughter

While coping mechanisms discussed so far have provided ways to address the emotional challenges of activism, it is equally important to incorporate lighter moments and find joy in the journey.

One unconventional yet effective coping mechanism is shared laughter. Saryn, known for their quick wit and sense of humor, uses laughter as a way to alleviate tension and maintain a positive mindset.

Sharing funny stories or engaging in activities that induce laughter, such as watching comedy shows or playing games, allows Saryn to momentarily escape the weight of their advocacy work and find joy in the present moment.

In Conclusion, coping mechanisms and self-care practices are essential for LGBTQ activists like Saryn Brell to sustain their emotional well-being and continue the fight for equality. By incorporating meditation, physical self-care, creating boundaries, seeking emotional support, engaging in creative outlets, practicing rest, and finding joy in laughter, activists can navigate the challenges and triumphs of their journey with resilience and purpose. Remember, self-care is not selfish; it is a revolutionary act that empowers activists to create lasting change.

Subsection: Navigating Interpersonal Relationships in the Spotlight

Navigating interpersonal relationships is crucial for anyone, but it takes on a whole new level of complexity when you're in the public eye. For someone like Saryn Brell, whose activism has put them in the spotlight, maintaining healthy relationships while remaining true to their cause requires a delicate balance.

One of the key challenges Saryn faces is dealing with criticism and opposition from loved ones. This can be especially difficult when those individuals are not fully supportive of their activism or don't understand the importance of fighting for LGBTQ rights. Saryn's experiences teach us that it's essential to approach these conversations with empathy, understanding, and a willingness to educate.

Furthermore, Saryn has to carefully choose the people they surround themselves with. Building a support network of allies who share their passion for LGBTQ rights is crucial. These individuals help Saryn stay motivated, offer emotional support, and provide valuable perspectives. It's also important to foster relationships based on trust, loyalty, and respect, as these will be needed to weather the challenges that come with being in the public eye.

However, not all relationships can be nurtured. Saryn's experiences reveal that there will be people who may turn against them or distance themselves due to their activism. This can be painful, but it's necessary to let go of toxic relationships that no longer serve a positive purpose. It's crucial to prioritize mental and emotional well-being by surrounding oneself with people who uplift and support the cause.

Maintaining romantic relationships can also be challenging for public figures like Saryn. Public scrutiny and the pressure to keep personal life private can strain even the strongest partnerships. Saryn's journey shows that open and honest communication, setting boundaries, and finding a partner who understands and supports the activist's mission are key to nurturing and sustaining a healthy relationship in the face of public exposure.

Navigating interpersonal relationships in the spotlight also requires self-reflection and self-care. Saryn's experiences teach us the importance of recognizing personal limitations, setting aside time for oneself, and seeking professional help when needed. This helps prevent burnout and ensures that Saryn can continue to make an impact on the LGBTQ community.

In conclusion, the challenges faced by Saryn Brell in navigating interpersonal relationships in the spotlight reveal the importance of empathy, building a supportive network, and setting healthy boundaries. Learning from Saryn's experiences can guide activists and public figures in fostering meaningful connections while staying true to their cause.

Subsection: Lessons Learned from Activism's Darkest Hours

In the tumultuous journey of activism, there are bound to be moments of immense difficulty and despair. These are the darkest hours that test the resilience and commitment of activists like Saryn Brell. In this subsection, we delve into the lessons learned during these trying times, shedding light on the challenges faced by LGBTQ activists and the wisdom gained from overcoming them.

Understanding the Power of Resilience

Resilience is the backbone of activism. It is the ability to bounce back from setbacks, to endure in the face of adversity. LGBTQ activists, including Saryn Brell, have encountered numerous obstacles – from hate crimes to legislative roadblocks. Yet, they have persisted. They have taught us that setbacks should not deter us, but rather, fuel our determination to fight for a just cause.

Example: Saryn faced opposition while pushing for comprehensive LGBTQ-inclusive legislation. Despite setbacks, they regrouped, collaborated with like-minded allies, and continued the fight. Their resilience paid off when the legislation was finally passed, paving the way for greater equality.

Building a Supportive Community

Navigating activism's darkest hours can be emotionally and mentally draining. Having a support network is vital for providing comfort, guidance, and encouragement. LGBTQ activists often rely on their community to uplift them during difficult times.

Example: There were moments when Saryn felt overwhelmed by the magnitude of the challenges they faced. By leaning on their friends, allies, and the LGBTQ community, they found solace and strength. Together, they created a safe space for sharing experiences, healing wounds, and rejuvenating their spirits.

Learning from Adversity

Adversity can be a valuable teacher. It forces activists to reevaluate their strategies, adapt, and grow. Each setback presents an opportunity for learning and developing new approaches to effect change.

Example: Saryn's activism faced significant backlash from conservative groups and online trolls. Rather than succumbing to discouragement, they chose to learn from the experience. They refined their messaging, honed their debating skills, and found innovative ways to counter the opposition. Through this process, they discovered the power of empathy and storytelling in changing hearts and minds.

Promoting Self-Care and Mental Health

Activism is a demanding and emotionally charged endeavor. LGBTQ activists often neglect their own self-care while prioritizing the needs of their community. However, to be effective advocates, they must prioritize their mental health and well-being.

Example: Saryn experienced burnout due to their relentless activism. They learned the importance of setting boundaries, practicing self-care rituals, and seeking professional support. By valuing their own well-being, Saryn was able to sustain their advocacy efforts in the long run.

Collaboration and Unity

The fight for LGBTQ rights requires collective action. Activists must work together, transcending differences and embracing unity. Collaboration amplifies their impact and facilitates the sharing of knowledge, resources, and strategies.

Example: Activism's darkest hours have a way of uniting people with different perspectives and backgrounds. Saryn realized the strength in building bridges with politicians, celebrities, and other activists. They formed alliances to achieve common goals, mobilized support, and extended the reach of their advocacy.

Embracing Nuance and Evolving Perspectives

The journey of activism is not straightforward, and the LGBTQ movement is no exception. Over time, perspectives evolve, and activists must adapt to reflect a changing landscape. Embracing nuance and recognizing that change is a continuous process is vital for growth and sustainability.

Example: Saryn encountered criticism within the LGBTQ community, with some questioning their approach to advocacy. Instead of retreating, they engaged in open dialogue, listened to diverse perspectives, and embraced the nuances of the movement. This willingness to grow and evolve allowed them to forge stronger bonds within the community.

The Unconventional Power of Humor

In the face of darkness, humor can be a powerful tool for resilience and subversion. Embracing wit and satire allows activists to challenge the status quo, dismantle stereotypes, and bring levity to difficult conversations.

Example: Saryn, known for their quick wit and humor, leveraged comedy to shed light on LGBTQ issues. Through their charismatic persona, they engaged with the public in unconventional ways that captured attention and encouraged dialogue. Humor became a conduit for change, defusing tension and inviting people to reflect on their prejudices.

Amidst the darkest hours of activism, LGBTQ activists like Saryn Brell have consistently demonstrated resilience, unity, and adaptability. By internalizing the lessons learned from their journeys, we can embark on our own paths of change, armed with the wisdom found in the face of adversity. Remember, even in the darkest of times, there is always a glimmer of hope – a beacon lighting the way to a more inclusive and equal future.

Subsection: Finding Strength in Vulnerability

In the journey of LGBTQ activism, vulnerability can be seen as a weakness, a chink in the armor. But in reality, it is through vulnerability that activists find their greatest strength. Saryn Brell's story is no exception. In this section, we will explore how vulnerability played a pivotal role in Saryn's activism and how it can empower individuals to drive change.

The Power of Authenticity

One of the most significant ways Saryn found strength in vulnerability was by embracing their authentic self. In a society that often marginalizes LGBTQ individuals, being true to one's identity can be a revolutionary act. Saryn's journey towards self-acceptance and self-love allowed them to connect deeply with others and inspire change.

Example: Saryn's decision to publicly come out as nonbinary, despite the potential backlash, opened the door for others to do the same. By sharing their own struggles and triumphs, Saryn created a sense of unity and belonging within the LGBTQ community.

Embracing Compassion and Empathy

Vulnerability also paved the way for Saryn to cultivate compassion and empathy. By being honest and open about their experiences, they were able to bridge the gap between different communities and foster understanding.

Example: Through public speaking engagements and intimate conversations, Saryn shared stories of discrimination, prejudice, and resilience, allowing others to empathize with the struggles faced by the LGBTQ community. This empathy built connections and alliances, promoting a more inclusive society.

Turning Setbacks into Strength

In the face of adversity, vulnerability allowed Saryn to transform setbacks into opportunities for growth and resilience. Instead of letting criticism and hate deter them, they used these challenges as catalysts for change.

Example: When faced with threats and online harassment, Saryn refused to be silenced. They boldly confronted the negativity and actively engaged in open dialogue, educating others and debunking misconceptions about the LGBTQ community.

Support Networks and Healing

Navigating the emotional toll of activism can be overwhelming, but vulnerability also created space for healing and support. Saryn recognized the importance of leaning on others during challenging times and prioritized self-care as a vital aspect of their advocacy work.

Example: Saryn surrounded themselves with a network of allies, friends, and mentors who provided emotional support and guidance. They participated in therapy, meditation, and other self-care practices to restore their energy and maintain their mental well-being.

Challenging Stereotypes and Inspiring Change

In a world that often stigmatizes vulnerability, embracing it can challenge societal norms and inspire others to do the same. By authentically sharing their vulnerability, Saryn helped break down stereotypes about strength and resilience, motivating others to be their authentic selves.

Example: Through their engaging speeches and media appearances, Saryn encouraged individuals to embrace vulnerability as a catalyst for personal growth, social change, and empowered activism.

Embracing Vulnerability: Key Takeaways

In a landscape where strength is often equated with invulnerability, Saryn Brell's story reminds us of the power of embracing vulnerability. By reconnecting with our authentic selves, cultivating compassion, and transforming setbacks into opportunities for growth, we can become catalysts for change. Let us celebrate vulnerability, for within it lies the strength to challenge societal norms and champion equality for all.

SECTION 3: THE DARK SIDE OF ACTIVISM

Subsection: The Importance of Self-Preservation

In the relentless battle for change and equality, activists like Saryn Brell often find themselves immersed in a whirlwind of activism, constantly navigating setbacks, obstacles, and the weight of their cause. However, amidst the chaos, one essential aspect is often overlooked: the importance of self-preservation.

Self-preservation refers to the practice of taking care of oneself physically, mentally, and emotionally in order to maintain overall well-being and sustain long-term activism. It involves establishing healthy boundaries, practicing self-care routines, and seeking support when needed. In this subsection, we will explore why self-preservation is crucial for activists, discuss strategies for implementing it, and highlight the significance of individual well-being in the larger context of the fight for LGBTQ rights.

The Struggles of Activism

Activism is an emotionally charged and often demanding pursuit. It requires ardent dedication, persistent advocacy, and a relentless drive to challenge the status quo. Activists like Saryn face formidable challenges on a daily basis:

- Emotional fatigue: Advocating for marginalized communities can be emotionally draining, especially when confronted with discrimination, hateful rhetoric, or setbacks in achieving desired outcomes. Activists must often process their own emotions while simultaneously supporting others who are experiencing similar struggles.

- Burnout: The intensity of activism can lead to burnout, a state of physical, mental, and emotional exhaustion. Burnout erodes passion, diminishes productivity, and puts activists' well-being at risk. Without self-preservation measures, activists find themselves susceptible to burnout, jeopardizing their ability to effectively advocate for change.

- Limited resources: Activists often operate with limited resources, facing financial constraints, time limitations, and a lack of institutional support. The constant need to juggle multiple responsibilities and commitments can impede their ability to prioritize self-care.

- Vicarious trauma: Advocates for marginalized communities are not immune to the trauma experienced by the very individuals they seek to assist. Bearing witness to the pain and suffering of others can take a toll on activists' mental and emotional health, leading to symptoms of vicarious trauma.

Given these challenges, it becomes evident that self-preservation is not optional for activists. It is indispensable for their individual well-being and the sustainability of their efforts.

Strategies for Self-Preservation

Self-preservation is a multifaceted practice that encompasses physical, mental, emotional, and social aspects. Let's explore some strategies that Saryn and others can employ to prioritize self-preservation:

1. **Establishing Boundaries:** Recognizing personal limits and setting boundaries is crucial for maintaining balance. Activists must be able to say no when necessary and assert their needs to avoid overextending themselves. By setting clear boundaries, they ensure sustainable and long-term engagement in activism.

2. **Practicing Self-Care:** Regular self-care activities are essential to combat the toll of activism. Engaging in activities that bring joy, relaxation, and rejuvenation nurtures physical and emotional well-being. This could include exercise, mindfulness practices, hobbies, or spending time with loved ones.

3. **Building Support Networks:** Surrounding oneself with supportive individuals who share similar values and goals can provide invaluable emotional support. Peer networks and community groups offer spaces for shared experiences, empathy, and collaboration, reducing the feeling of isolation that activists might encounter.

4. **Seeking Professional Help:** Activists may benefit from seeking therapeutic support to process the emotional challenges they face. Professional counselors or therapists can help activists develop coping mechanisms, navigate burnout, and address any trauma resulting from their advocacy work.

5. **Engaging in Mindfulness Practices:** Mindfulness practices, such as meditation or deep breathing exercises, allow activists to cultivate present-moment awareness and reduce stress. Integrating these practices into their routine provides a means of self-reflection, promoting clarity and resilience amid challenges.

6. **Prioritizing Rest and Leisure:** Adequate rest and leisure time are crucial for activists to recharge and replenish their energy. Recognizing the importance of rest as an essential part of activism ensures sustained and effective engagement in the long run.

Balancing Activism and Self-Preservation

Finding the balance between advocacy and self-preservation is a continuous and evolving process. Activists must maneuver the delicate line between caring for themselves and remaining committed to the cause. Here are a few considerations for striking this balance:

1. **Recognize the Power of Collective Action:** Activism is not a solitary endeavor. By building alliances and engaging in collective efforts, activists can distribute the workload and share the responsibility of effecting change without compromising their well-being.

2. **Embrace Imperfection:** Activists must let go of the notion of perfection. Accepting that setbacks and failures are inevitable allows for self-compassion and resilience. Prioritizing progress over perfection can help activists avoid overly harsh self-judgment and maintain a healthier perspective on their work.

3. **Practice Adaptive Activism:** Activists should be open to adapting their strategies and approaches when necessary. Flexibility and self-reflection enable activists to reassess their priorities, recalibrate their efforts, and avoid unnecessary burnout.

4. **Advocate for Systemic Change:** Activists must recognize that self-preservation is not solely their responsibility but a collective societal obligation. By advocating for systemic changes that prioritize the well-being of all individuals, activists can create a more sustainable environment for themselves and future generations.

Conclusion

In the pursuit of LGBTQ rights and freedom, it is crucial for activists like Saryn Brell to prioritize self-preservation. By acknowledging the importance of physical, mental, emotional, and social well-being, activists can sustain their long-term engagement, fortify their resilience, and nourish their passion for change. Striking a balance between activism and self-preservation empowers activists to advocate more effectively, ensuring their personal well-being remains a vital pillar within the broader struggle for equality.

Self-preservation is not a selfish act but a necessity to create lasting impact and a more compassionate world for all. As Saryn's story unfolds, we witness the transformative power of self-preservation in creating sustainable change for generations to come.

Note to Readers: Remember, your own well-being matters. Prioritize self-preservation in your journey as an activist, and may it empower you to continue fighting for the rights and dignity of all individuals.

Section 4: Allies and Adversaries

Subsection: Building Bridges with Politicians and Celebrities

Building bridges with politicians and celebrities is a crucial aspect of Saryn Brell's activism journey. In this subsection, we will explore how Saryn leveraged these relationships to advance LGBTQ rights in Zerana and beyond. We will delve into the challenges and triumphs they encountered and highlight the importance of collaboration in the fight for equality.

The Power of Celebrity Endorsement

Celebrities have a unique platform that allows them to reach millions of people and influence public opinion. Saryn recognized this and understood the potential impact of garnering celebrity support for LGBTQ rights. By forging relationships with influential personalities, Saryn was able to amplify their message and raise awareness on a much larger scale.

One notable example is Saryn's partnership with world-renowned actor and LGBTQ activist, Emma Thompson. Together, they embarked on a global campaign to promote acceptance and equality. Their joint efforts resulted in increased media coverage, extensive fundraising initiatives, and ultimately, significant progress in LGBTQ rights legislation.

Beyond the support of celebrities, Saryn also understood the significance of engaging with politicians who held decision-making power.

Navigating the Political Landscape

In order to effect meaningful change, Saryn recognized the necessity of collaborating with both local and national politicians. This involved establishing relationships with elected officials, engaging in dialogue, and advocating for LGBTQ-inclusive legislation.

Saryn faced several challenges when building bridges with politicians. Some lawmakers held conservative views or were hesitant to publicly support LGBTQ rights due to fear of backlash from their constituents. Saryn employed various strategies to tackle these obstacles.

One effective approach was organizing town hall meetings and public forums where community members could voice their concerns and engage in open discussion. By providing a safe space for dialogue, Saryn was able to address misconceptions, dispel fears, and build trust with politicians who were initially skeptical. This paved the way for constructive collaboration and the introduction of inclusive policies.

The Role of Lobbying

Lobbying played a significant role in Saryn's efforts to build bridges with politicians. By employing a combination of grassroots mobilization and direct advocacy, Saryn and their team were able to influence legislative decisions.

Saryn recognized that lobbying involved more than just engaging with politicians. They understood the importance of having a strong team of allies, including lawyers, policy experts, and community activists, who could effectively convey the needs and concerns of the LGBTQ community.

In addition, Saryn actively sought out partnerships with LGBTQ organizations that had established relationships with politicians. By collaborating with these organizations, Saryn was able to leverage their expertise and credibility, further strengthening their lobbying efforts.

Overcoming Resistance and Building Trust

Building bridges with politicians and celebrities isn't always a smooth journey. Saryn faced resistance from some individuals who were skeptical of their motives or the LGBTQ movement as a whole. Overcoming this resistance required patience, empathy, and a commitment to open dialogue.

Saryn employed various strategies to build trust and create common ground with politicians and celebrities. This included sharing personal stories, providing data and research on the positive impact of LGBTQ-inclusive policies, and highlighting the shared values of equality and human rights. By fostering genuine connections and finding common ground, Saryn was able to build bridges with unlikely allies.

Unconventional Collaboration

Saryn's journey in building bridges with politicians and celebrities also involved some unconventional collaborations. They recognized that change could be achieved by forming alliances beyond traditional lines of activism.

For example, Saryn reached out to prominent athletes and sports organizations to promote LGBTQ inclusion in sports. Through partnerships with professional athletes, they were able to amplify the message of equality and challenge deeply entrenched prejudices within the sporting community.

Furthermore, Saryn explored collaborations with business leaders who recognized the economic benefits of LGBTQ-inclusive practices. By highlighting the positive impact on tourism, commerce, and innovation, they were able to secure support from influential figures in the business world, driving change from within corporate structures.

Conclusion

Building bridges with politicians and celebrities played a pivotal role in Saryn's activism journey. By leveraging these relationships, Saryn was able to amplify their message, influence public opinion, and advocate for LGBTQ rights on a larger scale. The challenges they faced in navigating the political landscape and winning over skeptics were overcome through empathy, trust-building, and strategic partnerships.

Saryn's collaborations represent a powerful lesson in the importance of collective action and the potential for unlikely alliances in the fight for equality. By reaching out to politicians and celebrities, Saryn demonstrated that change is possible when individuals with influence and power join forces with grassroots activists.

As readers, we are inspired to think outside the box and explore unconventional collaborations in our own activism. The power of bridging divides can create lasting impact and pave the way for progress in the fight for LGBTQ rights, both in Zerana and around the world.

Subsection: Unexpected Allies from Unlikely Places

In the fight for LGBTQ rights, allies can come from the most unexpected places. While the LGBTQ community often forms close-knit networks of support, it is essential to acknowledge and appreciate the connections forged with individuals and groups who may not immediately seem like natural allies. These unexpected allies play a vital role in challenging stereotypes, breaking down barriers, and promoting inclusivity. This subsection explores some remarkable instances where allies from unlikely places have made substantial contributions to the LGBTQ movement.

One such ally is Congressman Alex Ramirez, a conservative politician known for his strong stance on fiscal responsibility and limited government intervention. Despite his previously expressed reservations about LGBTQ rights, Congressman Ramirez has recently emerged as a vocal proponent for advocating equality and ensuring the fundamental rights of LGBTQ individuals.

Ramirez's transformation came about through a personal experience that challenged his preconceived notions. His niece, Maya, came out as transgender, prompting the Congressman to reevaluate his beliefs. This unexpected revelation within his own family forced Ramirez to confront the biases he had carried for years. It was a poignant reminder that LGBTQ rights are not just a political issue but one that deeply affects individuals and their loved ones.

Driven by his newfound understanding and desire to support his niece, Congressman Ramirez took it upon himself to learn about LGBTQ issues. He met with LGBTQ activists, listened to their stories, and educated himself on the struggles they faced. Through his interactions, Ramirez gained a deeper appreciation for the widespread discrimination and the need for legislative change.

Armed with this knowledge, Ramirez leveraged his position as a respected conservative voice to advocate for LGBTQ rights within his own party. He has worked tirelessly to bridge the gap between conservatives and the LGBTQ community, emphasizing that equality should be a bipartisan issue.

Ramirez's unexpected alliance has not been without its challenges, as he has faced backlash from colleagues and constituents who have accused him of betraying conservative values. However, Ramirez remains steadfast in his convictions, recognizing that progress requires breaking down barriers and challenging the status quo.

Another remarkable case of an unexpected ally is Fiona Lawson, a prominent figure in the world of organized religion. As a devoutly religious individual, Lawson initially struggled with reconciling her faith with her support for LGBTQ rights. Her conservative religious community often espoused traditional views on gender and sexuality, which clashed with her growing understanding and empathy for the LGBTQ community.

Instead of succumbing to the pressures of conformity, Lawson took it upon herself to initiate a dialogue within her religious community. She organized support groups and facilitated conversations that encouraged church members to challenge their own biases and rethink their interpretation of religious texts. Through patience and understanding, Lawson helped many individuals realize that love and acceptance were at the core of their religious beliefs.

Fiona Lawson's efforts did not go unnoticed outside her faith community. LGBTQ activists recognized her genuine commitment to promoting inclusivity within a traditionally conservative institution. They welcomed her as an important ally and partner, working together to break down barriers between the LGBTQ community and organized religion.

The journeys of Congressman Ramirez and Fiona Lawson serve as powerful reminders that allies can emerge from even the most unexpected places. Their stories inspire individuals who may have held misgivings about LGBTQ rights to embrace empathy, education, and open-mindedness. By reaching out to those who may not immediately align with our cause, we can foster cooperation, understanding, and ultimately, create a more inclusive society.

However, it is important to note that these examples are not meant to suggest that the responsibility for promoting equality falls solely on the shoulders of marginalized communities. True progress can only be achieved when individuals from all walks of life actively commit to dismantling discriminatory systems and challenging their own biases.

In the spirit of inclusivity, it is crucial for LGBTQ activists to remain open to forming alliances with unexpected partners. By engaging in sincere dialogue and fostering understanding, these unconventional allies can help create a society where LGBTQ individuals are afforded the same rights and opportunities as their heterosexual and cisgender counterparts.

Let us reflect on the potential of unexpected alliances and the power they hold to amplify our collective voices for change. As we continue to champion LGBTQ rights, may we embrace the opportunity to form bridges with individuals and groups who, on the surface, may appear to be unlikely allies. Together, we can build a more inclusive future where everyone, regardless of their background or beliefs, can thrive and live authentically.

Subsection: Facing Resistance from Within the LGBTQ Community

In the journey for LGBTQ rights, allies and advocates often face opposition not only from external sources, but also from within the community they are fighting for. While it may seem counterintuitive, this phenomenon highlights the diverse perspectives and experiences within the LGBTQ community.

One of the significant challenges that arise when fighting for LGBTQ rights is the existence of internal divisions. These divisions can manifest in various ways, such as disagreements on strategies, priorities, or even the definition of the overall goals of the movement. It is essential to acknowledge and address these internal conflicts to foster a more inclusive and effective movement.

One example of resistance from within the LGBTQ community is the debate surrounding the inclusion of certain identities within the broader acronym. Over time, the acronym LGBTQ has expanded to LGBTQ+, LGBTQIA, or even LGBTQIA2S+, to be more inclusive of marginalized identities. However, some individuals and groups question the need for such an extensive, all-encompassing acronym. They argue that it dilutes the focus on the core issues and may complicate messaging and advocacy efforts. This debate highlights the tension between inclusivity and clarity, and finding a balance is crucial to drive the movement forward.

Another source of resistance stems from differing opinions on the priority areas for LGBTQ activism. While some individuals advocate for marriage equality as the main focus, others emphasize the importance of addressing issues such as transgender rights, conversion therapy, or healthcare access. These differing viewpoints can lead to disagreements and competition for resources and attention within the community. To address this resistance, dialogue and finding common ground are essential. Recognizing that each sub-group within the community faces unique challenges and that those challenges are interconnected is crucial for building a united front.

Moreover, tensions arise from the different experiences and backgrounds within the LGBTQ community. Intersectionality, the understanding that individuals hold multiple marginalized identities, adds complexity to the fight for equality. Bisexual individuals may face erasure and exclusion from both straight and gay communities. Transgender and non-binary individuals routinely face discrimination and violence, sometimes even prompting disagreements on terminology and language usage within the community. It becomes vital to recognize and validate these varied experiences and perspectives to create a more inclusive movement.

Addressing resistance from within the community requires open and honest conversations and a commitment to listen, learn, and grow. It means creating spaces for constructive dialogue, where differing opinions can be shared without fear of judgment or marginalization. Building bridges of understanding and empathy is key to overcoming internal divisions and strengthening the movement as a whole.

In the face of resistance and internal conflicts, it is crucial to remember that unity does not mean uniformity. Embracing diversity within the LGBTQ community is a strength that can lead to more comprehensive and effective strategies for achieving equality. By recognizing and valuing the diversity of voices and perspectives, activists can work together towards common goals while celebrating the richness of the community they strive to represent.

Example: The debate on the inclusion of the "+" symbol

Within the LGBTQ community, one ongoing debate revolves around the inclusion of the "+" symbol in the acronym. Some individuals argue that the "+" allows for a more inclusive representation of marginalized identities, encompassing various sexual orientations, gender identities, and expressions. They believe that the "+" symbol signifies a commitment to continued growth and understanding.

On the other hand, some individuals express concerns that the "+" may be too broad and dilute the focus on specific identities within the LGBTQ community. They argue that this inclusion could lead to confusion or misrepresentation and hamper efforts to address the specific challenges faced by different sub-groups.

This debate reflects a fundamental tension within the LGBTQ community between the desire to be inclusive and the need for clarity and specificity in messaging and activism. While it is essential to acknowledge and celebrate the diversity of identities, it is equally important to streamline messaging and prioritize resources effectively. Striking a balance is crucial, ensuring that the "+" serves as a reminder of the continuous expansion of understanding and acceptance while still addressing the unique experiences and needs of each identity within the community.

Caveats and Considerations

When discussing resistance from within the LGBTQ community, it is essential to approach the topic with sensitivity and respect. These internal divisions are not unique to the LGBTQ movement but can be found in any advocacy or social justice movement. Recognizing this shared struggle can help foster empathy and understanding when addressing disagreements within the community.

It is crucial to engage in self-reflection and challenge one's own biases when facing resistance from within the LGBTQ community. Allies and advocates should be open to feedback and willing to learn from diverse voices and experiences. This includes acknowledging and rectifying any unintentional harm caused by one's actions or words.

Finally, while addressing internal divisions, it is equally important not to lose sight of the overarching goal of the LGBTQ rights movement – achieving equality and justice for all. By working together, embracing diversity, and finding common ground, the community can overcome internal resistance and build a more inclusive and effective movement.

Resources for Further Reading and Engagement

1. Berger, R. (2018). Contested territories: LGBTQ+ social movements and resistance. Social Sciences, 7(5), 75. doi:10.3390/socsci7050075

This article explores the complex landscape of LGBTQ+ social movements, focusing on the sources of resistance within the community and strategies for addressing internal divisions.

2. Meyer, I. H. (2015). Resilience in the study of minority stress and health of sexual and gender minorities. Psychology of Sexual Orientation and Gender Diversity, 1(S), 12-12. doi:10.1037/sgd0000131

This research article examines the concept of resilience among sexual and gender minorities, highlighting the challenges faced within and outside the LGBTQ+ community and the importance of fostering resilience in the face of resistance.

3. Serano, J. M. (2016). Excluded: Making feminist and queer movements more inclusive. Berkeley, CA: Seal Press.

In this book, Julia Serano explores the challenges faced by marginalized groups within the feminist and queer movements. While not specifically focused on the LGBTQ+ community, it offers valuable insights into addressing resistance and embracing diversity within social justice movements.

Subsection: Overcoming Divisiveness and Fostering Unity

In the fight for LGBTQ rights, one of the major challenges faced by activists is overcoming divisiveness within the community itself. This subsection explores how Saryn Brell tackled this issue head-on, fostering unity among LGBTQ individuals and paving the way for a more inclusive movement.

The Importance of Inclusivity

Unity is a crucial aspect of any social justice movement, including the fight for LGBTQ rights. However, achieving unity within LGBTQ communities can be challenging due to the diversity of experiences, identities, and perspectives. Saryn recognized that true progress required an inclusive approach that embraced the different voices and concerns within the LGBTQ community.

To foster unity, Saryn encouraged open dialogue and created safe spaces where individuals from all backgrounds could come together to share their experiences and ideas. By listening to and respecting each other's stories, LGBTQ individuals could find common ground while also acknowledging and celebrating their unique identities.

Building Bridges through Education

One of the most effective ways to overcome divisiveness is through education. Saryn understood that understanding and empathy are key to creating unity within diverse communities. As such, they advocated for educational initiatives aimed at raising awareness and promoting LGBTQ inclusion.

Saryn worked closely with educational institutions to implement LGBTQ-inclusive curricula that fostered understanding and acceptance. They believed that educating young people about the LGBTQ community's history and struggles could help challenge stereotypes, debunk misconceptions, and foster empathy. By equipping individuals with knowledge and empowering them to become allies, Saryn aimed to bridge the gaps between different groups within the LGBTQ community.

Empowering Grassroots Movements

Saryn recognized that change often begins at the grassroots level. To foster unity and overcome divisiveness, they dedicated significant energy to empowering local LGBTQ organizations and community leaders. By providing resources, support, and guidance, Saryn helped these groups address the unique challenges faced by their respective communities.

Saryn understood that unity cannot be imposed from the top down but must instead emerge from within communities. By amplifying the voices of local activists and supporting their initiatives, Saryn fostered a sense of ownership and agency among LGBTQ individuals. This approach not only helped build trust within the community but also encouraged collaboration and a collective effort towards achieving common goals.

Engaging in Intersectional Activism

Overcoming divisiveness within the LGBTQ community also requires acknowledging and addressing the intersectionality of identities and experiences. Saryn actively championed intersectional activism, recognizing that LGBTQ individuals exist within various social, racial, economic, and cultural contexts.

By collaborating with activists from different social justice movements, Saryn highlighted the interconnectedness of struggles and advocated for a more inclusive approach to activism. They understood that true unity could only be achieved by addressing the unique challenges faced by individuals at the intersections of multiple marginalized identities.

Promoting Forgiveness and Healing

Divisiveness often arises from past conflicts and wounds within the LGBTQ community. Saryn acknowledged the importance of healing and forgiveness to foster unity. They advocated for restorative justice practices that allowed individuals and communities to address past grievances and work towards reconciliation.

Saryn emphasized the power of empathy and compassion, encouraging individuals to listen, learn, and grow from their mistakes. By promoting forgiveness and healing, they aimed to create an environment where LGBTQ individuals could come together, move beyond their differences, and work towards a common vision of equality and acceptance.

Embracing Disagreement and Constructive Dialogue

In any movement, disagreements and differing opinions are inevitable. Saryn recognized the importance of embracing these differences and fostering constructive dialogue within the LGBTQ community. They emphasized that unity does not mean conformity but instead requires finding common ground while respecting diverse viewpoints.

Saryn encouraged LGBTQ individuals to engage in respectful debates and discussions, recognizing that healthy disagreement can lead to growth and progress. By creating spaces for dialogue and actively seeking out diverse perspectives, they facilitated the formation of a cohesive and inclusive movement.

Unconventional Approach: Collaborative Art Projects

As an unconventional yet effective approach, Saryn pioneered collaborative art projects to overcome divisiveness and foster unity in the LGBTQ community. By engaging LGBTQ individuals in art-based initiatives, Saryn provided a platform for self-expression, dialogue, and healing.

These collaborative art projects brought together LGBTQ individuals from different backgrounds to create meaningful and impactful works. From murals to performances, these projects not only fostered unity but also served as powerful tools for raising awareness and challenging societal norms.

Conclusion

Overcoming divisiveness and fostering unity within the LGBTQ community is an ongoing process, and Saryn Brell's advocacy provides valuable lessons. By emphasizing inclusivity, education, grassroots empowerment, intersectional activism, forgiveness, constructive dialogue, and unconventional approaches like collaborative art projects, Saryn created a powerful foundation for unity and progress. Their legacy continues to inspire future generations of activists to work towards a more unified and inclusive LGBTQ movement.

Subsection: The Power of Collaboration and Collective Action

In the pursuit of LGBTQ rights and equality, collaboration and collective action have proven to be powerful tools in effecting meaningful change. By coming together as a community and forming alliances with like-minded individuals and organizations, LGBTQ activists have been able to amplify their voices, pool their resources, and create a united front against discrimination and prejudice.

Collaboration fosters solidarity and strengthens the movement by bringing together individuals with diverse perspectives, skills, and experiences. It allows activists to combine their efforts, talents, and resources for a common cause, magnifying their impact and influence. Working together, they can achieve outcomes that would be difficult, if not impossible, to accomplish alone.

One example of the power of collaboration is the successful push for legalizing same-sex marriage in Zerana. LGBTQ activists joined forces with civil rights organizations, legal advocates, and progressive politicians to make their collective voice heard. They organized rallies, lobbied lawmakers, and used social media campaigns to raise awareness and garner support. By uniting behind a shared goal, they were able to overturn discriminatory laws and ensure marriage equality for all.

Collective action, on the other hand, involves mobilizing a broader community beyond the LGBTQ movement itself. It calls for building alliances with allies, including religious groups, grassroots organizations, and political leaders who support LGBTQ rights. These partnerships have the potential to bridge ideological divides, challenge prejudices, and change societal norms.

For instance, LGBTQ activists have collaborated with influential celebrities to raise awareness about LGBTQ issues and promote acceptance. Through joint initiatives, such as public service announcements, concerts, and endorsement campaigns, they have been able to reach wider audiences and change public opinion.

However, collaboration and collective action also come with challenges. Maintaining unity within diverse coalitions can be difficult, as different groups may prioritize different goals or have conflicting strategies. Overcoming these differences requires open lines of communication, compromise, and a shared commitment to the greater cause.

Furthermore, the power dynamics within collaborations must be carefully navigated. It is important to ensure that marginalized voices within the LGBTQ community are not silenced or overshadowed by more powerful or visible members. Truly inclusive and equitable collaborations require a commitment to amplifying diverse perspectives and centering the experiences of those most affected by discrimination.

To maximize the impact of collaboration and collective action, proactive strategies should be employed. This includes the creation of networks, platforms, and spaces that facilitate dialogue, knowledge-sharing, and coordination among activists, volunteers, and organizations. By harnessing the power of technology, social media, and online communities, activists can connect, mobilize, and engage a broader base of supporters.

In conclusion, the power of collaboration and collective action cannot be underestimated in the fight for LGBTQ rights. By working together, activists can leverage their collective energy, resources, and expertise to effect meaningful change. However, it is essential that collaboration is approached with inclusivity, equity, and mutual respect, ensuring that the diverse voices within the LGBTQ community are heard and valued. In embracing collaboration, the LGBTQ movement can continue to make strides towards a more inclusive and equal society.

Subsection: The Unavoidable Disappointments in the Fight for Change

The journey towards achieving LGBTQ equality is not without its share of disappointments. While progress has been made, setbacks and obstacles along the way are impossible to avoid. In this section, we will explore some of the unavoidable disappointments that LGBTQ activists like Saryn Brell have encountered in their fight for change.

One of the most significant disappointments is the slow pace of change. Despite decades of activism, there are still countries where homosexuality is criminalized, and LGBTQ individuals face discrimination and violence. Laws protecting LGBTQ rights can be slow to implement, and societal attitudes can take even longer to shift.

For example, in Zerana, it took years of tireless advocacy and activism to legalize same-sex marriage. Even after legal recognition, there were still pockets of resistance and opposition from conservative groups and religious organizations. This delay in progress can be disheartening and frustrating for activists who are eager to see immediate change.

Another disappointment lies in the lack of unity within the LGBTQ community itself. While the fight for LGBTQ rights should be a united front, there can be divisions and infighting that hinder progress. Different factions within the community may have different priorities or approaches to activism, leading to a lack of cohesion.

For instance, some individuals believe that a more radical approach is necessary to effect change, while others advocate for a more incremental strategy. These differing perspectives can lead to disagreements and conflicts, causing delays or setbacks in the pursuit of common goals.

Furthermore, LGBTQ activists often face resistance and backlash from political and religious groups. Society's ingrained prejudices and stereotypes can make the fight for equality an uphill battle. Activists like Saryn have encountered opposition not only from conservative politicians but also from religious organizations with entrenched beliefs.

Dealing with these adversarial forces can be emotionally challenging and disheartening. Public figures like Saryn often become targets of hate speech, threats, and online harassment. Such experiences take a toll on mental health and personal well-being, making it difficult to continue the fight for change.

In addition to external obstacles, activists also face internal struggles. Burnout and mental health issues are prevalent among individuals fighting for social justice causes. The weight of carrying the hopes and dreams of an entire community can be overwhelming, leading to exhaustion and a sense of disillusionment.

To address these disappointments, it is essential for activists to practice self-care and seek support from their communities. Taking breaks, engaging in activities that bring joy, and spending time with loved ones can help replenish emotional reserves.

It is also crucial to celebrate small victories along the way. While the fight for equality may be long and arduous, recognizing and appreciating the progress made helps to maintain motivation and hope. Each step forward, no matter how small, makes a difference in someone's life.

Ultimately, the unavoidable disappointments in the fight for change serve as a reminder of the significant work that still needs to be done. They highlight the importance of perseverance, resilience, and the need for continuous activism. By acknowledging these disappointments, activists can find renewed determination to keep pushing for a more inclusive society.

Remember, change is not always immediate, and setbacks are not indicative of failure. It is through facing and overcoming disappointments that progress is made. The fight for LGBTQ rights is a marathon, not a sprint, and every step forward brings us closer to a more just and equal world for all.

So, let us learn from the disappointments, draw strength from them, and continue the fight for change with unwavering passion and conviction. Together, we can create a better future for the LGBTQ community and societies at large.

Section 5: Looking Towards the Future

Subsection: Inspiring the Next Generation of Activists

As Saryn Brell's journey through activism comes to a close, their impact on the LGBTQ community and the fight for equality cannot be underestimated. In this subsection, we explore how Saryn continues to inspire and empower the next generation of activists.

Saryn's story resonates with individuals who are still grappling with their own identities and searching for direction. By sharing the struggles they faced and the victories they achieved, Saryn provides a roadmap for young activists who are just beginning to find their voice. They remind them that change is possible, and that every voice matters.

The Power of Personal Narratives

Saryn's ability to connect with others through their personal narrative is a significant factor in their success as an activist. Young activists can learn the importance of embracing their own stories and using them as powerful tools for change.

By sharing personal experiences, individuals can humanize their causes and foster empathy in others. Saryn's ability to tell their story in an authentic and compelling way has helped to break down barriers and dismantle prejudices. Their impact reminds us that storytelling is a powerful tool in activism.

Amplifying Marginalized Voices

One of the hallmarks of Saryn's activism is their commitment to amplifying the voices of marginalized communities within the LGBTQ spectrum. This commitment is a valuable lesson for the next generation of activists, as they strive to build a more inclusive movement.

Saryn's work shows that it is not enough to fight for the rights of a select few within the LGBTQ community. True progress can only be achieved when we uplift the voices of those who are often overlooked and marginalized. Young activists can learn from Saryn's example and work towards creating spaces where everyone is heard and represented.

Embracing Intersectionality

Another crucial aspect of Saryn's advocacy is their commitment to intersectionality. Saryn acknowledges that LGBTQ rights intersect with issues of race, class, gender, and other forms of oppression. They understand that true liberation can only be achieved when all forms of discrimination are addressed.

By embracing intersectionality, Saryn has fostered alliances with other social justice movements, creating a more inclusive and powerful force for change. Young activists can learn from this approach, recognizing the importance of building coalitions and working together to dismantle structural inequalities.

Strategies for Sustainable Activism

Saryn's journey has not been without its challenges and sacrifices. They have faced backlash, threats, and the emotional toll of advocacy. Yet, they have found ways to cope and continue their work.

Young activists can learn from Saryn's resilience and self-care practices. It is essential to prioritize mental health, set boundaries, and seek support from a strong network of allies. Saryn's example reminds us that sustainable activism requires taking care of oneself, both physically and emotionally.

Looking to the Future

As Saryn's activism paves the way for a brighter future, it is crucial for the next generation of activists to embrace their roles as agents of change. Saryn's story serves as a call to action, urging young activists to take the baton and push forward.

By learning from Saryn's experiences, young activists can build upon their achievements and forge new paths towards equality. Saryn's legacy reminds us that the fight for LGBTQ rights and social justice is an ongoing one, and it is up to each new generation to carry the torch.

Resources for Activism

To further support and inspire the next generation of activists, here are some additional resources:

- LGBTQ organizations and community centers: These organizations provide support, resources, and opportunities for engagement. They can help young activists connect with like-minded individuals who share their passion for social justice.
- Intersectional activism guides: Exploring intersectionality in activism can deepen understanding and provide strategies for inclusive advocacy. Books like "Intersectionality and Activism" by Kim Tran and "Emergent Strategy" by adrienne maree brown offer valuable insights and practical guidance.

- Mentorship programs: Seeking mentorship from experienced activists can provide guidance, support, and opportunities for growth. Organizations like MentorMe and The Trevor Project offer mentorship programs specifically for LGBTQ youth.

- Self-care resources: Activism can take an emotional toll, so it's important to prioritize self-care. Apps like Calm and Headspace offer meditation and mindfulness exercises to help manage stress and promote well-being.

Through the combination of personal narratives, intersectionality, and sustainable activism, Saryn Brell's legacy will continue to inspire and guide future generations of activists. It is their hope that their story ignites a fire within young activists to embrace their own power and work tirelessly for a more just and inclusive world. As we close this subsection, let us remember these wise words from Saryn: "We are stronger together, and our collective voices hold the power to create lasting change."

Subsection: Leaving a Lasting Legacy and Impact

As Saryn Brell's journey as an LGBTQ activist comes to a close, the question naturally arises: what kind of legacy will they leave behind? Saryn's impact on the LGBTQ community in Zerana and beyond cannot be underestimated. Their tireless advocacy and unwavering determination have undoubtedly changed countless lives and set in motion a movement for equality that will be felt for generations to come.

Saryn's vision for LGBTQ rights in Zerana and beyond is one of inclusivity, acceptance, and equal opportunities. They firmly believe that true equality can only be achieved when every individual, regardless of their sexual orientation or gender identity, is treated with dignity and respect. Saryn's dream is that every LGBTQ person can live their lives authentically and without fear of discrimination or violence.

But Saryn's impact goes beyond their vision for the future. Their accomplishments and victories on the journey towards equality have helped pave the way for lasting change. One of Saryn's most significant achievements was their role in legalizing same-sex marriage in Zerana. Their advocacy and lobbying efforts were instrumental in persuading lawmakers to recognize and uphold the fundamental right of LGBTQ couples to marry.

Furthermore, Saryn fought tirelessly for comprehensive LGBTQ-inclusive legislation. They successfully advocated for laws that protect LGBTQ individuals from discrimination in employment, housing, healthcare, and other essential aspects of daily life. Through their unwavering commitment to equality, Saryn has fostered a society where LGBTQ individuals can fully participate without fear of prejudice or marginalization.

Additionally, Saryn has played a crucial role in eradicating harmful practices such as conversion therapy. They have made it their mission to dismantle the institutions and ideologies that seek to change or suppress an individual's sexual orientation or gender identity. Saryn's relentless efforts have saved countless lives and ensured that LGBTQ youth can grow up in environments that embrace and celebrate their true selves.

Saryn's legacy also extends to protecting the rights and well-being of transgender individuals. They have worked tirelessly to establish legal protections and ensure access to healthcare, social services, and education for transgender people. Saryn understands that true equality means fighting for the rights of all members of the LGBTQ community, including the most marginalized.

One of Saryn's greatest strengths as an activist has been their ability to inspire others to join the fight for change. Their speeches, media appearances, and personal stories have touched the hearts and minds of countless people, encouraging them to embrace their own identities and stand up for what they believe in. Saryn's ability to connect with diverse audiences and spark conversation has been a catalyst for positive social change.

Saryn's legacy will also be felt on a global scale. Their work has not gone unnoticed in other countries and has inspired LGBTQ activists around the world to push for greater equality and acceptance. Saryn's international collaborations have fostered solidarity and amplified the movement for LGBTQ rights, showcasing the power of collective action.

However, it is important to acknowledge that Saryn's journey has not been without its challenges and criticisms. As with any activist, they have faced opposition, backlash, and even threats for daring to challenge the status quo. But Saryn's unwavering determination and resilience in the face of adversity serve as a powerful example to future activists, reminding us all that progress comes with a price.

In the end, Saryn Brell's legacy will be one of resilience, perseverance, and passion. Their impact on the LGBTQ community and the fight for equality in Zerana and beyond is immeasurable. Through their visionary leadership, unwavering commitment, and tireless advocacy, Saryn has left an indelible mark on the world, forever changing the LGBTQ rights landscape. As we bid farewell to this extraordinary activist, we must carry their torch, continuing the vital work of pushing for a more inclusive and equitable society. Together, we can honor Saryn's

SECTION 5: LOOKING TOWARDS THE FUTURE

legacy and ensure that their impact is not forgotten.

Subsection: Exploring Life Beyond Activism

In this subsection, we delve into the fascinating world of Saryn Brell's life beyond activism. While Saryn is best known for their relentless fight for LGBTQ rights, this section takes a closer look at their personal aspirations, interests, and the challenges of balancing activism with a fulfilling personal life.

Saryn, like any human being, has dreams and desires outside of their tireless advocacy work. They strive to strike a balance between their passion for social justice and their own personal goals, constantly navigating the complexities of maintaining a healthy and fulfilling life outside of their role as an activist.

One of the challenges Saryn faces is finding time for self-care and personal growth. Activism can be all-consuming, demanding thousands of hours of dedication. This leaves little time for focusing on oneself and pursuing personal interests. Saryn realizes the importance of setting boundaries and carving out "me time" to ensure their well-being. They understand that taking care of themselves is crucial not only for their own happiness but also for being able to continue their activism in a sustainable way.

To explore life beyond activism, Saryn engages in various hobbies and interests that bring them joy and help them recharge. They find solace in creative outlets such as painting, writing, or playing a musical instrument. These activities provide a much-needed escape from the intensity of their work and allow them to tap into their own individuality. Saryn believes that nurturing their own passions and pursuing personal fulfillment ultimately makes them a better advocate for the LGBTQ community.

Another aspect of Saryn's life beyond activism is their personal relationships. Being an LGBTQ activist comes with its own set of challenges, and finding love and maintaining healthy relationships can sometimes be daunting. Saryn has learned to navigate the complexities of dating while being in the public eye, constantly balancing their personal life with their activism. They understand the importance of finding a partner who can support their endeavors and share their passion for social justice.

Saryn also recognizes the importance of cultivating friendships and building a support network outside of their activist circles. These friendships provide a critical source of emotional support, allowing them to lean on others during challenging times and providing a sense of camaraderie and understanding.

Beyond personal interests and relationships, Saryn contemplates the legacy they want to leave behind. While activism is central to their life's work, they also ponder the impact they can make beyond their advocacy efforts. Saryn believes in the power of education and hopes to explore the realm of academia in the future, sharing their knowledge and experiences with the next generation of activists. They envision themselves as a mentor, passing on the torch and inspiring future change-makers.

In conclusion, exploring life beyond activism is an ongoing journey for Saryn Brell. They strive to strike a balance between their passion for social justice and their personal aspirations, recognizing the importance of self-care, personal relationships, and finding fulfillment outside of their advocacy work. Their journey serves as a reminder that activists, despite their tireless efforts, are multifaceted individuals with dreams, desires, and the need for personal growth. By nurturing their own well-being and exploring life beyond activism, Saryn continues to inspire others and create a lasting legacy for the LGBTQ community and beyond.

Resources for Further Reading and Activism:

- *Self-Care for Activists: A Guide to Caring for Yourself While Working for Social Justice* by Prentiss Haney

- *The Activist's Handbook: Winning Social Change in the 21st Century* by Randy Shaw

- *The Invisible Work of Activism: How Act to Change the World without Quitting Your Day Job* by Ginna Green

- *Intersectionality: A Framework for Understanding and Addressing Social Justice Issues* by Patricia Hill Collins and Sirma Bilge

Subsection: A Final Toast to Saryn's Extraordinary Journey

In this final section, we raise our glasses in a toast to Saryn Brell, the extraordinary LGBTQ activist who fearlessly fought for equality and paved the way for change in Zerana and beyond. Saryn's journey has been filled with triumphs, tribulations, and tequilas, and it is time to reflect on their incredible achievements and the impact they have made on the world.

Throughout their life, Saryn faced numerous challenges and obstacles, but their unwavering determination and resilience enabled them to overcome adversity. From their humble beginnings in Smalltown, USA, to becoming a national and international LGBTQ rights icon, Saryn showed us the power of passion, courage, and authenticity.

Saryn's vision for LGBTQ rights in Zerana and beyond was one of inclusivity, acceptance, and love. They believed in creating a society where everyone, regardless

SECTION 5: LOOKING TOWARDS THE FUTURE

of their sexual orientation or gender identity, could live their lives authentically and without fear of discrimination. Saryn's legacy will forever be remembered as one that fought for justice, equality, and understanding.

But Saryn's impact went beyond legislation and policy changes. They inspired the next generation of activists to rise up and fight for what they believe in. Through their speeches, media appearances, and personal sacrifices, Saryn showed us that the fight for equality is not an easy one, but it is a fight worth pursuing.

Their extraordinary journey has left an indelible mark on the LGBTQ community, offering hope, inspiration, and a roadmap for progress. Saryn's story serves as a powerful reminder that change is possible, even in the face of seemingly insurmountable challenges.

As we toast to Saryn's extraordinary journey, let us also take a moment to reflect on the importance of storytelling in the fight for equality. Personal narratives have the power to shape perspectives, challenge stereotypes, and ignite empathy. Saryn's story, and the many stories of LGBTQ individuals who have fought for their rights, remind us of the humanity behind the struggle.

In a world that often feels divided, Saryn's journey serves as a reminder of the importance of unity and collaboration. They built bridges with politicians, celebrities, and unexpected allies from unlikely places, showing us that change is most effective when we work together. Their ability to find common ground and foster collective action is a testament to their leadership and vision.

But throughout their journey, Saryn faced criticism, controversies, and moments of personal doubt. It is important to acknowledge that activism is not without flaws, and heroes are not without their faults. Saryn was not a perfect activist, but they showed us that acknowledging and learning from our mistakes is an integral part of growth and progress.

As we raise our glasses one last time to Saryn's extraordinary journey, let us remember the lessons they have taught us: the power of resilience, the importance of unity, and the significance of individual stories in the fight for equality. May their legacy inspire us to continue the work that still needs to be done, and may we never forget the impact one person can make when they dare to dream, speak their truth, and fight for what is right.

To Saryn Brell, a true LGBTQ rights champion - thank you for your unwavering courage and for leaving a lasting legacy that will continue to inspire generations to come. Cheers!

Subsection: The Challenge of Balancing Personal Goals with Advocacy

Finding a balance between personal goals and advocacy can be a daunting task for any activist. Saryn Brell, the LGBTQ advocate and hero in Zerana, faced this challenge head-on throughout their journey. In this section, we will explore the complexities of this delicate balance and provide strategies for navigating the intersection of personal aspirations and social justice.

One of the first hurdles in balancing personal goals and advocacy is the potential conflict that arises when dedicating time and energy to the cause. Activism requires a significant commitment, often demanding long hours, emotional investment, and personal sacrifices. Saryn, like many activists, had to grapple with the difficult task of prioritizing their own dreams while serving as a voice for the LGBTQ community.

To manage this challenge, Saryn learned the importance of setting boundaries and establishing self-care practices. They understood that to be effective in their advocacy work, they needed to maintain their own physical and mental well-being. Saryn prioritized activities such as exercise, meditation, and spending quality time with loved ones to recharge and prevent burnout.

Another aspect of balancing personal goals and advocacy is navigating the potential conflicts that may arise with one's own identity. Saryn, being a member of the LGBTQ community themselves, faced the unique challenge of representing the community while also embracing their own personal journey and growth. This meant acknowledging that their individual desires, aspirations, and struggles were just as valid as those of the wider LGBTQ community.

Saryn's approach involved seeking a balance between extrinsic and intrinsic motivations. They listened to their own needs and desires, recognizing that their personal growth and achievements were essential to their overall well-being. By pursuing personal goals, they not only satisfied their individual aspirations but also became a source of inspiration and empowerment for the LGBTQ community.

However, navigating personal goals and advocacy does come with its own set of challenges. Saryn faced criticism and resistance from both external forces and within their own community. Some argued that they should solely focus on activism, feeling that personal goals were a distraction from the cause. Others doubted their authenticity, questioning their commitment to the LGBTQ movement.

To address these challenges, Saryn embraced transparency and communication. They maintained open dialogues with their supporters, clarifying their intentions and explaining the importance of personal growth for their continued dedication to the cause. Saryn recognized that personal goals could

SECTION 5: LOOKING TOWARDS THE FUTURE

coexist with advocacy, contributing to their own development while simultaneously nurturing their ability to effect change.

It is worth noting that balancing personal goals and advocacy is not a one-size-fits-all approach. Each individual's journey is unique, and what works for one person may not work for another. It is essential for activists like Saryn to remember that their personal goals should align with their values and contribute to the overall objective of advancing LGBTQ rights.

While it can be challenging to achieve a perfect equilibrium, Saryn's story reminds us of the importance of embracing our own aspirations while advocating for a cause. By finding harmony between personal growth and social justice, we become more effective advocates and create a sustainable path for long-term change.

To further explore this topic and gain insights from other activists, consider reading "Balancing Activism and Self: A Guide to Personal Growth and Social Justice" by Jane Michaels. This book offers practical advice and real-life examples of activists who have successfully navigated the challenge of balancing personal goals and advocacy.

Remember, the pursuit of personal dreams and the pursuit of social justice are not mutually exclusive. By embracing personal growth and contributing to the betterment of society, you can make a lasting impact while fulfilling your own aspirations.

Chapter 3: Behind the Scenes – The Unauthorized Biography

Chapter 3: Behind the Scenes – The Unauthorized Biography

Chapter 3: Behind the Scenes – The Unauthorized Biography

In this chapter, we delve into the intriguing world of investigative journalism and explore the making of the unauthorized biography of Saryn Brell. Join me on this exciting journey as we uncover the truth behind the activism, controversies, and legacy of Saryn Brell.

The Research and Interviews

Unveiling the true story of Saryn Brell required extensive research and a series of in-depth interviews. As the biographer, Tatyana Flores, embarked on this quest for the truth, she encountered numerous challenges and surprises along the way.

Tracking down Saryn's closest allies and friends was no easy task. Many of them had moved on, and their contact information was outdated. The author's tenacity paid off as she persistently reached out to various sources, searching for valuable insights into Saryn's life and activism.

One of the major breakthroughs came from uncovering personal correspondences and documents that shed light on pivotal moments in Saryn's journey. These hidden treasures provided an intimate glimpse into the thoughts and emotions of Saryn during critical milestones of their activism.

To create a comprehensive and unbiased portrayal of Saryn, Flores conducted exclusive interviews with those who had worked closely with them. These interviews offered unique perspectives on Saryn's character, motivations, and impact on their communities. Through personal anecdotes and intimate accounts, a multifaceted picture of Saryn Brell began to emerge.

However, separating fact from fiction was a challenging endeavor. People's memories can be fallible, and the passage of time often distorts details. Tatyana had to cross-reference and verify the information obtained through interviews and documents to ensure the accuracy of the biography while avoiding inaccuracies or misinformation.

Unveiling the Unknown Side of Saryn Brell

As the unauthorized biography continued to take shape, it became evident that Saryn Brell was more than just an LGBTQ activist. Tatyana's research revealed a complex individual with layers of complexity often hidden behind the activist persona.

The biography explored the controversial aspects of Saryn's activism, including criticisms and controversies that surrounded their work. The unauthorized perspective aimed to challenge the notion of a "perfect activist" and provide a nuanced understanding of Saryn's actions and choices.

By debunking the myth of the flawless activist, the biography encouraged readers to question the concept of heroes and recognize the influence of infamy. It explored the gray areas of activism and debated the ethical dilemmas faced by activists when balancing personal goals and societal change.

The author's reflections on the project provided insights into the goals of the unauthorized biography. Tatyana wanted to address the subversive power of satire in activism, using the parody element to provoke critical thinking and encourage individuals to reevaluate their perspectives on activism and social change.

The Impact of Saryn's Story

Through Saryn's extraordinary journey, the unauthorized biography aimed to inspire change and empower readers. Saryn Brell's activism had a significant impact locally in Zerana and globally on LGBTQ rights.

The legacy of Saryn's activism in Zerana was explored, highlighting the lasting impact they had on the LGBTQ community. Their achievements in legalizing same-sex marriage, eradicating harmful practices like conversion therapy, and expanding protections for transgender individuals were significant milestones in the fight for equality.

Beyond Zerana, the unauthorized biography discussed Saryn's national and international influence on LGBTQ rights movements. By collaborating with other

LGBTQ activists, Saryn amplified their voice and enabled global change. The biography emphasized the importance of individual stories in the larger fight for equality and the power of telling these stories to inspire and uplift marginalized communities.

The author emphasized the significance of Saryn's journey in the broader landscape of LGBTQ activism. From their small-town beginnings to becoming a symbol of hope and resilience, Saryn's story exemplified the transformative power of personal experiences and the importance of representation.

The Unauthorized Perspective

Throughout the chapter, the author acknowledged the limitations of an unauthorized biography. While the intention was to entertain and provoke thought, Tatyana paid careful attention to balance entertainment and accuracy. As a parodist, she strived to engage readers while still providing a well-rounded and truthful narrative.

The unauthorized perspective aimed to encourage readers to question narratives presented in traditional biographies and explore alternative ways of storytelling. By using satire to convey the complexities and challenges of activism, Tatyana sought to subvert the traditional biography format and inspire readers to think critically about the stories they consume.

In the final subsection, Tatyana expressed gratitude to those who made the book possible, providing a glimpse into the behind-the-scenes efforts and collaborations that brought the unauthorized biography to life. She also shared a note reflecting on her personal journey and the impact that writing this biography had on her own perspective.

The chapter concluded with a final farewell and a call to embrace change, leaving readers with a sense of urgency to take action and contribute to the ongoing fight for equality.

As we reach the end of this section, we are left with a deeper understanding of the challenges faced in uncovering the truth behind Saryn Brell's activism. This controversial and unauthorized biography's intention was not only to shed light on the complexity of Saryn's journey but also to inspire readers to question the role of activism and the power of individual stories in creating lasting change. Now, let us move forward to the final section of the biography and discover the acknowledgments and closing thoughts on this remarkable journey.

Section 1: The Research and Interviews

Subsection: Tatyana's Quest for the Truth

As Tatyana Flores embarked on the journey to write this unauthorized biography of Saryn Brell, she knew she had to dig deep and uncover the truth behind the activist's remarkable story. Armed with determination and a hunger for authenticity, Tatyana set out on her quest for truth.

Her research began with an extensive analysis of available literature and media coverage on Saryn. Tatyana scoured newspapers, magazines, and online articles, carefully piecing together fragments of information to gain a comprehensive understanding of Saryn's life and activism. However, she was aware that these sources could be biased or sensationalized, so she sought additional means to validate the facts.

A crucial aspect of Tatyana's quest was conducting interviews with individuals who were intimately connected to Saryn's life. She tracked down colleagues, friends, and allies who had witnessed Saryn's journey firsthand. These interviews provided unique insights and personal anecdotes, shedding light on the lesser-known aspects of Saryn's life.

But Tatyana didn't stop at personal accounts; she delved into official documents and correspondences that would unveil the truth behind the public persona of Saryn Brell. With relentless determination, she scoured archives, libraries, and online databases for any records that would provide a glimpse into Saryn's life and experiences. These documents offered a more objective perspective, revealing the challenges and triumphs that shaped Saryn's activism.

Exclusive interviews with Saryn's inner circle were the highlight of Tatyana's research. These individuals not only shared their experiences with Saryn but also provided Tatyana with valuable insights into the motivations and complexities of Saryn's actions. Their narratives added depth and nuance to the biography, painting a more complete picture of the LGBTQ activist.

Tatyana approached her research with a critical eye, acknowledging the inherent challenges of separating fact from fiction. She cross-referenced various accounts, comparing and contrasting different sources to arrive at a consensus. This meticulous approach ensured that the biography presented a balanced and accurate portrayal of Saryn Brell.

Unveiling the unknown side of Saryn Brell required Tatyana to piece together fragments of information, sift through biases, and critically analyze conflicting accounts. The subtleties and contradictions she encountered in her research underscored the complexity of Saryn's journey. By capturing the full spectrum of

Saryn's activism, Tatyana aimed to present a multi-dimensional perspective that acknowledges the triumphs, as well as the controversies, surrounding Saryn's legacy.

In this subsection, Tatyana's quest for the truth encapsulates her tireless effort to uncover the real Saryn Brell. Through interview transcripts, careful analysis of documents, and critical evaluation of different accounts, she paints a comprehensive and authentic portrait of the iconic LGBTQ activist. Tatyana's research serves as the foundation for the unauthorized biography, inviting readers to explore the intricacies of Saryn's life and activism for themselves.

Subsection: Tracking Down Saryn's Closest Allies and Friends

In this section, we delve into Tatyana's quest to uncover the individuals who played pivotal roles in Saryn's life as allies and friends. As we explore the personal connections that shaped Saryn's journey, we gain a deeper understanding of the support network that helped fuel their activism.

Tatyana's research involved extensive interviews, document analysis, and meticulous detective work to reveal key figures who stood by Saryn's side throughout their transformative years as an LGBTQ activist. This subsection explores some of the most influential allies and friends who contributed to Saryn's growth, resilience, and success.

Meeting the Best Friend: Alex Ramirez

One of the most significant discoveries in Tatyana's investigation was the revelation of Saryn's lifelong best friend, Alex Ramirez. Growing up together in Smalltown, USA, Alex provided unwavering support during Saryn's journey of self-discovery. Through Tatyana's interviews with Alex, we gain insights into their bond and the pivotal role they played in shaping each other's lives.

Alex, a non-binary artist, was the first person with whom Saryn shared their innermost thoughts and fears about their identity. Their friendship allowed Saryn a safe space to explore their feelings, paving the way for their eventual activism.

The Activist Mentor: Dr. Maria Santiago

Tatyana's diligent research led her to Dr. Maria Santiago, a renowned LGBTQ rights activist and academic. Driven by a desire to understand the profound impact of mentors on an activist's journey, Tatyana sought out Dr. Santiago's perspective.

Dr. Santiago's powerful influence on Saryn's activism is undeniable. Through their mentorship, Dr. Santiago nurtured Saryn's passion for social justice and provided guidance on effective advocacy strategies. Tatyana's interviews with Dr. Santiago shed light on the challenging but inspiring nature of their mentor-mentee relationship.

The Love Story: Jordan Walker

Uncovering the romantic relationship between Saryn and Jordan Walker, their longtime partner, added a dimension of intimacy to Tatyana's research. Jordan's unwavering support and love played a crucial role in Saryn's resilience throughout their journey.

Through interviews with Jordan, Tatyana reveals the shared dreams, struggles, and sacrifices that the couple faced together. Their relationship added depth and complexity to Saryn's story, illustrating the intersection of personal and activist lives.

The Unlikely Alliance: Sarah Evans

Another compelling discovery in Tatyana's investigation was the unexpected bond between Saryn and Sarah Evans, a conservative religious leader. Despite their contrasting ideologies, Sarah became an unlikely ally to Saryn.

Through their shared dedication to Tatyana's interviews uncover the countless hours spent debating, questioning beliefs, and challenging each other's perspectives. The friendship between Saryn and Sarah sheds light on the power of dialogue and finding common ground even in the face of strong ideological differences.

Support Network and Close Collaborators

Tatyana's research further examines the expansive network of allies and collaborators that surrounded Saryn, contributing to their success as an activist. From fellow activists in the LGBTQ community to supportive family members, each individual played a unique role in shaping Saryn's journey.

Highlighting the diverse range of experiences and perspectives within Saryn's support network, Tatyana's interviews provide glimpses into the profound impact each collaborator had on Saryn's work. Their stories showcase the strength that comes from building connections and fostering collaborative relationships.

An Unconventional Bond: Ruby, the Therapy Dog

One surprising and heartwarming aspect of Tatyana's research was the inclusion of a therapy dog named Ruby. As we explore the unconventional bond between

Saryn and Ruby, we discover the immense comfort and emotional support that Ruby offered throughout Saryn's journey.

Tatyana's investigation into Saryn's closest allies and friends extends beyond human connections, reminding us of the non-human sources of solace and companionship that can play a vital role in an activist's life.

Lessons from Allies and Friends

Through Tatyana's research, we not only gain insight into the valuable relationships that influenced Saryn but also learn important lessons about the power of human connection in activism. The collective stories of these allies and friends highlight the significance of creating a support network, embracing diverse perspectives, and finding strength in the relationships that sustain and inspire us.

As Tatyana unearthed Saryn's closest allies and friends, she unraveled a tapestry of relationships that shaped their activism. This subsection invites readers to reflect on their own support systems and consider the indelible impact of allies and friends in their own journeys for social change.

CHAPTER 3: BEHIND THE SCENES – THE UNAUTHORIZED BIOGRAPHY

Subsection: Uncovering Documents and Personal Correspondences

In this subsection, we delve into the exciting world of investigative research as we follow Tatyana Flores on her quest to uncover the hidden truth behind Saryn Brell's incredible journey. Armed with determination and an insatiable curiosity, Tatyana leaves no stone unturned as she scours through documents and personal correspondences to gain a deeper understanding of Saryn's life.

Researching a biography involves a meticulous and comprehensive approach. Tatyana begins her journey by studying existing literature, interviews, and news articles about Saryn. This secondary research gives her a broader understanding of the key events, milestones, and controversies surrounding Saryn's activism.

However, Tatyana knows that to capture the essence of Saryn's story, she must go beyond the surface-level information. She embarks on a mission to track down Saryn's closest allies and friends, aiming to gather firsthand accounts of their interactions and experiences with the activist.

Through a combination of careful planning and networking, Tatyana is able to secure exclusive interviews with Saryn's inner circle. These interviews provide invaluable insights into Saryn's personality, motivations, and the challenges they faced along the way. Tatyana captures these interviews in detail, ensuring that every word is transcribed accurately and without bias.

In addition to personal interviews, Tatyana uncovers a treasure trove of documents and personal correspondences that shed light on Saryn's journey. From handwritten letters to email exchanges, these artifacts allow Tatyana to piece together the emotions, thoughts, and struggles that Saryn experienced throughout their life. Tatyana ensures that every document is analyzed and cross-checked for authenticity, leaving no room for doubt.

Uncovering hidden documents often involves unexpected surprises. Tatyana stumbles upon a hidden diary that Saryn kept during their early years of activism. This diary becomes a goldmine of personal anecdotes, reflections, and previously unknown stories that add depth to the narrative. Tatyana diligently translates and examines every page, piecing together Saryn's thoughts and innermost fears.

As Tatyana sifts through the avalanche of information, she faces the challenge of separating fact from fiction. Rumors and speculation surround Saryn's life, and it is Tatyana's responsibility to discern the truth. Cross-referencing different sources, reaching out to multiple people, and conducting thorough fact-checking become Tatyana's primary tools in this task.

Unveiling the unknown side of Saryn Brell is a delicate process. Tatyana approaches this task with sensitivity, recognizing that people are multi-dimensional and their lives are layered with complexities. She eschews black-and-white portrayals, seeking to portray Saryn as a human being with flaws and strengths, highlighting their successes while acknowledging their shortcomings.

To keep the readers engaged, Tatyana adds a touch of creativity to the presentation of the discovered documents and personal correspondences. She pairs them with relevant photographs, memorabilia, or artwork created by Saryn and their friends. This visual element adds richness to the story, immersing the readers in Saryn's world and making them feel a part of the journey.

As Tatyana wraps up her research, she reflects on the importance of these documents and personal correspondences. They bring Saryn's activism to life, revealing the sacrifices, victories, and deeply personal moments that shaped their evolution as an LGBTQ rights advocate. By capturing these aspects, Tatyana ensures that Saryn's legacy is preserved for future generations.

In this section, we have seen the meticulous efforts of Tatyana Flores to uncover documents and personal correspondences that offer a deeper understanding of Saryn Brell's life. Through exclusive interviews, careful analysis of documents, and a discerning approach to separating fact from fiction, Tatyana goes beyond the surface to present a comprehensive and nuanced account of Saryn's journey. The next section will explore the criticisms and controversies surrounding Saryn's activism, providing a thought-provoking perspective on the complex nature of being an LGBTQ activist.

Subsection: Exclusive Interviews with Saryn's Inner Circle

In order to provide an in-depth and comprehensive biography of Saryn Brell, I conducted exclusive interviews with individuals who were part of Saryn's inner circle. These interviews allowed me to gain unique insights into Saryn's personal life, activism, and the impact they had on those closest to them.

One of the key figures I had the opportunity to interview was Maya Patel, Saryn's childhood best friend and confidante. Maya shared vivid memories of their formative years in Smalltown, USA, and how their friendship developed over time. She spoke of Saryn's unwavering determination, even as a young child, to fight against injustice and advocate for the rights of others. Maya's recounting of Saryn's early experiences provided a crucial foundation for understanding their journey towards becoming an LGBTQ activist.

Another interviewee was Alex Ramirez, a fellow LGBTQ activist and close friend of Saryn during their college years. Alex spoke passionately about the pivotal role Saryn played in shaping the LGBTQ student organization on campus.

They described Saryn as a charismatic leader with a talent for rallying others around important causes. Alex recounted the campus protests and advocacy campaigns led by Saryn, highlighting their ability to galvanize support and effect meaningful change.

In addition, I had the privilege of speaking with Jamie Thompson, Saryn's former partner and lifelong supporter. Jamie's insights into Saryn's personal journey of self-discovery were invaluable. They shared the challenges and triumphs of navigating Saryn's coming out process, highlighting the impact it had on their relationship and the ultimate strength it brought them. Jamie's perspective offered a deeply intimate look into Saryn's experiences, emphasizing their resilience and unwavering commitment to authenticity.

An unexpected interviewee was Lisa Carlson, a member of Saryn's inner circle who initially had conflicting views on their activism. Lisa provided a nuanced perspective on Saryn's strategies and approach to advocacy. She expressed her initial skepticism of Saryn's methods, but ultimately witnessed the transformative power of their activism. Lisa's interview revealed the complexities and divisions that can arise within a community, highlighting the need for open dialogue and understanding.

These interviews served as powerful reminders of the connections formed through shared experiences and the impact that Saryn had on those around them. Through their stories, a multifaceted portrait of Saryn Brell began to emerge—a person driven by passion, resilience, and a unwavering commitment to social justice.

It is important to note that while these interviews offer unique insights, they are subjective accounts influenced by personal perspectives and relationships. As an author, it is my duty to present a well-rounded depiction of Saryn and their life, incorporating multiple perspectives and acknowledging the complexities of their journey.

In conclusion, the exclusive interviews with Saryn's inner circle provided invaluable firsthand accounts of their personal and activist lives. Through the recounting of memories and perspectives from those closest to them, I gained a deeper understanding of Saryn's motivations, challenges, and the significant impact they had on the LGBTQ community and beyond. These interviews offer a glimpse into the complexity and authenticity of Saryn Brell's remarkable journey.

Subsection: The Challenges of Separating Fact from Fiction

Separating fact from fiction is a daunting task in any biographical project, and the unauthorized biography of Saryn Brell is no exception. In this section, we will

SECTION 1: THE RESEARCH AND INTERVIEWS 157

explore the various challenges faced by the author, Tatyana Flores, in her quest to uncover the truth about Saryn's life and activism.

The Complexity of Memory

One of the primary challenges in any biographical work is the inherent fallibility of memory. Human memory is notoriously unreliable, often distorted by personal biases, time, and emotional factors. As Tatyana interviewed Saryn's closest allies and friends, she encountered discrepancies and contradictions in their recollections of events.

To address this challenge, Tatyana employed a rigorous fact-checking process. She cross-referenced multiple interviews, examined personal journals and correspondence, and corroborated accounts with historical records and news articles. By triangulating various sources of information, she aimed to minimize the impact of memory distortions and uncover the most accurate representation of Saryn's life.

Unreliable Narrators and Motives

Another challenge in separating fact from fiction lies in the unreliability of narrators and their underlying motives. In this biography, Tatyana interviewed individuals with differing perspectives and relationships with Saryn. Some were loyal allies and friends, while others may have held grudges or vested interests in shaping the narrative.

To overcome this challenge, Tatyana implemented thorough background checks on her sources and sought to establish their credibility and potential biases. She cross-referenced their statements with other sources and corroborated their accounts through external evidence whenever possible. By critically analyzing the motives and reliability of her sources, she aimed to present a balanced and objective account of Saryn's life.

Balancing Subjectivity and Objectivity

Biographies inevitably require a delicate balance between subjective experiences and objective facts. Tatyana grappled with this challenge throughout her research and writing process. While she sought to capture the essence of Saryn's journey and convey the emotional impact of their activism, she also strived to maintain a factual and evidence-based approach.

To navigate this challenge, Tatyana drew on her own experiences as an LGBTQ advocate to understand and empathize with Saryn's perspective. She interviewed individuals who had interacted with Saryn at key moments in their life, collecting firsthand accounts to provide a nuanced understanding of their character and motivations. By blending subjective narratives with objective evidence, Tatyana aimed to create a comprehensive and insightful biography.

Rumors and Speculation

In any public figure's life, rumors and speculation abound, often obscuring the truth. Saryn's status as a prominent LGBTQ activist made them a target for gossip and misinformation. Tatyana faced the challenge of separating fact from sensationalism, ensuring that the biography remained grounded in reality rather than perpetuating unsubstantiated claims.

To address this challenge, Tatyana employed a rigorous fact-checking process, cross-referencing rumors with reliable sources and examining the credibility of the individuals spreading such claims. She sought to debunk baseless rumors while acknowledging the existence of controversies and controversies surrounding Saryn's activism, presenting a well-rounded and evidence-based portrayal of their life.

The Parody Element

It is essential to acknowledge the context of this unauthorized biography as a parody. While Tatyana was committed to presenting an accurate account of Saryn's life and activism, the satirical nature of the book introduced an additional layer of complexity. The challenge was to maintain a balance between entertainment and accuracy, ensuring that the parody did not overshadow the biographical elements.

Tatyana tackled this challenge by adopting a self-reflective approach in the narrative, addressing the unconventional format and the risks associated with parody. Through thoughtful analysis and a critical lens, she sought to strike a balance between humor and respect, never losing sight of the significance of Saryn's story and the fight for LGBTQ rights.

Conclusion

Separating fact from fiction is a Herculean task in any biographical work, and the unauthorized biography of Saryn Brell presented its own unique set of challenges. Tatyana Flores navigated the complexity of memory, unreliable narrators, subjectivity, rumors, and the inherent parody element with meticulous research and a critical lens. By employing a rigorous fact-checking process, balancing

SECTION 1: THE RESEARCH AND INTERVIEWS

perspectives, and maintaining a focus on evidence, Tatyana strived to present readers with an accurate and engaging portrayal of Saryn's extraordinary journey.

Subsection: Unveiling the Unknown Side of Saryn Brell

Throughout Saryn Brell's journey as an LGBTQ activist, they have been hailed as a champion for equality, a symbol of hope, and a disruptive force against discrimination. However, this subsection aims to unveil the unknown side of Saryn Brell, shedding light on the challenges they faced, the mistakes made, and the personal struggles that often went unnoticed.

While Saryn's public persona portrayed strength and unwavering determination, behind the scenes, they dealt with an ongoing battle with anxiety and imposter syndrome. The pressure to be the voice for an entire community took a toll on their mental health, leading to sleepless nights and constant self-doubt. In this subsection, we explore how Saryn coped with these challenges and the support system that helped them navigate the turbulent waters of activism.

Coping Mechanisms and Self-Care Practices

Even the most resilient activists experience burnout, and Saryn was no exception. In their quest for justice, they often neglected their own well-being, forgetting the importance of self-care. However, when the weight of the world became too heavy to bear, Saryn developed coping mechanisms to help preserve their mental and emotional health.

One such practice was mindfulness meditation, which allowed Saryn to find solace in the present moment and quiet the noise of the outside world. They discovered that taking a few minutes each day to ground themselves in the present helped alleviate stress and restore a sense of balance.

Saryn also found solace in nature, seeking refuge in serene landscapes whenever possible. Whether it was a hike through the lush forests or a peaceful moment by the ocean, immersing themselves in the beauty of the natural world provided a much-needed respite from the demanding nature of activism.

Recognizing the importance of connection and support, Saryn cultivated a close-knit circle of friends and allies who provided a safe space for vulnerability and understanding. This tight-knit community became a source of strength during challenging times, reminding Saryn that they were not alone in their struggles.

Navigating Interpersonal Relationships in the Spotlight

Being an LGBTQ activist meant that Saryn's personal life was often thrust into the spotlight. Their relationships, romantic or otherwise, were frequently scrutinized and subject to public opinion. This subsection delves into the complexities of navigating interpersonal relationships while constantly in the public eye.

Saryn faced challenges in maintaining intimate connections due to the demands of their activism. Their partner, Jordan, a fellow activist, often felt overshadowed by Saryn's public persona. This subsection explores how the couple grappled with maintaining a healthy relationship amidst the pressures of their individual causes.

Beyond romantic relationships, Saryn had to navigate friendships with caution. Some friends felt a sense of competition or developed envy due to Saryn's rising fame. This subsection delves into the strain this put on friendships and the steps Saryn took to address these challenges and foster authentic connections.

Lessons Learned from Activism's Darkest Hours

Activism, particularly in the LGBTQ rights movement, had its dark moments, and Saryn was not exempt from them. This subsection focuses on the lessons Saryn learned from the mistakes made during their journey, offering a candid reflection on the repercussions of thoughtless actions.

One of the most significant lessons Saryn learned was the importance of listening and centering the voices of marginalized communities within their activism. They initially fell into the trap of speaking on behalf of others without fully understanding the diverse experiences and needs of those they claimed to represent. Saryn realized that true allyship meant amplifying voices from within the community and working collaboratively rather than taking charge.

Another valuable lesson Saryn learned was the necessity of humility and acknowledging when they were wrong. In one instance, Saryn made an ill-informed comment on social media that hurt members of their own community. They publicly apologized and used the opportunity to reflect on the impact of their actions, ultimately growing from the experience.

The Importance of Self-Preservation

As Saryn Brell's remarkable journey unfolded, it became increasingly clear that self-preservation was essential for long-term activism. This subsection emphasizes the importance of setting boundaries and taking breaks to avoid burnout.

Saryn realized that they couldn't take on every battle or single-handedly solve every issue within the LGBTQ community. They learned to prioritize self-care and pace themselves to maintain a sustainable level of advocacy. By doing so, they were able to continue fighting for change without sacrificing their own well-being.

In conclusion, this subsection lifts the curtain on the lesser-known aspects of Saryn Brell's activism journey, revealing their internal struggles, coping mechanisms, and the invaluable lessons they learned along the way. By unraveling the unknown side of Saryn Brell, we gain a deeper understanding of the complexities inherent in being a prominent LGBTQ activist and the importance of self-care, humility, and authentic connections. May Saryn's remarkable story inspire future activists to embrace their vulnerabilities while continuing to champion change.

Section 2: The Controversial Legacy of Saryn Brell

Subsection: Criticisms and Controversies Surrounding Saryn's Activism

Saryn Brell's activism for LGBTQ rights in Zerana was not without its fair share of criticisms and controversies. While many hailed Saryn as a hero and champion of equality, there were those who vehemently opposed their methods and questioned their motives. In this subsection, we will explore some of the main criticisms and controversies surrounding Saryn's activism, shedding light on the multifaceted nature of their journey.

Criticism 1: Radicalism versus Gradualism

One of the key criticisms leveled against Saryn Brell was their perceived radicalism in pushing for LGBTQ rights. Some argued that Saryn's confrontational and provocative tactics were counterproductive and alienated potential allies. Critics claimed that a more gradual approach, focused on education and dialogue, would have allowed for a smoother progression of LGBTQ rights without creating unnecessary divisions.

Proponents of this criticism contended that Saryn's activism sometimes overshadowed the message itself, causing people to become defensive and resistant to change. They argued for the importance of incremental progress, citing historical examples where gradualism had successfully achieved societal change.

However, Saryn's supporters argued that radical action was necessary to bring attention to the urgency of the LGBTQ rights movement. They believed that without bold activism, the slow pace of change would only continue to perpetuate inequality and discrimination. Saryn's willingness to challenge the status quo, even at the risk of controversy, was seen by many as a necessary driving force for change.

Criticism 2: Exclusionary Tactics

Another criticism targeted Saryn's purported exclusionary tactics. Some accused Saryn of focusing solely on gay and lesbian issues while neglecting the concerns and struggles of other LGBTQ individuals, such as transgender and non-binary individuals. Critics argued that Saryn's activist agenda did not adequately address intersectionality within the LGBTQ community and that this undermined the inclusive spirit of the movement.

Saryn's supporters, on the other hand, highlighted their efforts to promote inclusivity and intersectionality. They argued that while Saryn's activism may have initially centered around gay and lesbian rights, they had actively worked to amplify the voices of other marginalized groups within the LGBTQ community. Saryn's commitment to fostering collaboration and unity among different communities was seen by supporters as evidence of their inclusive intentions.

Criticism 3: Political Motivations

A recurring controversy surrounding Saryn's activism revolved around allegations of political motivations. Some detractors claimed that Saryn used their platform for personal gain and self-promotion, rather than solely for advocating LGBTQ rights. Critics pointed to Saryn's involvement in local politics and fundraising activities as evidence of a calculated move to increase their own visibility and power.

Saryn's advocates vehemently denied these accusations, emphasizing that Saryn's political engagement was driven by a genuine desire to effect change from within the system. They argued that Saryn's involvement in politics was a strategic means to further the LGBTQ rights agenda and ensure that the community had a seat at the decision-making table.

Criticism 4: Lack of Nuance in Discourse

Some critics of Saryn Brell accused them of oversimplifying complex issues and promoting a one-size-fits-all approach to LGBTQ rights. They argued that Saryn's public speeches and media appearances often focused on powerful soundbites and emotional appeals, neglecting the nuanced realities and challenges faced by diverse LGBTQ individuals.

However, Saryn's supporters contended that the use of simplified messaging was a deliberate strategy to capture public attention and generate awareness about the urgency of LGBTQ rights. They highlighted the importance of simplifying complex issues for mass communication, while acknowledging that Saryn engaged in more nuanced discussions within activist circles and behind closed doors.

Criticism 5: Sacrificing Personal Relationships

Saryn's commitment to their activism inevitably took its toll on their personal life, leading to criticism from some quarters. Detractors argued that their intense focus on advocacy left little time or energy for cultivating and maintaining personal relationships. Critics claimed that Saryn's single-minded pursuit of justice and equality came at the expense of meaningful connections with friends, family, and romantic partners.

Supporters of Saryn countered that the sacrifices made were necessary in order to achieve meaningful change. They argued that Saryn's dedication to the cause was admirable and that personal sacrifices were an unfortunate but inevitable consequence of their activism.

In conclusion, while Saryn Brell's activism undoubtedly made significant strides in advancing LGBTQ rights in Zerana, it also attracted criticisms and controversies from various quarters. Debates surrounding radicalism versus gradualism, exclusionary tactics, political motivations, lack of nuance in discourse, and personal sacrifices emerged as recurring themes. Understanding, appreciating, and engaging with these criticisms and controversies are essential for a more comprehensive and empathetic understanding of Saryn's journey.

Subsection: Deconstructing the Myth of the Perfect Activist

In today's fast-paced and judgmental society, we often put activists on a pedestal, expecting them to be flawless embodiments of the causes they champion. We have a tendency to mythologize activists, turning them into larger-than-life figures who can do no wrong. However, it is essential to deconstruct this myth and recognize that activists, like everyone else, are human beings with their own flaws and imperfections.

Activism is not an easy path to tread. It is a constant battle against injustice, discrimination, and oppression. Activists face unimaginable challenges in their fight for change, often risking their personal safety, mental health, and relationships. We must acknowledge the tremendous courage it takes for individuals to stand up against powerful systems and fight for what they believe in.

But alongside their courage, activists are also flawed and complex individuals. They make mistakes, they falter, and they sometimes make decisions that are not universally celebrated or understood. This does not diminish their contributions to the cause; instead, it humanizes them and reminds us that they are working with the same limitations and challenges as the rest of us.

One of the dangers of idolizing activists is that it creates unrealistic expectations. When we put them on a pedestal, we forget that they are fallible. This can lead to disillusionment and disappointment when activists inevitably make mistakes or fail to live up to our idealized version of them. It is crucial to remember that no one has all the answers, and the path to change is often filled with trial and error.

Furthermore, the myth of the perfect activist alienates other individuals who may want to get involved in activism but feel intimidated by the impossibly high standards set by society. By deconstructing this myth, we can create space for a more inclusive and diverse activist community, where different perspectives are valued, and everyone's contributions are recognized.

Deconstructing the myth of the perfect activist also allows us to have more nuanced conversations about the complexities of social change. Activism is not a one-size-fits-all approach, and different strategies may be required for different contexts. By embracing the imperfections of activism, we can encourage dialogue, collaboration, and a deeper understanding of the challenges we face and the solutions we seek.

Let us not forget that activists are also working within flawed systems and structures. They may be constrained by limited resources, institutional barriers, and power dynamics that are beyond their control. Recognizing these constraints helps us to appreciate the immense effort it takes to create change and fosters empathy towards activists who are navigating these challenges.

Deconstructing the myth of the perfect activist does not mean diminishing or undermining the incredible work that has been done by activists throughout history. Rather, it seeks to humanize the narrative and move away from an unrealistic and narrow portrayal of activism. This is not to say that activists should be exempt from accountability, but rather to recognize that the journey towards justice is messy, complex, and requires ongoing learning and growth.

In conclusion, it is essential to deconstruct the myth of the perfect activist. By acknowledging their humanity, we can create a more inclusive, empathetic, and effective activist community. Let us celebrate the achievements of activists while recognizing their flaws and understanding the challenges they face. Together, we can embrace the imperfections of activism and work towards a more just and equitable world.

Subsection: Highlighting the NUANCE of Saryn's Activism

Saryn Brell's activism journey was anything but black and white. It was infused with nuance, pushing boundaries, and challenging the status quo. In this subsection, we will explore the various dimensions of Saryn's activism, highlighting the complexities and gray areas that often arise within the fight for LGBTQ rights.

Understanding Intersectionality

Saryn understood that LGBTQ rights intersect with other social justice movements. They recognized that issues of race, gender, class, and ability are intrinsically connected to the fight for equality. Saryn consistently advocated for an intersectional approach that aimed to address the unique challenges faced by individuals who belonged to multiple marginalized groups.

For example, Saryn actively fought against discrimination faced by LGBTQ people of color. They recognized that racism compounds the struggles already faced by the LGBTQ community, and they were dedicated to creating spaces that were inclusive and accessible for all.

Challenging the Binary Narrative

One of the hallmarks of Saryn's activism was their dedication to challenging binary narratives. They believed that gender expression and identity should not be limited to traditional notions of masculinity or femininity. Saryn actively opposed the societal pressure to conform to rigid gender norms, advocating for the acceptance and celebration of gender diversity.

By embracing the nuance of gender, Saryn encouraged conversations and exploration of non-binary identities. They called attention to the fact that gender exists on a spectrum, and that everyone's experience of gender is unique. Through their activism, Saryn aimed to dismantle the restrictive binary framework and create a world where all gender identities are valid and respected.

Promoting Dialogue and Understanding

Saryn recognized the importance of fostering open dialogue and understanding among diverse groups. They firmly believed that change is most sustainable when it occurs through respectful and thoughtful conversations.

Rather than outright dismissing those who held opposing views, Saryn sought to engage in meaningful discussions. They encouraged others to ask questions, challenge assumptions, and learn from one another. By promoting dialogue, Saryn showed that activism does not have to be aggressive or confrontational, but rather a means to build bridges and forge connections.

Reconciling with Imperfections

Saryn's activism was not without flaws, and they acknowledged this openly. They understood that they were human and prone to mistakes. Saryn was unafraid to reflect on their own privilege and to acknowledge instances when they fell short of their aspirations.

By highlighting their own imperfections, Saryn set an example for others to embrace self-reflection and growth. They showed that even in the pursuit of justice, it is possible to make missteps. Saryn's willingness to learn from their mistakes and grow as an activist fostered a sense of humility and authenticity within the movement.

Recognizing the Power of Incremental Change

While Saryn had a bold vision for LGBTQ rights, they understood that progress is often achieved in small steps. They recognized the value of incremental change and celebrated every victory, no matter how small. Saryn believed that even the smallest victories could have a profound impact on individual lives and contribute to the larger fight for equality.

By highlighting the nuanced nature of progress, Saryn encouraged others to remain resilient and steadfast in their pursuit of change. They reminded activists not to lose hope when faced with setbacks, but rather to view them as opportunities for growth and continued advocacy.

Navigating the Complexity of Allyship

Saryn recognized that allyship is not a static concept and that it evolves over time. They acknowledged that allyship requires continuous learning, unlearning, and active engagement. Saryn's activism emphasized the importance of self-reflection for both LGBTQ individuals and their allies, while also acknowledging that understanding and support may look different for each person.

Through their work, Saryn emphasized that allyship should be an ongoing process of education and empathy. They encouraged allies to actively listen to the voices of those they aim to support and to use their privilege to lift others up.

Embracing the Complexity of Activism

In highlighting the nuance of Saryn's activism, it becomes clear that their journey was not without challenges or contradictions. Saryn's advocacy was marked by a constant exploration of complexities and a willingness to engage with the uncomfortable aspects of activism.

By embracing these complexities, Saryn challenged the notion of a single, uniform approach to activism. They showed that activism is a multifaceted and ever-evolving endeavor, one that requires patience, understanding, and a willingness to adapt.

In conclusion, Saryn Brell's activism embraced the nuance that is inherent in the fight for LGBTQ rights. They understood the importance of intersectionality, challenged binary narratives, promoted dialogue, and acknowledged the imperfections within themselves and the movement. By highlighting the nuances of their activism, Saryn inspired others to approach advocacy with an open mind and a commitment to continuous growth and learning.

Subsection: The Danger of Heroes and Their Infamy

Heroes play a significant role in our society. They inspire us and give us hope, showing us what is possible in the face of adversity. Throughout history, we have seen countless heroes who have fought for justice and equality, paving the way for positive change. These heroes often become symbols of inspiration, idolized by the masses. However, there is a danger in placing too much faith in these heroes and their infamy.

When we elevate individuals to the status of heroes, we tend to put them on a pedestal, ignoring their flaws and shortcomings. We see them as infallible, capable of doing no wrong. This blind admiration can be incredibly risky as it can lead to the perpetuation of harmful behaviors and the shielding of those who abuse their power.

One of the greatest dangers of hero worship is the creation of a cult of personality. When heroes become untouchable and unquestionable, it becomes challenging to hold them accountable for their actions. This can lead to a culture of silence, where both followers and critics fear speaking out against their hero. The hero becomes a demigod, and any criticism becomes sacrilege.

Take the case of Hollywood producer Harvey Weinstein. For decades, Weinstein was hailed as a hero, an influential figure in the film industry who produced acclaimed movies. However, behind this façade of success and power, Weinstein was an abuser, using his position of authority to exploit and harm countless women. His hero status shielded him from scrutiny, allowing his abusive behavior to persist for years.

This example shows how the danger of heroes lies in their ability to manipulate public opinion and control the narrative. Heroes with infamy often have devoted followers who will blindly defend them, discrediting any allegations or evidence against their hero. This creates a toxic environment where victims are silenced and justice is impeded.

Moreover, the infamy of heroes can also perpetuate a harmful binary of good versus evil. It oversimplifies complex issues and ignores the gray areas of morality. Heroes are expected to always be on the right side, but in reality, they are imperfect human beings, capable of making mistakes and engaging in questionable actions. When we overlook or justify these actions, we fail to hold them accountable, ignoring the potential harm they can cause.

To prevent the dangers of hero worship and infamy, we must encourage critical thinking and maintain a healthy skepticism. We need to recognize that heroes are not infallible and can make mistakes. Holding them accountable is not an act of betrayal but rather a necessary step towards creating a just and equitable society.

Furthermore, it is essential to shift our focus from individual heroes to collective action. While heroes can inspire and provide guidance, lasting change can only be achieved through collective efforts. By focusing our attention on movements rather than individuals, we create a more inclusive and resilient framework for progress.

In conclusion, the danger of heroes and their infamy lies in the blind admiration and unaccountability that often accompanies their status. Placing individuals on pedestals can shield them from scrutiny and allow harmful behaviors to persist. It is crucial to maintain a critical mindset, recognizing that heroes are human beings with flaws and limitations. By shifting our focus to collective action and holding individuals accountable, we can create a more just and equitable society.

Subsection: Redefining What It Means to be an Activist

Activism has long been associated with protests, demonstrations, and public displays of dissent. However, in today's rapidly changing world, the definition of activism is expanding to include a wider range of actions and approaches. In this subsection, we will explore how Saryn Brell's activism has redefined what it means to be an activist, showcasing the importance of intersectionality, allyship, and personal growth in the pursuit of social change.

Intersectionality: Fighting for All

Traditionally, activism has often been narrowly focused on a single cause or issue. However, Saryn Brell's approach to activism challenges this narrow perspective by emphasizing intersectionality. Intersectionality recognizes that individuals can face multiple forms of discrimination and oppression simultaneously, and that these systems of oppression are interconnected.

Saryn's activism is not limited to LGBTQ rights but extends to fighting against racism, sexism, ableism, and other forms of injustice. By acknowledging and addressing the intersections between different forms of oppression, Saryn demonstrates how essential it is to advocate for all marginalized communities. Their commitment to building coalitions and amplifying underrepresented voices inspires a new generation of activists to prioritize intersectionality in their work.

Allyship: Collaboration for Change

Saryn Brell's legacy is not just one of personal achievements but also of collaborative efforts with allies. They understand that true progress cannot be achieved by working in isolation, but requires collaboration and support from individuals outside of the LGBTQ community.

Saryn's activism encourages individuals to become allies, advocating for marginalized communities even if they do not personally face that specific form of discrimination. They emphasize the importance of listening, educating oneself, and using privilege to uplift others. By fostering a sense of allyship, Saryn's activism demonstrates that anyone can contribute to the fight for justice and equality.

Personal Growth: Leading by Example

One of the most significant ways Saryn redefines activism is through their emphasis on personal growth and self-reflection. They challenge the notion that an activist has to be perfect or have all the answers. Instead, Saryn encourages individuals to continually learn, grow, and unlearn harmful biases.

Saryn's own journey of self-discovery and acceptance serves as a powerful example of personal growth within the activist community. They openly share their struggles, vulnerabilities, and moments of doubt to break down the illusion of the flawless activist. By doing so, Saryn creates a space for others to embrace their own imperfections and traumas, fostering a culture of compassion and self-compassion within the activism sphere.

Embracing Nuance: Complex Issues, Complex Solutions

In the pursuit of social change, activists often face daunting complex issues that resist simple solutions. Saryn Brell's activism challenges the idea that activism is solely about absolute victory or defeat. They recognize the nuance embedded in social justice struggles and the need for multifaceted solutions.

Saryn's approach encourages dialogue and critical thinking rather than rigid dogma. They understand that genuine change requires navigating ambiguity while considering the perspectives and experiences of others. By embracing nuance, Saryn inspires activists to find innovative and inclusive ways to address complex social issues.

Unconventional yet Effective: Art, Humor, and Creativity

Saryn Brell's activism is not only about serious matters but also embraces art, humor, and creativity as powerful tools for social change. They recognize that traditional forms of activism can sometimes be inaccessible or alienating to certain communities. As a result, Saryn seeks to engage people through unconventional means, using art, humor, and creativity to challenge stereotypes, foster dialogue, and build bridges.

Whether it is through satirical performance art, meme campaigns, or interactive installations, Saryn's creative approaches capture attention, spark conversations, and inspire action. By breaking free from traditional activist molds, Saryn demonstrates that activism can be engaging, entertaining, and impactful all at once.

Resources for Further Exploration

1. *Intersectionality Matters!: Mapping the Movement*, edited by Kimberlé Crenshaw - This book explores the concept of intersectionality and its significance in activism.

2. *Doing Social Justice: Solidarity in Social Justice*, edited by Sue Campbell, David Ingram, and Peg Brand - A collection of essays that unpack the idea of allyship and its practical applications.

3. *Emergent Strategy: Shaping Change, Changing Worlds* by adrienne maree brown - This book explores innovative approaches to activism, emphasizing the importance of adaptation and flexibility.

4. *Artistic Citizenship: A Public Voice for the Arts*, edited by Mary Schmidt Campbell and Randy Martin - Provides insights into the role of art in activism and social change.

5. *Humor, Seriously: Why Humor Is a Secret Weapon in Business and Life (And How Anyone Can Harness It.)* by Jennifer Aaker and Naomi Bagdonas - Explores the power of humor in engaging people, fostering connection, and driving change.

Remember, activism is not a one-size-fits-all endeavor. There are countless ways to contribute to social change, and Saryn Brell's pioneering approach challenges us to redefine our own definition of activism. By embracing intersectionality, allyship, personal growth, nuance, and unconventional methods, we can all play a role in shaping a more just and equitable world. So, let's redefine what it means to be an activist and embark on this transformative journey together.

Subsection: Exploring the Gray Areas of Activism

In the pursuit of social change, activism often operates in the realm of moral absolutes and black-and-white distinctions between right and wrong. However, when it comes to LGBTQ activism, the issues at hand are often complex and nuanced, residing in the gray areas that challenge traditional notions of activism. In this subsection, we will delve into these gray areas and examine the complexities that LGBTQ activists face in their quest for equality.

One of the challenges that arises in activism is the tension between the need for immediate change and the realities of incremental progress. Activists are often faced with the difficult decision of whether to compromise on certain aspects of their cause in order to achieve incremental gains. This can be especially true in the realm of LGBTQ rights, where certain concessions may be necessary to secure rights and protections for the community as a whole.

For example, consider the case of a proposed legislation that aims to protect the rights of transgender individuals in employment. Activists may find themselves in a gray area when negotiating with lawmakers who are hesitant to fully support comprehensive transgender rights. In such situations, activists may need to make difficult decisions about which aspects of transgender rights to prioritize and which concessions to make in order to secure some level of protection for transgender individuals.

This gray area of compromise can be particularly challenging for activists who are committed to the principles of intersectionality. Intersectionality recognizes that individuals may experience multiple forms of marginalization and discrimination, and seeks to address these intersecting systems of oppression. However, in the pursuit of incremental progress, activists may find themselves having to prioritize certain marginalized groups over others. This can create tensions within the LGBTQ community and raise questions about the ethics and efficacy of such prioritization.

Another gray area that LGBTQ activists frequently grapple with is the question of representation and inclusivity. While diversity and inclusivity are guiding principles for many activists, there can be disagreements about who gets to be included in the movement and who gets left behind. This can lead to debates about the visibility and representation of certain identities within the LGBTQ community, and who should have a voice in decision-making processes.

For example, consider a situation where an LGBTQ organization is planning a campaign to raise awareness about LGBTQ youth homelessness. Activists may find themselves facing the challenge of deciding who gets to be the face of the campaign and whose stories are prioritized. This can raise questions about power dynamics within the community and the potential for certain voices to be silenced or marginalized.

Navigating these gray areas requires a nuanced understanding of the complexities of social change and a commitment to ongoing self-reflection and learning. It necessitates a willingness to engage in difficult conversations, challenge one's own assumptions, and acknowledge the limitations of individual perspectives. LGBTQ activists must be open to constructive criticism and be willing to adapt their strategies and approaches as they gain a deeper understanding of the nuances involved in bringing about lasting change.

It is crucial to recognize that the gray areas of activism should not be seen as obstacles or weaknesses, but rather as opportunities for growth and progress. Embracing the complexities of activism allows us to have a more comprehensive understanding of the issues at hand and empowers us to engage in more effective and inclusive advocacy.

In conclusion, exploring the gray areas of activism is essential for LGBTQ activists who seek to navigate the complexities of social change. It requires a willingness to compromise, a commitment to intersectionality, an examination of representation and inclusivity, and an ongoing process of self-reflection and learning. By embracing these complexities, activists can forge a path forward that is more inclusive, effective, and resilient in the fight for LGBTQ equality.

Section 3: The Impact of Saryn's Story

Subsection: Inspiring Change and Empowering Others

In this subsection, we explore how Saryn Brell's activism has inspired change and empowered countless individuals in their journey towards equality. Saryn's story reminds us that one person can make a difference and that collective action has the power to bring about meaningful social change.

Inspiring with Personal Stories

One of the most powerful tools in Saryn's activism arsenal has been their ability to share personal stories and experiences. By openly discussing their own struggles and triumphs, Saryn breaks down barriers and helps others feel seen and validated. They highlight the diversity within the LGBTQ community and

SECTION 3: THE IMPACT OF SARYN'S STORY 173

emphasize the importance of embracing intersectionality. Saryn's ability to connect on a personal level inspires others to share their stories and advocate for change.

Creating Safe Spaces

Saryn's activism goes beyond raising awareness and advocating for policy change. They have also played a crucial role in creating safe spaces for LGBTQ individuals. Through their work, Saryn has helped establish support groups, helplines, and community centers where LGBTQ individuals find solace, acceptance, and guidance. These safe spaces provide a sense of belonging and community, inspiring others to seek support and become agents of change themselves.

Encouraging Education

Education is a powerful tool in the fight for equality, and Saryn understands this well. They have been instrumental in promoting LGBTQ-inclusive curricula in schools, colleges, and universities. By pushing for accurate and comprehensive education, Saryn helps create a more understanding and accepting society. Their efforts have resulted in young people gaining a better understanding of LGBTQ issues, which in turn inspires them to become advocates for change within their own communities.

Leading by Example

Saryn's leadership style is rooted in leading by example. They actively encourage others to step up and lead in their own communities. Saryn recognizes that lasting change requires a collective effort and encourages others to take action and fight for their rights. By showcasing their own courage and determination, Saryn inspires a new generation of activists to step forward and make their voices heard.

Promoting Intersectionality

Saryn's activism goes beyond advocating for LGBTQ rights alone. They emphasize the importance of intersectionality and recognize the interconnectedness of various social justice movements. By collaborating with advocates from diverse backgrounds, Saryn amplifies the voices of marginalized communities and showcases the power of allyship. Their commitment to intersectionality inspires others to forge alliances across social justice movements and work together towards a more inclusive world.

Empowering Through Representation

Representation matters, and Saryn recognizes this at every turn. Through their visibility as an LGBTQ activist, Saryn provides hope and inspiration to individuals who may feel marginalized or invisible. By challenging stereotypes and promoting positive LGBTQ representation in the media, they empower others to embrace their identities and become advocates for change. Saryn's work reminds us all of the importance of visibility and representation in empowering marginalized communities.

In conclusion, Saryn Brell's activism has inspired change and empowered others by sharing personal stories, creating safe spaces, encouraging education, leading by example, promoting intersectionality, and empowering through representation. Their dedication to the cause and unwavering commitment to equality continue to inspire a new generation of activists. Saryn's story serves as a reminder that each person has the power to make a difference and that together, we can create a more inclusive and just society.

Subsection: The Legacy of Saryn's Activism in Zerana

Saryn Brell's activism in Zerana has left an indelible mark on the LGBTQ community, sparking a wave of change that continues to reverberate across the nation. Through tireless advocacy and fearless leadership, Saryn has not only transformed the lives of countless individuals but also shaped the landscape of LGBTQ rights in Zerana and beyond. In this subsection, we will explore the profound impact of Saryn's activism, examining the milestones achieved, the social and legal changes implemented, and the lasting legacy that continues to inspire generations to come.

Milestones for LGBTQ Rights

Saryn's relentless pursuit of equality has paved the way for significant milestones in LGBTQ rights. One of the most notable achievements was the legalization of same-sex marriage in Zerana. In the face of staunch opposition, Saryn mobilized activists and galvanized public support, leading to a historic Supreme Court decision that recognized the fundamental right for all couples to marry, regardless of gender.

Furthermore, Saryn played a pivotal role in driving comprehensive LGBTQ-inclusive legislation. Working in collaboration with lawmakers, they championed bills that prohibited discrimination based on sexual orientation and gender identity in employment, housing, and public accommodations. These legislative victories provided crucial protections and ensured equal opportunities for LGBTQ individuals throughout Zerana.

Another significant milestone in Saryn's legacy was the eradication of conversion therapy and other harmful practices targeting the LGBTQ community. Through rigorous advocacy efforts, Saryn exposed the dangers and pseudoscience behind these damaging therapies, leading to statewide bans that protected vulnerable individuals from harm. The elimination of conversion therapy was a crucial step towards affirming the rights and dignity of LGBTQ individuals in Zerana.

Expanding Protections for Transgender Individuals

Recognizing the unique challenges faced by transgender individuals, Saryn shifted the focus towards expanding legal protections and societal acceptance. They played an integral role in advocating for legislation that enabled transgender individuals to update their identification documents, without undue burdens or invasive requirements. These legal reforms allowed transgender individuals to assert their true identities, reducing discrimination and ensuring equal treatment under the law.

Moreover, Saryn's activism fostered greater understanding and visibility for transgender issues. By sharing personal stories and raising awareness, they humanized the experiences of transgender individuals, challenging stereotypes and promoting inclusion. Saryn's efforts sparked a social transformation, encouraging Zerana's society to embrace and uplift transgender voices, leading to increased acceptance and support.

Inspiring Advocacy Beyond Zerana

While Saryn's impact was undoubtedly profound within Zerana, their activism also resonated far beyond its borders. Their unwavering commitment to equality and human rights has inspired a new generation of LGBTQ activists worldwide. Saryn's boldness in confronting political opposition, challenging religious ideologies, and debunking societal prejudice has set a precedent for grassroots advocacy and activism in the global LGBTQ community.

Through international speaking engagements and collaborations with other prominent LGBTQ activists, Saryn expanded their reach, advocating for LGBTQ rights on the world stage. Their speeches resonated with audiences, challenging oppressive systems and inspiring millions to stand up and fight for justice. By uniting activists from different countries and cultures, Saryn helped forge a global movement that is driving progress and pushing for LGBTQ equality across continents.

The Personal and Emotional Impact

Despite the remarkable progress achieved, Saryn's activism also came at a personal cost. The constant challenges, backlash, and threats took a toll on their mental and emotional well-being. Burnout became an ever-present danger, as Saryn's tireless commitment often exceeded their personal capacity. Their struggles with mental health further highlighted the need for self-care and support within the activist community.

Saryn's legacy also serves as a reminder of the importance of self-preservation and balance. Their experiences shed light on the complex dynamics of interpersonal relationships in the spotlight, the sacrifices made for the cause, and the need for personal growth beyond activism. By sharing their vulnerabilities and lessons learned, Saryn has provided a valuable blueprint for activists to navigate the challenges of advocacy while maintaining their overall well-being.

The Call to Continue Saryn's Work

As we reflect on Saryn's legacy, it is clear that their impact extends far beyond their time in the public eye. Their indomitable spirit, unwavering determination, and groundbreaking achievements have left an enduring imprint on the LGBTQ rights movement. Saryn's legacy serves as a rallying cry for continued action and progress, inspiring activists to carry the torch and push for further advancements in equality.

By embracing the lessons of Saryn's journey, we can effectively address the complexities of activism and shape a future that is more inclusive, understanding, and just. Let us honor Saryn's life by standing up against discrimination, challenging the status quo, and working towards a world where every individual, regardless of their sexual orientation or gender identity, can live free from prejudice and discrimination.

In the words of Saryn Brell, "We must never forget that our fight for equality is not only about changing laws; it is about changing hearts and minds. It is about creating a world where everyone can live and love openly, without fear or shame. And that is a fight worth fighting."

Subsection: Global Recognition and Influence on LGBTQ Rights

Saryn Brell's impact on LGBTQ rights extends far beyond the borders of Zerana. Their dedication to activism and unwavering commitment to equality have garnered them global recognition. This subsection explores the worldwide influence of Saryn's work and how it has shaped the landscape of LGBTQ rights across different countries and societies.

1. The Ripple Effect of Saryn's Activism: Saryn's activism in Zerana has served as a catalyst for similar movements around the world. Their unwavering determination to challenge discrimination and fight for equality has inspired countless individuals, organizations, and even governments to take action. Saryn's

story has provided hope and encouragement to LGBTQ individuals everywhere, empowering them to embrace and assert their rights.

2. International LGBTQ Rights Advocacy: Saryn's engagement with international organizations and advocacy groups has further amplified their impact. They have become a prominent voice in global conversations on LGBTQ rights, advocating for comprehensive and inclusive legislation worldwide. Saryn has participated in numerous international conferences, delivering impassioned speeches that challenge discriminatory policies and promote acceptance and equality.

3. Collaboration with Global Activists: Recognizing that the fight for LGBTQ rights is a global struggle, Saryn has actively collaborated with activists from different countries. By sharing knowledge, strategies, and experiences, Saryn has fostered international solidarity among LGBTQ activists. Together, they have taken the fight to multinational corporations, religious institutions, and governments, advocating for fair treatment and equal rights for LGBTQ individuals globally.

4. Legalizing Same-Sex Marriage: Saryn's influence on LGBTQ rights has been instrumental in the push for marriage equality worldwide. By successfully advocating for the legalization of same-sex marriage in Zerana, they have set a precedent that has reverberated across the globe. Countries and regions have looked to Zerana as an example of progress, leading to the repeal of discriminatory laws and the recognition of same-sex marriages in various jurisdictions.

5. Changing Public Opinion: Saryn's unwavering commitment to visibility and representation has helped change public opinion about LGBTQ rights on a global scale. Their charismatic personality and powerful speeches have reached millions, dispelling stereotypes and promoting understanding and acceptance. This shift in public opinion has paved the way for greater LGBTQ inclusion and rights in communities worldwide.

6. Addressing Homophobia and Transphobia: Saryn's influence extends to challenging and dismantling discriminatory beliefs and practices. Through their activism, they have exposed and confronted homophobia and transphobia at both individual and systemic levels. Saryn's advocacy for inclusive education, workplace policies, and healthcare services has inspired change and helped shape more inclusive societies globally.

7. Inspiring Legislative Change: Saryn's relentless advocacy has led to significant legislative victories for LGBTQ rights worldwide. By partnering with politicians and leveraging their influence, they have contributed to the passage of comprehensive anti-discrimination laws, the ban on conversion therapy, and the expansion of rights for transgender individuals. Their impact on legislation has been transformative, serving as a guiding light for lawmakers committed to progress.

8. Media Influence: Through their media appearances and interviews, Saryn has captured the attention of audiences worldwide. By bravely sharing their personal journey and experiences, they have humanized LGBTQ issues and made them relatable to diverse audiences. This increased visibility has fostered empathy and understanding, transforming the narrative around LGBTQ rights globally.

In conclusion, Saryn Brell's impact on LGBTQ rights extends well beyond their native country of Zerana. Their activism has resonated with marginalized communities globally, inspiring change, challenging discriminatory practices, and advocating for equal rights. By collaborating with international activists, challenging oppressive systems, and changing public opinion, Saryn has left an indelible mark on the fight for LGBTQ equality around the world. The legacy of Saryn Brell serves as a constant reminder that collective action and unwavering dedication can lead to meaningful, positive change for LGBTQ individuals globally.

Subsection: Lessons to be Learned from Saryn's Journey

Saryn Brell's journey as an LGBTQ activist in Zerana is not just a story of personal triumph and societal change; it is also a source of valuable lessons that can inspire and guide future activists. Let us delve into the lessons that can be learned from Saryn's remarkable journey.

1. Persistence and Resilience: Saryn's story teaches us the significance of persistence and resilience in the face of adversity. Throughout their activism, Saryn faced numerous challenges, from discrimination to threats and backlash. Despite these obstacles, they remained determined and continued their fight for equality. This unwavering dedication reminds us that progress does not happen overnight. To bring about real change, we must be prepared for setbacks and be resilient in the face of adversity.

2. Collaboration and Community: Another lesson we can learn from Saryn's journey is the power of collaboration and the importance of community support. Saryn continuously sought allies, built a strong support network, and collaborated with other LGBTQ activists. By working together, they were able to amplify their voices, share resources, and increase their impact. Saryn's story teaches us that unity and collective action are crucial in effecting meaningful change.

3. Intersectionality and Inclusivity: Saryn's activism was marked by their commitment to intersectionality and inclusivity. They understood that the LGBTQ community is not a monolith and actively worked to address the diverse needs and experiences within the community. Saryn's emphasis on recognizing and lifting up the voices of marginalized groups teaches us the importance of inclusivity

and fighting for the rights of all individuals, regardless of their race, gender, or socioeconomic background.

4. Utilizing and Challenging Institutions: Saryn's journey demonstrates the both the power and limitations of utilizing and challenging existing institutions. They navigated the political landscape, leveraging positions of power to push for LGBTQ-inclusive legislation. At the same time, they were keenly aware of the need to challenge and disrupt oppressive systems that perpetuated discrimination and marginalization. Saryn's story inspires us to not only work within existing structures but also to question and overhaul them when necessary.

5. Personal Sacrifices and Self-Care: Activism can be emotionally and physically demanding, and Saryn's journey reminds us of the importance of self-care. They faced personal sacrifices and endured the toll that comes with fighting for change. However, Saryn also recognized the need to prioritize their own well-being, coping mechanisms, and self-care practices. This lesson emphasizes the significance of striking a balance between advocating for others and taking care of oneself.

6. Embracing nuance and complexity: Saryn's activism was multifaceted and involved engaging with a wide range of perspectives. They tackled controversial issues, confronted opposition, and held nuanced conversations about the complexities of LGBTQ rights. Saryn's journey teaches us that progress is not a black-and-white issue, and it requires us to embrace uncomfortable conversations, challenge our own biases, and navigate the complexities of social change.

7. Inspiring the next generation: Finally, Saryn's story serves as a powerful reminder that one person can make a lasting impact and inspire future generations. Their work laid the foundation for continued progress and paved the way for future activists. By sharing their story and highlighting the importance of activism, Saryn inspires us to find our own voice, stand up for what we believe in, and create a better world for future generations.

In conclusion, Saryn Brell's journey as an LGBTQ activist offers valuable lessons for aspiring activists. These lessons encompass persistence and resilience, collaboration and community, intersectionality and inclusivity, utilizing and challenging institutions, personal sacrifices and self-care, embracing nuance and complexity, and inspiring the next generation. By internalizing these lessons and applying them to our own lives, we can continue the fight for LGBTQ rights and work towards a more inclusive and equitable society.

Subsection: A Call to Action for Readers and Activists Alike

As we reach the final stretch of Saryn Brell's captivating journey, it's crucial to reflect on the impact of their life and activism. Saryn's story serves as a reminder that true change can only be achieved through collective action. In this subsection, we will explore the call to action for readers and activists alike, offering practical steps and inspiring examples to motivate you to join the fight for LGBTQ equality.

Understanding the Power of Individual Actions

While it's easy to feel overwhelmed by the magnitude of societal change, it's important to remember that even the smallest actions can make a difference. Each voice raised, each act of solidarity, and each conversation challenging bigotry adds momentum to the journey toward equality. Whether you identify as LGBTQ or an ally, your support is invaluable.

Take the time to educate yourself about LGBTQ history, rights, and the current challenges faced by the community. Learning about the struggles and achievements of LGBTQ activists can deepen your understanding and help you become a more effective advocate.

Using Your Platform and Privilege

Whether you have a large social media following or influence within your community, everyone has a platform they can use to amplify marginalized voices. Use your privilege to support and uplift LGBTQ voices, highlight LGBTQ stories, and challenge discriminatory beliefs. Speak out against hateful rhetoric and discrimination whenever you encounter it, whether it's online or in your daily interactions.

Being an Ally

To be an effective ally, it's crucial to listen and learn from LGBTQ individuals. Engage in heartfelt conversations, ask questions, and validate their experiences. Actively seek out LGBTQ voices in literature, media, art, and activism to expand your perspective and challenge your own biases.

Support LGBTQ-owned businesses, organizations, and events. Attend pride parades, fundraisers, and community gatherings to show your solidarity. By actively engaging with the LGBTQ community, you can build meaningful connections and have a tangible impact.

Advocating for LGBTQ-Inclusive Policies

Political engagement is a powerful way to enact change. Research political candidates' stances on LGBTQ rights and support those who are committed to advancing equality. Vote in local, state, and national elections to elect officials who will champion LGBTQ-inclusive legislation.

Write letters to your elected representatives urging them to support LGBTQ equality. Attend town hall meetings and community forums to voice your support for inclusive policies. By actively participating in the political process, you can ensure that the voices of the LGBTQ community are represented and heard.

Supporting LGBTQ Organizations and Activists

Donate your time, skills, or resources to LGBTQ organizations that champion equality and provide essential support and resources to queer individuals. Volunteer at LGBTQ community centers, shelters, or helplines. Offer your expertise in marketing, legal support, or event planning to help these organizations better serve their communities.

In addition to supporting established organizations, consider starting your own initiatives to address specific needs or gaps in your community. By taking direct action at the grassroots level, you can make a tangible difference in the lives of LGBTQ individuals.

Creating Safe Spaces

Be intentional about creating safe and welcoming spaces for LGBTQ individuals in your everyday life. Educate yourself about inclusive language and be mindful of the impact your words can have. Practice empathy and respect, honoring people's pronouns and identities. By cultivating inclusive environments, you can ensure that LGBTQ individuals feel seen, heard, and valued.

Continuing the Conversation

The fight for LGBTQ equality is far from over, and the call to action extends beyond the pages of this book. It's essential to engage in ongoing dialogue about LGBTQ rights, challenging prejudice and discrimination wherever you encounter it.

Encourage open conversations with friends, family, and colleagues about LGBTQ issues. By sharing personal stories and experiences, you can humanize the struggles faced by the community and inspire empathy and understanding.

Taking Care of Yourself

While advocating for LGBTQ rights is vital, it's essential to prioritize self-care and well-being. Activism can be emotionally draining, so establish healthy boundaries and recognize when you need to take a step back and recharge. Surround yourself with a supportive community of fellow activists who understand the challenges you face and provide a space for collective healing.

Remember, change takes time, and setbacks are inevitable. Celebrate the progress made along the way and draw inspiration from the resilience and determination of activists like Saryn Brell. Together, we can create a more inclusive and equitable world for all.

Conclusion

As we conclude this subsection, I invite you to take the call to action to heart. Embrace your power as a reader and activist and use it to dismantle systemic discrimination and create a more inclusive society. Saryn's extraordinary journey serves as a reminder that, with dedication and collective effort, we can bring about meaningful change. Let us march forward, hand in hand, towards a future where LGBTQ individuals can live, love, and thrive without fear of discrimination.

The Significance of Individual Stories in the Fight for Equality

In the fight for equality, the power of individual stories cannot be underestimated. These personal narratives have the ability to evoke empathy, challenge stereotypes, and inspire change. By sharing their experiences, LGBTQ individuals can create a human connection that resonates with people from all walks of life. This subsection will explore the significance of individual stories in the fight for equality, highlighting their impact and the challenges they face.

Empathy and Understanding

One of the most powerful aspects of individual stories is their ability to foster empathy and understanding. When we hear someone's personal journey, we are more likely to connect on an emotional level and see them as individuals rather than just labels or statistics. This emotional connection can help break down barriers and biases, allowing people to see the common humanity in others.

For example, imagine a heterosexual person, who has never personally experienced discrimination based on their sexual orientation, listening to the story of a gay individual who was denied housing or fired from their job because of their identity. By hearing about the challenges and injustices faced by LGBTQ individuals, this person can gain insight into the systemic issues that perpetuate inequality and become motivated to take action.

Challenging Stereotypes

Individual stories have the power to challenge stereotypes and misconceptions about the LGBTQ community. By sharing diverse experiences, we can break down the often monolithic representation of LGBTQ people in the media and educate others about the complexities and nuances of sexual orientation and gender identity.

For instance, consider a bisexual individual sharing their story of bisexuality being dismissed as a phase or being told they are just confused. By dispelling the myth that bisexuality is not valid or that it equates to indecisiveness, they can challenge preconceived notions and pave the way for greater acceptance and understanding.

Inspiring Change

Individual stories also serve as catalysts for change. When we hear about the resilience, courage, and determination of LGBTQ individuals, it can inspire others to join the fight for equality. These stories can ignite a spark within individuals, encouraging them to question the status quo and advocate for a more inclusive society.

For example, hearing a transgender person's journey of self-discovery and the obstacles they faced along the way can motivate others to fight for trans rights and push for policies that protect transgender individuals from discrimination. Their story becomes a driving force that empowers others to take action and create change.

Challenges and Vulnerability

Sharing individual stories is not without its challenges. LGBTQ individuals who choose to share their experiences often expose themselves to vulnerability and potential backlash. There is a risk of discrimination, harassment, and even violence. These risks, however, should not deter individuals from sharing their stories.

It is important to create a supportive and safe environment for LGBTQ individuals to share their stories. This includes providing resources and platforms for them to express themselves authentically and ensuring their voices are heard and respected. Allies also play a vital role in amplifying these stories and being vocal supporters of the LGBTQ community.

The Power of Unity

While individual stories are impactful, it is also essential to recognize that they are just one piece of the puzzle. The fight for equality requires collective action and unity. By connecting individual stories, we can build a comprehensive narrative that highlights the common threads and shared experiences within the LGBTQ community.

By bringing these stories together, we can showcase the diversity within the community, break down internal divisions, and foster a sense of solidarity. It is through unity that we can advocate for systemic change and create a society that respects and values the rights and dignity of all individuals.

Moving Forward

In the fight for LGBTQ equality, individual stories have the power to transform hearts and minds. They embody the spirit of activism by humanizing the struggle for equality and inspiring change on a personal and societal level. However, it is crucial to remember that while these stories are significant, they must be accompanied by concrete actions and policy changes to create lasting impact.

As individuals, we should actively seek out and listen to the stories of LGBTQ individuals with an open heart and mind. By doing so, we can educate ourselves, challenge our own biases, and become allies in the fight for equality. Together, through the power of individual stories, we can build a more inclusive and just world for all.

Section 4: The Unauthorized Perspective

Subsection: Balancing Entertainment and Accuracy

When writing a biography, especially one that is meant to entertain as well as inform, striking a balance between entertainment and accuracy can be a challenging task. In the case of the unauthorized biography of Saryn Brell, this challenge is magnified by the parody element of the book. In this subsection, we will explore the delicate dance between entertainment and accuracy and discuss some strategies for achieving this balance.

One of the key considerations when balancing entertainment and accuracy in a biography is to ensure that the essence of the subject's story and message is preserved. While adding entertaining elements can make the book more engaging for readers, it is important not to sacrifice the truth and integrity of the story. As a biographer, it is crucial to maintain accurate facts and events, while finding creative ways to present them.

To strike this balance, it is essential to conduct thorough research and interviews with people close to the subject. In the case of the unauthorized biography of Saryn Brell, the author, Tatyana Flores, embarked on a quest for the truth. She tracked down Saryn's allies, friends, and acquaintances, uncovering documents and personal correspondence that shed light on Saryn's life and activism. By relying on primary and reliable sources, the author ensures that the information presented in the book is accurate and credible.

However, it's worth noting that a biography can sometimes be limited by the available information and the perspective of the sources. This is where the creative element comes into play. The unauthorized biography of Saryn Brell embraces a parody style, allowing the author to add entertaining elements to the narrative while still staying true to the essence of Saryn's story. By using humor, wit, and satire, the author can engage readers and present the biography in an entertaining and engaging manner.

It is important to keep in mind that while the unauthorized biography of Saryn Brell is a work of parody, it is essential to maintain the utmost respect for the subject and the LGBTQ community. While satire and parody can be powerful tools for social commentary, they should never belittle or undermine the struggles and accomplishments of LGBTQ activists. Striking a balance between entertainment and respect is crucial to ensure that the book does not perpetuate harmful stereotypes or undermine the significance of the activism portrayed.

In addition, it is important to maintain transparency with readers about the intention behind the parody elements. The unauthorized biography of Saryn Brell includes a section dedicated to addressing the parody element, explaining the author's reflections on the project and the intention behind it. By openly discussing the parody element, the author ensures that readers understand the purpose and context of the entertaining elements, while still appreciating the accuracy and integrity of the biography.

Ultimately, striking a balance between entertainment and accuracy in a biography requires careful consideration, diligent research, and a deep understanding of the subject and their message. By maintaining accurate facts and events while using creative and entertaining storytelling techniques, an unauthorized biography can captivate readers while staying true to the story it aims to tell.

Subsection: Addressing the Parody Element of the Biography

In this subsection, we will discuss the use of parody in the unauthorized biography of Saryn Brell. Parody is a powerful tool that can effectively convey a message while also providing entertainment value. However, it is important to recognize that parody may not be suitable for all subjects or situations. In the case of Saryn Brell, the use of parody allows us to approach the topic of LGBTQ activism with a lighthearted and humorous tone, while still acknowledging the serious nature of the issues at hand.

Parody provides a unique way to engage readers and spark their interest in the subject matter. By using humor and satire, we can captivate readers who may not have initially been drawn to a traditional biography. Through the lens of parody, we can explore the challenges faced by LGBTQ activists in an entertaining and thought-provoking manner.

It is crucial to strike a balance between comedy and sensitivity when utilizing parody. While humor can be a powerful tool for addressing serious social issues, it is important not to trivialize or diminish the struggles faced by the LGBTQ community. Therefore, throughout the biography, we ensure that the jokes and humorous elements are carefully crafted to maintain respect for the subject matter and the individuals involved.

Additionally, it is important to acknowledge that parody might not resonate with everyone. Humor is subjective, and what one person finds funny, another may not. We understand that our approach may not be embraced by all readers, and that's perfectly fine. The goal is to engage and educate as many individuals as possible, and we recognize that different approaches and perspectives are necessary to achieve this.

In order to avoid misunderstandings or misinterpretations, we provide clear cues and context to signal when we are using parody. This helps readers differentiate between the factual elements of Saryn's life and the satirical commentary we layer on top. We want readers to understand that while we may take certain creative liberties, we are still committed to showcasing the significant contributions and challenges faced by LGBTQ activists, like Saryn Brell.

It is also important to address any potential criticisms that may arise from the use of parody. Some may argue that parody diminishes the seriousness of the subject matter or undermines the efforts of LGBTQ activists. However, it is crucial to remember that parody can be a powerful tool for highlighting social issues and attracting wider attention to important causes. By using humor and satire, we can reach audiences who may not be familiar with or interested in LGBTQ activism. This can potentially lead to increased awareness, empathy, and support for the cause.

In conclusion, the use of parody in the unauthorized biography of Saryn Brell allows us to present her story in an entertaining and engaging manner. We recognize the gravity of the subject matter and strive to strike a balance between humor and sensitivity. Parody provides an opportunity to captivate readers, evoke thought, and spark a broader conversation about LGBTQ activism.

Subsection: The Subversive Power of Satire in Activism

Satire has long been a powerful tool in social and political commentary, using humor and irony to expose the flaws and contradictions of society. In the realm of activism, satire can be a particularly effective means of challenging the status quo and sparking conversations about important issues. With its ability to engage, entertain, and provoke thought, satire has the potential to break down barriers, dismantle oppressive systems, and create positive change.

The subversive power of satire lies in its ability to confront societal norms and expectations through humor. By presenting serious issues in a lighthearted and often exaggerated manner, satire allows activists to discuss sensitive topics without triggering defensiveness or resistance. This approach disarms the audience, making them more receptive to the underlying message and more likely to question their own beliefs and biases.

One of the key strengths of satire is its ability to reach a wide audience. Unlike traditional forms of activism that may appeal primarily to like-minded individuals, satire has the potential to capture the attention of a broader range of people, including those who may not typically engage in discussions about social justice. Through its humorous and entertaining nature, satire can draw in diverse audiences and spark interest in topics that may have been overlooked or dismissed in more serious forms of advocacy.

However, it is important to recognize that satire is not without its challenges and limitations. Satirical content can sometimes be misinterpreted or misunderstood, leading to unintended consequences. It requires a delicate balance of wit and sensitivity to ensure that the message is conveyed effectively without causing harm or perpetuating stereotypes. Satirists must be mindful of the potential for their work to be co-opted or weaponized by those who may seek to undermine the activist's cause.

To harness the subversive power of satire effectively, activists should consider the following strategies and principles:

1. **Understanding the Target:** Satire works best when it targets the powerful and privileged, exposing their hypocrisy and challenging their authority. By

critiquing the actions and beliefs of those in power, activists can use satire to advocate for those who are marginalized and oppressed.

2. **Punching Up, Not Down:** Satire should be aimed at those with more power, rather than vulnerable groups. It is important to avoid reinforcing harmful stereotypes or perpetuating further harm. Satire should uplift marginalized voices and challenge the systems and structures that perpetuate inequality.

3. **Cultivating Empathy:** Satire has the potential to create empathy by presenting issues in a relatable and accessible way. By using humor, activists can provoke thought and encourage individuals to see the world from a different perspective. This empathetic approach can foster understanding and promote meaningful conversations.

4. **Fostering Dialogue:** Satire can open the doors to important discussions that may otherwise be met with resistance or defensiveness. Instead of outright confrontation, satire can create a space for dialogue and reflection, allowing individuals to reconsider their beliefs and challenge the status quo.

5. **Amplifying Marginalized Voices:** Satire can provide a platform for marginalized voices that are often silenced or overlooked. By incorporating the experiences and perspectives of those affected by social injustice, activists can use satire to give voice to those who are most impacted.

6. **Subverting Expectations:** Satire challenges societal norms and expectations by presenting alternative narratives and perspectives. By subverting the expected, satirical activism prompts individuals to question ingrained biases and assumptions, leading to a broader understanding of the issues at hand.

To illustrate the subversive power of satire in activism, let's consider a fictional example. Imagine an LGBTQ rights activist who creates a satirical video series showcasing the absurdity of arguments against same-sex marriage. Through witty dialogue, exaggerated characters, and humorous scenarios, the activist manages to highlight the irrationality and discrimination present in anti-LGBTQ rhetoric. By using satire, the activist disarms opposition and engages a broader audience, prompting them to reflect on their own beliefs and prejudices.

In conclusion, the subversive power of satire in activism lies in its ability to challenge societal norms, foster dialogue, and create empathy. When used effectively, satire can be a powerful tool for activists to dismantle oppressive systems, amplify marginalized voices, and advocate for positive change. However, it is crucial to approach satire with care, ensuring that it punches up rather than down, amplifies marginalized voices, and fosters meaningful dialogue. Satire has the potential to break down barriers, inspire action, and pave the way for a more inclusive and equitable society. So, let us embrace the subversive power of satire in our activism and dare to challenge the status quo with a smile on our faces.

Subsection: The Author's Reflections on the Project

As I come to the end of this unauthorized biography on Saryn Brell, I find myself reflecting on the journey that has brought me here. Writing this book has been an incredible and eye-opening experience, one that has challenged and inspired me in more ways than I could have imagined. In this section, I want to take a moment to share my personal reflections on the project and what it has meant to me.

When I set out to write this biography, I wanted to pay homage to the remarkable work that Saryn Brell has done as an LGBTQ activist and advocate for freedom in Zerana. But I also wanted to inject a sense of humor and satire into the narrative, using the entertaining writing style of John Krasinski to engage readers and make them think about the complexities of activism.

Throughout the process, I aimed to strike a delicate balance between providing an entertaining read and delivering accurate information. I understood the importance of maintaining the integrity of the facts while incorporating the humorous elements. This meant conducting extensive research, interviewing key individuals in Saryn's life, and unearthing documents to piece together the most comprehensive and authentic account possible.

However, I also recognized the challenge of separating fact from fiction when it comes to Saryn's story. A figure as influential and controversial as Saryn is susceptible to myths and misconceptions, which can be perpetuated even in well-intentioned biographies. That's why I made a conscious effort to approach this project with nuance and to explore the gray areas of activism.

Activism is a messy and complicated endeavor, and it cannot be neatly packaged into a hero's journey narrative. Saryn's story is no exception. While I admire their accomplishments and dedication, I also acknowledge the criticisms and controversies surrounding their work. It was important for me to deconstruct the myth of the perfect activist and to highlight the flaws and challenges that come with fighting for change.

In writing this biography, I hope to inspire readers to critically examine the stories and narratives that are presented to them. It is crucial that we challenge the notion of infallible heroes and explore the diversity of perspectives and experiences within the LGBTQ community. If this book achieves anything, I hope it encourages readers to redefine what it means to be an activist and to embrace the complexity and messiness of this work.

As I close this chapter and bring this unauthorized biography to an end, I want to express my gratitude to Saryn Brell for their courageous legacy. Their impact on LGBTQ rights in Zerana and beyond cannot be overstated, and I feel honored to have been able to share their story, albeit through a satirical lens.

I also want to thank all the individuals who made this book possible. From the researchers who helped me gather information, to the publishers who took a chance on this unconventional project, to the readers who have supported and engaged with the book – your contributions have been invaluable.

Finally, I want to emphasize the importance of individual stories in the fight for equality. It is through the sharing and amplification of personal experiences that we can create understanding, empathy, and ultimately, change. I hope that this book prompts readers to reflect on their own roles in this ongoing struggle for LGBTQ freedom and inspires them to take action in their own lives and communities.

In conclusion, as I put the pen down and say goodbye to Saryn Brell, I am left with a sense of awe and admiration for the remarkable journey they have undertaken. Their activism has left an indelible mark on Zerana and has paved the way for progress in LGBTQ rights. May their story continue to inspire future generations of activists, and may we all remember the power of individual stories in the quest for a more inclusive and equal world.

Thank you for coming along on this unauthorized journey with me. May we embrace change, challenge the status quo, and continue to push for a better future for all.

Subsection: Thank You, Saryn Brell, for Your Courageous Legacy

In this final subsection, I want to take a moment to express our deepest gratitude to Saryn Brell for their courageous and unwavering commitment to LGBTQ rights. Saryn, your legacy is one that will continue to inspire generations to come.

Throughout the pages of this unauthorized biography, we have explored the remarkable journey of a small-town individual who transformed into a powerful advocate for freedom and equality. Saryn, your story is a testament to the power of authenticity, resilience, and the unwavering belief in the inherent worth and dignity of every individual.

Your journey started in the unremarkable beginnings of Smalltown, USA, where you first discovered your interest in politics and social justice. As you navigated the challenges of coming to terms with your own identity, you faced not

SECTION 4: THE UNAUTHORIZED PERSPECTIVE

only friends and allies, but also enemies along the way. It was during these formative years that the first seeds of your activism were sown.

As you found your voice in college, you joined the LGBTQ student organization and became an influential force in campus protests and advocacy. Your iconic look emerged as a symbol of defiance, challenging the status quo and sparking conversations that were uncomfortable yet necessary. We admire your ability to confront the unspoken challenges of being an LGBTQ activist on campus, as you paved the way for future generations to feel empowered and supported.

Beyond the campus walls, you answered the call to action. Saryn, your ability to build a support network and organize the first LGBTQ Pride Parade in Zerana has left an indelible mark on the community. You fearlessly confronted discrimination and pushed for equality, playing an influential role in local politics. But let us not forget the personal sacrifices you made, facing backlash and threats with unwavering bravery.

Your activism did not stop at local borders. Saryn, you took the fight to the national and international stage, collaborating with other LGBTQ activists and using your platform to speak truth to power. Your speeches and media appearances had a profound impact, inspiring change and challenging societal norms. Your influence on LGBTQ rights in Zerana and beyond cannot be understated.

In our exploration of your remarkable journey, we also delved into the dark side of activism. Saryn, you faced burnout and mental health struggles, highlighting the importance of self-care and finding strength in vulnerability. We learned about the complexities of navigating interpersonal relationships in the spotlight and felt the weight of the emotional toll your advocacy took on you. Your journey reminds us all of the need for self-preservation and the importance of maintaining one's well-being.

In your pursuit of change, you garnered allies and faced adversaries. Politicians, celebrities, and unexpected supporters from unlikely places rallied behind you, helping to build bridges and foster unity. But you also encountered resistance from within the LGBTQ community and experienced disappointments along the way. Your ability to maintain an unwavering focus on the bigger picture and the power of collaboration and collective action sets you apart as a true leader.

As we look towards the future, Saryn, your vision for LGBTQ rights in Zerana and beyond is an inspiration to us all. We are grateful for your unwavering dedication to inspiring the next generation of activists and leaving a lasting legacy of impact. Your extraordinary journey will continue to push the boundaries of change and serve as a reminder that each individual story holds immense significance in the fight for equality.

Through the pages of this unauthorized biography, we have aimed to capture the essence of your extraordinary life and activism. We approached this project with a blend of entertainment and accuracy, using the subversive power of satire to shed light on the flaws and complexities of activism. It is our hope that readers will not only be entertained but also inspired to take action and make a difference.

In closing, we extend our deepest gratitude to Saryn Brell for their tireless efforts, sacrifices, and courage. Your legacy will forever shape the landscape of LGBTQ rights, and we are honored to have had the opportunity to share your story. Thank you, Saryn, for being an extraordinary voice for LGBTQ freedom and a true inspiration to us all.

Subsection: The Intention behind the Parody

As an unauthorized biography, it is important to acknowledge the intention behind the parody in this book. While we have sought to entertain readers throughout, it is crucial to remember that this work is a work of fiction and not an accurate representation of Saryn Brell's life.

The use of humor and satire in this book is meant to shed light on the flaws and complexities of activism, while providing a thought-provoking and engaging read. It is not meant to undermine or diminish the real struggles faced by LGBTQ activists or to trivialize the immense courage displayed by individuals like Saryn Brell.

It is our hope that by infusing this biography with an element of parody, readers will be encouraged to question and critically analyze the heroes and figures we hold in society. While Saryn Brell's story, as presented in this unauthorized biography, may be fictional, it is a reflection of the broader themes and challenges faced by LGBTQ activists worldwide.

Throughout the book, we have aimed to strike a balance between entertainment and accuracy, always mindful of the impact our words may have. We hope that readers will find this unauthorized biography both entertaining and thought-provoking, and that it may inspire discussions about the nuances and complexities of activism.

Please remember that this book should be approached with a sense of humor and an open mind, and should not be taken as a factual representation of Saryn Brell's life and activism.

Subsection: The Possibility of Future Unauthorized Biographies

This unauthorized biography has been a labor of love, a chance to explore the life and legacy of Saryn Brell in a unique and entertaining way. It is our hope that this book will pave the way for future unauthorized biographies that challenge the conventional norms of the genre and provide engaging and thought-provoking narratives.

The field of unauthorized biographies has often been plagued by sensationalism, exaggeration, and distortions of truth. By embracing humor and satire, we have attempted to bring a fresh perspective to the genre, encouraging readers to think critically about the stories we tell and the figures we idolize.

As new figures emerge in the fight for justice and equality, we envision a future where unauthorized biographies continue to provide alternative narratives, shining a light on both the triumphs and tribulations of remarkable individuals. These stories have the potential to humanize our heroes, highlighting their flaws and complexities, while inspiring us to strive for a better world.

In the spirit of this unauthorized biography, we encourage readers to challenge the traditional notions of heroism and to seek out diverse perspectives. By embracing the power of storytelling, we can continue to learn from the past, celebrate the present, and shape a future that is more inclusive, empathetic, and just.

Subsection: Acknowledgments and Final Thoughts

I would like to express my sincerest gratitude to everyone who played a part in making this unauthorized biography possible. To Saryn Brell, although this work is fictional, your story is an inspiration that deserves to be shared. To the friends, allies, and enemies who shaped Saryn's journey, thank you for lending your voices and making this biography come to life.

I would also like to extend a special thank you to all the researchers and interviewees who generously shared their insights and knowledge. Your dedication to uncovering the truth and illuminating the complexities of activism has been invaluable.

To the readers, thank you for joining us on this unauthorized journey. It is our hope that this book has entertained, challenged, and inspired you to reflect on the power of activism and the incredible individuals who lead the charge for change.

Finally, I would like to thank Saryn Brell themselves for their courageous legacy. Your unwavering commitment to equality and justice continues to shape the world we live in. As this unauthorized biography comes to a close, let us raise a glass and toast to Saryn Brell, a true icon and a beacon of hope for the LGBTQ community and beyond.

Cheers, and may we all find the strength to fight for our beliefs and create a world where everyone can live as their true selves.

Subsection: The Intention behind the Parody

In this subsection, we explore the intention behind the parody aspect of this unauthorized biography on LGBTQ activist Saryn Brell. Parody, as an art form, allows us to take a lighthearted approach to serious subjects and challenge the social norms through humor and satire. Through this parody, we hope to engage readers in a thought-provoking and entertaining manner while shedding light on the complexities and nuances of activism.

The purpose of this parody is twofold. Firstly, it aims to entertain readers and provide a refreshing take on the traditional biographical genre. By adopting the writing style of John Krasinski, known for his wit and charm, we inject humor into the narrative, making it engaging and enjoyable to read. This approach appeals to a broader demographic, capturing the attention of readers who may not typically gravitate towards activist biographies.

Secondly, the parody allows us to explore the layers of Saryn Brell's activism and the LGBTQ movement in a subversive manner. By blending facts and fictitious elements, we can push the boundaries of conventional storytelling and draw attention to the constraints and challenges faced by activists.

It is important to note that while parody allows for a certain level of exaggeration and fictionalization, our intention is never to undermine the significance of Saryn's activism or the struggles faced by the LGBTQ community. We honor their fight for equality and their contributions to society. The humor and satire employed in this parody are meant to engage readers in a meaningful way, not to diminish the importance of the cause.

This unauthorized biography seeks to highlight the power of storytelling and the role it plays in activism. By presenting Saryn Brell's journey through a lens of entertainment, we hope to reach a wider audience and spark conversations about LGBTQ rights and social justice. It serves as a reminder that the fight for equality is not always serious and somber; it can also be filled with laughter, camaraderie, and unexpected twists.

While this parody may deviate from the standard format of a biography, it ultimately seeks to capture the essence of Saryn Brell's activism and the experiences faced by LGBTQ activists globally. Through humor and satire, we hope to challenge preconceived notions, inspire readers, and ignite their own passion for social change.

In the spirit of the parody, we encourage readers to delve deeper into Saryn's remarkable journey and explore the real-life stories of LGBTQ activists who have paved the way for progress. Let this unauthorized biography serve as a gateway to learning, reflection, and a renewed commitment to fighting for equality for all.

Together, let us embrace the power of storytelling and continue advocating for a world that celebrates diversity, acceptance, and love.

Section 5: Acknowledgments and Final Thoughts

Subsection: Gratitude for Those Who Made This Book Possible

As I reach the end of this unauthorized biography on the life and activism of Saryn Brell, it's essential to recognize and extend gratitude to the individuals who have made this book possible. Writing a comprehensive and engaging biography is a collaborative effort, and I am incredibly thankful for the support and contributions of various people throughout this journey.

First and foremost, I would like to express my deepest gratitude to Saryn Brell themselves. Without their courage, resilience, and dedication to LGBTQ rights, there would be no story to tell. Saryn's unwavering commitment to justice and freedom has inspired countless individuals, and their willingness to share their life experiences has been truly remarkable. Thank you, Saryn, for your trust and for allowing me to bring your story to life.

I would also like to extend my thanks to the members of Saryn's inner circle, including their friends, family, and fellow activists. Their insights, perspectives, and personal anecdotes have added depth and nuance to this biography. From sharing memories of Saryn's early years in Smalltown, USA, to recounting pivotal moments in their activism, each interviewee has provided invaluable contributions that have helped shape this book.

Furthermore, my gratitude extends to the researchers who have tirelessly worked behind the scenes to gather information and uncover hidden documents. Their meticulous efforts have helped unravel the complexities of Saryn's journey and have contributed to a more nuanced understanding of their life and activism. Without their commitment to accuracy and thorough research, this biography would lack the factual foundation it needs to inform and engage readers.

I would also like to acknowledge the countless LGBTQ activists and allies who have fought alongside Saryn in the struggle for equality. Their unwavering dedication, whether in the form of protests, advocacy work, or coalition-building, has played an instrumental role in advancing LGBTQ rights. It is their collective effort and resilience that have paved the way for change, and their contributions should not be overlooked.

Additionally, I want to express my appreciation to the readers of this unauthorized biography. Your interest and support are what make this book possible. By engaging with Saryn's story, you are not only honoring their legacy but also contributing to the ongoing dialogue and fight for LGBTQ rights. Your willingness to learn and grow alongside the activists and visionaries who have come before us is what propels our collective progress.

Finally, I would like to thank the team at the publishing company. Their unwavering support, guidance, and expertise in bringing this project to fruition have been instrumental. From the editors and designers who have meticulously crafted the pages of this book to the marketing and publicity team who have helped share Saryn's story with the world, I am incredibly grateful for your professionalism and dedication.

In conclusion, "Saryn Brell: A Voice for LGBTQ Freedom in Zerana – Unauthorized" would not have been possible without the contributions of many individuals. To each and every person who has played a part in this project, whether directly or indirectly, I extend my sincerest gratitude. It is through our collective efforts that we continue to amplify the voices of activists, create lasting change, and strive towards a more inclusive and accepting world.

Subsection: Additional Content

Here, I want to take a moment to provide some additional content related to the section above. Specifically, I want to highlight some lesser-known LGBTQ activists who have made significant contributions to the fight for equality.

1. Marsha P. Johnson: Known as an outspoken advocate for transgender rights and one of the leading figures in the Stonewall Uprising, Marsha P. Johnson was a key player in the LGBTQ rights movement. Her activism and dedication to supporting the most marginalized members of the community continue to inspire activists today.

2. Harvey Milk: As the first openly gay elected official in California, Harvey Milk made history in the late 1970s. His unwavering dedication to LGBTQ rights, particularly in the realms of anti-discrimination legislation and visibility, laid the groundwork for future progress in the fight against homophobia and for equal rights.

3. Sylvia Rivera: Another key figure in the Stonewall Uprising, Sylvia Rivera was an advocate for transgender rights and fought tirelessly for the inclusion of transgender individuals within the LGBTQ rights movement. Her work as a self-identified drag queen and transgender activist paved the way for greater visibility and acceptance of transgender people.

4. Bayard Rustin: A behind-the-scenes force in the civil rights movement, Bayard Rustin was instrumental in organizing the groundbreaking March on Washington in 1963. As an openly gay African American man, he faced significant

challenges but remained committed to intersectional activism, advocating for the rights of both the Black community and the LGBTQ community.

These are just a few examples of the many remarkable activists who have dedicated their lives to fighting for LGBTQ rights. While their stories may not be as widely known or celebrated, it is crucial to recognize and honor their contributions in the ongoing struggle for equality.

Subsection: Exercises

To further engage with the content of this section, I invite readers to consider the following exercises:

1. Reflect on your own experiences with gratitude. Take a moment to document three people who have made a significant impact on your life and write a letter expressing your appreciation to them.

2. Research a local LGBTQ activist in your community or country who has made notable contributions to LGBTQ rights. Write a short biography outlining their activism, the challenges they have faced, and the impact they have made.

3. Imagine you are organizing a community event to celebrate LGBTQ activists and allies. Design a promotional poster that showcases different activists and highlights their accomplishments. Consider using quotes, imagery, and engaging design elements.

4. Engage in a discussion with friends or classmates about the importance of recognizing and celebrating LGBTQ activists who may not receive mainstream recognition. Explore the potential consequences of overlooking their contributions and how acknowledging their work could lead to a more inclusive narrative of LGBTQ history.

5. Take the time to reach out to LGBTQ activists or organizations in your area and offer support. This could involve volunteering your time, making a donation, or amplifying their message through social media. Reflect on the impact that your support can have on their work and the broader fight for equality.

Remember, activism and the fight for equality are ongoing endeavors that require collective effort and support. By engaging with these exercises and recognizing the contributions of activists, we can actively contribute to a more inclusive and accepting society.

Subsection: A Note from Tatyana Flores, Author and Parodist

Dear Readers,

CHAPTER 3: BEHIND THE SCENES – THE UNAUTHORIZED BIOGRAPHY

Welcome to this unauthorized biography of LGBTQ activist Saryn Brell. As the author and parodist, I want to take a moment to introduce myself and shed some light on the intentions behind this project.

First and foremost, my name is Tatyana Flores, and I am both a writer and an LGBTQ ally. I have been deeply inspired by the incredible work that activists like Saryn Brell have done to advance equality and fight for the rights of the LGBTQ community.

This biography is intended to be a light-hearted and entertaining homage to Saryn's journey, while also offering a critical perspective on the complexities of activism. By using the writing style of John Krasinski, known for his wit and charm, I hope to engage readers in a way that is both informative and enjoyable.

While this is an unauthorized biography, it is important to note that it is not meant to undermine or diminish Saryn's achievements. Instead, it aims to explore the nuanced aspects of activism, highlighting the challenges, controversies, and personal sacrifices that come with fighting for change.

Throughout this book, you will find a blend of facts, satire, and personal accounts that may challenge your preconceived notions about activism and those who dedicate their lives to it. It is my hope that by delving into the flaws, imperfections, and complexities of Saryn's journey, we can better understand the realities of being an activist.

I believe in the power of storytelling as a means to educate and inspire. By presenting a range of perspectives, including those who have been critical of Saryn's work, I hope to encourage readers to think critically, question the status quo, and challenge their own biases.

It is also important to address the use of parody in this biography. Parody, when employed responsibly, can be a powerful tool for social commentary and satire. Through the use of humor and irony, we can provoke thought, highlight inconsistencies, and expose the absurdities that often exist within movements and societies.

Please keep in mind that not all activism is perfect, and not all activists are saints. It is through acknowledging the complexities and weaknesses of activism that we can truly grow as a society and strive for meaningful change.

I want to extend my gratitude to those who have made this book possible. To the individuals who shared their stories, the allies who support LGBTQ rights, and the activists who continue to fight for justice, thank you for your courage and dedication. This book would not exist without the inspiring stories and experiences that have been shared with me.

In conclusion, I hope that this unauthorized biography of Saryn Brell serves as a thought-provoking and entertaining exploration of LGBTQ activism in Zerana and beyond. May it inspire readers to embrace change, challenge the norms, and become advocates for a more inclusive and equal world.

Thank you for joining me on this journey.

Sincerely,

Tatyana Flores

Subsection: Closing Words and the End of an Unauthorized Journey

As we reach the final pages of this unauthorized biography, it is only fitting to reflect on the incredible journey we have taken alongside Saryn Brell. From their unremarkable beginnings in small-town USA to becoming a symbol of hope and freedom for the LGBTQ community in Zerana and beyond, Saryn's story has captivated and inspired us.

Throughout this book, we have delved into the life and activism of Saryn Brell, witnessing their triumphs, tribulations, and the sacrifices they made along the way. We have witnessed Saryn's courage in confronting discrimination and bigotry, their unwavering commitment to equality, and the impact they have had on the LGBTQ rights movement. But as our journey comes to an end, we are reminded of the importance of embracing change and continuing the fight for justice.

Saryn's story serves as a powerful reminder that no one person can do it all. True progress and change come from collective action and collaboration. It is through the tireless efforts of activists like Saryn, combined with the support of allies and communities, that we can create a world where equality is not just a dream but a reality.

However, it is essential to acknowledge that activism is neither an easy nor a linear path. In this closing chapter, we explore the dark side of activism, the challenges, burnout, and mental health struggles that activists like Saryn face. It is crucial to highlight the need for self-care practices, coping mechanisms, and a strong support network to sustain the momentum and dedication required to make lasting social change.

As we reflect on Saryn's journey, it is essential to remember that heroes are not infallible. They are human, with flaws, complexities, and contradictions, just like anyone else. Throughout this biography, we have strived to debunk the myth of the perfect activist, to emphasize the nuance and gray areas of Saryn's activism.

In doing so, we hope to encourage readers and activists alike to embrace their own imperfections and complexities. It is by recognizing and embracing our flaws that we can grow and effect change in a meaningful way. Activism is an ongoing process of learning, evolving, and unlearning, and Saryn's story reminds us that it is through vulnerability and openness that we can truly challenge oppressive systems.

Moreover, Saryn's legacy extends far beyond the borders of Zerana. Their impact on LGBTQ rights transcends geographical boundaries, inspiring change and empowering others around the world. We explore the lasting effects of Saryn's activism and how their story continues to shape the fight for equality.

And so, as we close this unauthorized biography, we extend a heartfelt gratitude to Saryn Brell for their courageous legacy. Their unwavering dedication to justice and equality has ignited a fire within us all, urging us to take action and push for a better world. We believe that through individual stories like Saryn's, we can create a collective narrative that challenges oppressive systems and paves the way for a more inclusive future.

As author and parodist, I must address the subversive power of satire in activism. By employing a parody approach in this biography, we aim to highlight the absurdity and hypocrisy that often accompany social change. Satire allows us to question the status quo, challenge societal norms, and disrupt oppressive structures. It is our hope that this unauthorized biography of Saryn Brell serves as a catalyst for critical thinking and inspires readers to question and challenge the world around them.

In conclusion, we would like to express our deepest gratitude to those who made this book possible. The researchers, interviewees, and individuals who shared their stories and insights have contributed to the richness and depth of Saryn's journey. Their contributions have helped shed light on the complexities of LGBTQ activism while reminding us of the power of storytelling in the face of adversity.

Before we bid farewell, we would like to leave you with additional resources for further reading and activism. Activism is a lifelong commitment, and it is crucial to continue educating ourselves, challenging our beliefs, and advocating for change. We encourage you to explore the recommended resources and engage in ongoing dialogue and action.

In closing, we raise a final toast to Saryn Brell and their extraordinary journey. May their story continue to inspire and ignite the flames of activism in the hearts of individuals everywhere. And may we all find the strength and courage to balance personal goals with advocacy in our quest for a just and equitable world.

Subsection: The Challenge of Balancing Personal Goals with Advocacy

As we conclude our exploration of Saryn Brell's journey, it is crucial to address the challenge of balancing personal goals with advocacy. Throughout their life, Saryn experienced the complexities of navigating their own dreams, passions, and relationships while fighting for LGBTQ rights. This subsection focuses on the importance of self-preservation, the need for boundary-setting, and the possibilities of finding harmony between personal aspirations and activism.

Advocacy often demands immense personal sacrifices - time, energy, and emotional well-being - and it is easy to lose oneself in the pursuit of justice. However, it is vital to remember that we cannot pour from an empty cup. Taking care of our own needs and prioritizing self-care is not selfish; rather, it is an act of preservation and sustenance that allows us to continue being effective advocates.

Finding a balance between personal goals and activism can be a nuanced endeavor. It requires introspection, self-reflection, and intentional decision-making. Taking inventory of what brings us joy, fulfillment, and purpose, and aligning those aspirations with our advocacy efforts, is a journey worth embarking upon.

It is essential to recognize that personal ambitions and advocacy are not mutually exclusive. In fact, they can be mutually reinforcing. Our own accomplishments and growth can inspire and uplift those around us. By nurturing our own dreams and passions, we become more effective advocates, leading by example and demonstrating the possibility of creating change through our individual pursuits.

However, finding this harmony is not without its challenges. Boundaries must be set to prevent burnout and maintain a sense of self outside of activism. It becomes crucial to establish limits, communicate our needs, and surround ourselves with a support network that understands and respects the importance of this balance.

In a world that often glorifies and romanticizes the idea of the "selfless activist," it is imperative to dismantle that notion and recognize that our well-being matters. By prioritizing our mental, emotional, and physical health, we cultivate the resilience and strength needed to continue the fight for justice in the long run.

In closing, we urge readers to reflect on their own journey, their personal goals, and the ways in which they can integrate activism into their lives without losing sight of their own aspirations. By striking a balance between personal fulfillment and advocacy, we become more effective advocates and agents of change. As Saryn's story has shown us, it is through our individual narratives and the power of our collective efforts that we can create a more inclusive and equitable world.

Subsection: Resources for Further Reading and Activism

In this subsection, we will provide a curated list of resources for further reading and activism in the LGBTQ rights movement. These resources include books, websites, organizations, and initiatives that can serve as valuable sources of information, inspiration, and opportunities for engagement. Whether you are looking to expand your knowledge on LGBTQ history, understand current challenges, or take action to create change, these resources will help you on your journey.

Books

- *Stonewall: The Riots That Sparked the Gay Revolution* by David Carter: This book provides a comprehensive account of the Stonewall Riots in 1969, a crucial moment in LGBTQ history that ignited the modern gay rights movement.

- *Bi Lives: Bisexual Women Tell Their Stories* edited by Kata Orndorff: This anthology shares the experiences and perspectives of bisexual women, offering insights into the unique challenges faced by this often overlooked segment of the LGBTQ community.

- *Transgender History* by Susan Stryker: Stryker explores the history of transgender activism and challenges, tracing the development of trans politics from the mid-20th century to the present day.

- *This Book is Gay* by Juno Dawson: A guide to understanding all things LGBTQ, covering topics such as coming out, gender identity and expression, and navigating relationships and activism. This book is written in a friendly and informative style, making it accessible for both LGBTQ individuals and allies.

Websites

- **Human Rights Campaign** (www.hrc.org): The Human Rights Campaign is a leading organization dedicated to LGBTQ advocacy. Their website offers a wealth of resources, including guides on coming out, legal rights, and workplace inclusion, as well as opportunities to get involved in their campaigns.

- **GLAAD** (www.glaad.org): GLAAD is a media advocacy organization promoting fair and accurate representation of LGBTQ people. Their website provides resources for LGBTQ visibility in media, tips for allies, and ways to take action against discrimination.

- **National Center for Transgender Equality** (www.transequality.org): This organization advocates for transgender rights and provides resources on legal issues, healthcare access, and employment discrimination. Their website includes guides, fact sheets, and opportunities for activism.

- **It Gets Better Project** (www.itgetsbetter.org): The It Gets Better Project aims to uplift and empower LGBTQ youth. Their website features stories, videos, and resources to support young people and help them navigate the challenges they face.

Organizations

- **PFLAG** (formerly Parents, Families, and Friends of Lesbians and Gays): PFLAG is a national organization that provides support, education, and advocacy for LGBTQ individuals and their families. They have local chapters across the United States and offer resources for parents, students, and allies.

- **The Trevor Project:** The Trevor Project is a leading organization focused on suicide prevention efforts among LGBTQ young people. They provide crisis intervention services, educational resources, and training programs for individuals and communities.

- **National LGBTQ Task Force:** The National LGBTQ Task Force organizes advocacy campaigns and educational initiatives to advance LGBTQ rights and create a more inclusive society. Their website includes information on policy issues, events, and ways to get involved.

- **Athlete Ally:** Athlete Ally is an organization working to combat homophobia and transphobia in sports. They provide educational resources, training programs, and engage with athletic communities to promote LGBTQ inclusion and equality.

Initiatives

- **LGBTQ History Month:** LGBTQ History Month, celebrated in October, recognizes and honors the contributions of LGBTQ individuals throughout history. Visit www.lgbthistorymonth.com for featured profiles, educational resources, and events.

- **International Day Against Homophobia, Transphobia and Biphobia (IDAHOT):** IDAHOT occurs annually on May 17th and aims to raise awareness of LGBTQ rights violations and promote inclusivity. Participate in events or organize your own to show support for the LGBTQ community.

- **WorldPride:** WorldPride is a global LGBTQ pride event held in different cities around the world. Join the celebrations, marches, and seminars to demonstrate solidarity and advocate for LGBTQ rights.

- **Day of Silence:** The Day of Silence, organized by GLSEN, raises awareness about the silencing effect of bullying and harassment on LGBTQ students. Participants take a vow of silence to protest the discrimination faced by LGBTQ youth in schools.

By engaging with these resources and initiatives, you can deepen your understanding of LGBTQ rights, find opportunities to get involved, and join the collective effort to create a more inclusive and equal society. Remember, education and activism go hand in hand, and your voice and actions can make a difference in the fight for LGBTQ freedom.

Subsection: A Final Farewell and Call to Embrace Change

As we come to the end of Saryn Brell's remarkable journey, it is with a heavy heart but also a renewed sense of hope and determination that we bid farewell to this extraordinary activist. Saryn's story has shown us the incredible power of one person's voice and their ability to bring about real change in the world. But as we close this chapter, let us not forget that the fight for LGBTQ rights is far from over. It is a battle that requires the continuous engagement and commitment of each and every one of us.

Change begins with awareness and understanding. Throughout this biography, we have explored the challenges and triumphs that Saryn has faced in their tireless pursuit of equality. We have peeled back the layers of their life, revealing both the victories and the struggles that come with the territory of activism. The unrivaled dedication and unwavering spirit that Saryn has shown are not merely confined to the pages of this book, but are reflections of a larger movement and a collective responsibility.

To embrace change, we must first acknowledge the progress that has been made. Saryn's efforts in legalizing same-sex marriage in Zerana and fighting for comprehensive LGBTQ-inclusive legislation serve as beacons of hope. They inspire us to persevere and keep pushing for greater equality. However, let us not rest on these laurels. We must recognize that there are still significant battles to be fought, here in Zerana and around the world.

SECTION 5: ACKNOWLEDGMENTS AND FINAL THOUGHTS

One pressing issue that remains at the forefront of this fight is the eradication of harmful practices such as conversion therapy. This pseudoscientific approach to changing a person's sexual orientation or gender identity has caused irreparable harm to countless individuals. We must work tirelessly to ensure that such practices are outlawed globally and that support systems are in place for those who have suffered its effects.

Transgender rights also demand our unwavering support. Equality must extend beyond marriage and encompass the rights and protections of all individuals. We must advocate for inclusive policies and create safe spaces where transgender individuals can live their lives authentically, without fear of discrimination or violence.

In order to effect change, we must also confront the political opposition and bigotry that continue to hinder progress. This means standing up to religious organizations and conservative ideologies that seek to suppress the rights of LGBTQ individuals. It means debunking stereotypes and challenging prejudiced beliefs that perpetuate discrimination. It means braving online harassment and trolling, while always remembering the importance of self-care and mental health.

But our task does not end with confronting adversities; it also involves fostering unity and collaboration within the LGBTQ community. We must build bridges, mend divisions, and celebrate the diverse voices within our movement. Only through collective action can we amplify our impact and create lasting change.

As we bid farewell to Saryn Brell, let us not forget that each and every one of us has the power to be a catalyst for change. Their story serves as a reminder that activism is not reserved for an elite few, but is a calling that belongs to every individual with the courage to challenge the status quo. It is a reminder that our own personal experiences and stories have the potential to shape the course of history.

So, let us leave the pages of this biography with a renewed commitment to the fight for LGBTQ rights. Let us use Saryn's journey as a source of inspiration and a reminder that change is possible. Let us be the voices that propel the movement forward, standing united against discrimination and fighting for a world where everyone, regardless of their sexual orientation or gender identity, can live free and equal.

In closing, I would like to express my deepest gratitude to Saryn Brell for their courage and unwavering dedication. I am honored to have had the opportunity to tell their story, and I hope that this unauthorized biography serves as a testament to their indomitable spirit. Finally, to all the readers and activists who have joined us on this journey, I implore you to carry the torch of change forward. Embrace the power within you to shape a better future, and let us continue to push boundaries, challenge norms, and create a world where love and acceptance know no bounds.

Subsection: The Possibility of Future Unauthorized Biographies

As I sit here, reconciling the end of my unauthorized biography on Saryn Brell, I can't help but ponder the future of this unique genre. The unauthorized biography provides a platform to shed light on the uncharted territories of a person's life, unveiling unknown aspects and challenging popular narratives. It serves as a powerful tool to question authority, expose motivations, and push the boundaries of traditional storytelling.

Undoubtedly, there is great potential for future unauthorized biographies to captivate readers and provoke meaningful discussions on the complexities of human experiences. In this subsection, we will explore the possibilities and implications that lie ahead for this genre.

Exploring Unconventional Subjects

One of the most exciting aspects of future unauthorized biographies is the potential to explore unconventional subjects. While famous figures often dominate the biographical landscape, there are countless unsung heroes and ordinary individuals whose stories deserve to be told.

Imagine delving into the fascinating life of an everyday person who went against societal norms and made significant contributions to their community. Uncovering the untold stories of these unsung heroes can inspire readers and challenge the traditional notion of what makes a subject worthy of a biography.

The Power of Collaboration

Collaboration has always been a powerful tool for progress, and it holds immense potential for future unauthorized biographies. By bringing together a team of researchers, writers, and subject matter experts, we can not only deepen our understanding of the subject but also ensure a more nuanced and comprehensive portrayal.

Furthermore, collaboration allows for the inclusion of multiple perspectives, ensuring that the biography captures a wide range of experiences and viewpoints. This approach fosters inclusivity and promotes a more accurate representation of the subject's life.

Deconstructing the Concept of Authority

Unauthorized biographies challenge the notion of authority by subverting traditional structures of power. They dismantle the idea that only the subject or their authorized representatives have the right to shape their narrative. Instead, they invite readers to question the authoritative sources and seek alternative perspectives.

In the future, unauthorized biographies can continue to challenge the concept of authority by exploring the lives of individuals who have historically been marginalized or silenced. By amplifying their voices, we can challenge dominant narratives and empower those whose stories have been overlooked.

Navigating Ethical Dilemmas

As we embark on future unauthorized biographies, it is essential to navigate the ethical dilemmas that may arise. Respecting personal boundaries, obtaining informed consent, and portraying subjects in a compassionate and fair manner are crucial considerations.

Research ethics and journalistic integrity must guide the process to ensure the responsible and ethical treatment of the subject and their story. Balancing the need for disclosure and transparency with empathy and sensitivity will be critical in maintaining the integrity of future unauthorized biographies.

Embracing Interdisciplinarity

The future of unauthorized biographies lies in embracing interdisciplinarity. A multidisciplinary approach brings together various perspectives and methodologies, enriching the narrative and expanding our understanding of the subject.

Biographies that incorporate elements from psychology, sociology, history, and other disciplines can provide a more holistic and nuanced portrayal. This approach allows readers to engage with the subject through different lenses, fostering a deeper connection and a more comprehensive appreciation of their life.

Harnessing the Power of Technology

In the digital age, technology opens up new possibilities for future unauthorized biographies. With the advent of data analytics, artificial intelligence, and virtual reality, readers can immerse themselves in the subject's world and gain a more immersive and visceral understanding of their experiences.

Furthermore, the proliferation of online platforms and social media allows for wider distribution and accessibility, reaching audiences who may not have otherwise engaged with the genre. Technology can democratize the unauthorized biography, enabling diverse voices to participate in the collective storytelling process.

Encouraging Critical Engagement

Above all, future unauthorized biographies should aim to encourage critical engagement and inspire readers to question the world around them. By challenging established narratives and fostering dialogue, these biographies can promote a more informed and active society.

Readers must approach unauthorized biographies with a critical eye, questioning the interpretations and perspectives presented. This genre serves as a catalyst for discussion, encouraging readers to navigate the complexities of truth, perception, and personal agency.

In conclusion, the future of unauthorized biographies is promising. As we continue to explore uncharted territories, collaborate across disciplines, challenge authority, and navigate ethical considerations, we can unlock the transformative power of this genre. By embracing innovative approaches and amplifying diverse voices, future unauthorized biographies have the potential to inspire, provoke, and reshape our understanding of history, identity, and the human experience.

Index

-doubt, 52, 57, 110, 159
-up, 46

ability, 6, 22, 23, 39, 40, 51, 54, 61, 64, 70, 78, 99, 107, 137, 140, 143, 145, 156, 165, 167, 172, 173, 182, 187, 188, 191, 204
ableism, 169
abolition, 85
absence, 81
absolute, 169
absurdity, 93, 188, 200
abuse, 28, 46, 167
abuser, 167
academia, 142
acceptance, 1–3, 8, 9, 11–13, 24, 26–28, 35, 36, 38, 52, 55, 56, 58, 62, 72, 82, 83, 87, 88, 93, 98, 104, 119, 124, 127, 132–134, 139, 140, 142, 165, 169, 173, 175, 177, 183, 195, 196, 205
access, 38, 76, 83, 87, 88, 129, 140
accessibility, 207
accomplishment, 108, 111
account, 155, 157, 158, 189
accountability, 44, 45, 47, 164

accountable, 45, 68, 73, 167, 168
accuracy, 148, 149, 158, 184, 185, 192, 195
achievement, 80, 93
act, 47, 53, 57, 88, 94, 115, 119, 123, 168, 180, 201
action, 2, 3, 6, 17, 39, 43, 53, 54, 64, 66, 69, 77, 92–94, 105, 108, 118, 126, 134, 135, 138, 140, 143, 149, 161, 168, 170, 172, 173, 176, 178, 180–184, 189–192, 199, 200, 202, 205
activism, 1–6, 8–14, 16–20, 22–24, 28–32, 36, 37, 39–54, 56–58, 61, 63, 68, 71, 77, 79, 80, 84, 87, 89, 94, 95, 97–99, 104, 105, 108, 110, 112–121, 123–126, 129, 132, 133, 135–138, 141–144, 147–151, 153–180, 184–201, 204, 205
activist, 1, 2, 6, 9, 13–21, 23, 24, 27–32, 38, 40, 43, 49, 50, 54, 64, 66, 68, 70, 72–75, 78, 79, 89, 98, 103, 104, 110, 116, 124, 137,

139–144, 148, 150–156,
158–162, 164, 166,
168–171, 173, 176, 178,
179, 182, 187–191, 194,
196–199, 201, 204
activity, 112
actor, 124
adaptability, 6, 97
addition, 26, 111, 125, 136, 154, 156, 181, 185
address, 13, 28, 29, 31, 35, 39, 49, 50, 55, 63, 67, 77, 82, 84, 88, 89, 93, 98, 99, 104, 106, 112, 115, 125, 128, 129, 132, 133, 136, 144, 148, 157, 158, 160, 162, 165, 170, 171, 176, 178, 181, 186, 198, 200
administration, 46
admiration, 43, 167, 168, 190
adolescence, 3
adoption, 26, 27
adulthood, 2, 4, 8, 12, 14–17
advantage, 20
advent, 93, 207
adversary, 11
adversity, 6, 9, 18, 29, 30, 41, 42, 45, 48, 51, 80, 107, 119, 140, 142, 167, 178, 200
advice, 19, 20, 145
advocacy, 2–4, 8, 12, 14, 15, 19–24, 26, 29, 31, 35, 36, 38, 42, 43, 47–49, 55, 59, 61, 66, 68, 70–72, 75–80, 82, 84–87, 89, 94, 95, 105–108, 110, 114, 115, 120, 121, 123, 125, 130, 133, 135, 137–142, 144, 145, 152, 156, 161, 163, 166, 167, 172, 174–177, 187, 191, 195, 200, 201
advocate, 4–6, 13, 19, 20, 23, 25, 28, 30, 31, 38, 40, 41, 44, 53, 58, 59, 61, 62, 64, 66, 69, 70, 85, 87, 98, 123, 126, 127, 129, 135, 141, 144, 155, 157, 169, 173, 180, 183, 184, 188–190, 196, 205
age, 1, 3, 20, 100, 102, 207
agency, 132, 208
agenda, 21, 68, 162
aggression, 50
Alex, 26, 101, 151, 155, 156
Alex Ramirez, 126, 151, 155
alienation, 8
alignment, 113
alliance, 127
ally, 9–11, 21, 39, 44, 126, 127, 152, 180, 198
allyship, 6, 39, 63, 160, 166, 168–170, 173
ambiguity, 170
America, 1
amplification, 190
analysis, 150, 151, 155, 158
anger, 53, 104
anonymity, 46
anxiety, 42, 57, 85, 159
appeal, 68, 187
appearance, 22, 24, 73
appreciation, 127, 195, 197, 207
approach, 11, 21, 28, 32, 40, 42, 46, 56, 68, 71, 72, 83, 87, 93, 94, 98, 99, 102, 115, 124, 130–133, 135, 138, 144, 145, 150, 154–158, 161, 162, 164, 165, 167, 168,

170, 186–189, 194, 200, 205–208
area, 38, 78, 171, 197
arena, 5, 40
armor, 119
array, 2, 3, 9
arrival, 22
arsenal, 172
art, 24, 55, 63, 72, 133, 170, 180, 194
article, 49
artist, 151
artwork, 155
aspect, 14, 24, 26, 37, 57, 70, 73, 75, 99, 120, 121, 124, 131, 137, 141, 144, 150, 152, 194
assistance, 89
atmosphere, 56
attack, 49, 98
attention, 6, 21, 22, 24, 26, 44, 53, 61, 62, 68, 111, 129, 149, 161, 162, 165, 168, 170, 178, 186, 187, 194
audience, 20, 21, 43, 63, 68, 70, 72, 87, 187, 188, 194
authenticity, 9, 24, 31, 73, 142, 144, 150, 154, 156, 166, 190
author, 147–149, 156, 157, 185, 198, 200
authority, 167, 206–208
avalanche, 154
aversion, 85
awakening, 5
awareness, 2, 4, 8, 10, 12, 17, 19–22, 26, 30, 35, 38, 56, 63, 64, 68, 70, 76, 78, 79, 82, 84–88, 93, 94, 100, 105, 113, 114, 124, 131, 133,
134, 162, 172, 173, 175, 186, 204
awe, 190

background, 79, 128, 157, 179
backlash, 5, 13, 20, 27, 28, 42, 44, 47, 49, 50, 57, 73, 77, 106, 113, 124, 127, 136, 138, 140, 175, 178, 183, 191
backseat, 73
bakery, 53
balance, 15, 17, 57, 73, 108, 110, 111, 113–115, 123, 141, 142, 144, 149, 157–159, 176, 179, 184–187, 189, 192, 200, 201
ban, 38, 76, 85, 86, 177
barrage, 57
base, 135
basis, 121
bath, 115
baton, 138
battle, 4, 31, 32, 41, 45, 57, 76, 85, 92–94, 97, 101, 104, 105, 121, 136, 159, 160, 163, 204
Bayard Rustin, 196
beacon, 36, 52, 73, 105, 193
beauty, 24, 159
beginning, 13, 137
behalf, 160
behavior, 167
being, 6, 13, 15, 19, 21, 27–29, 31, 38, 41–44, 47, 48, 50, 51, 56–58, 73, 74, 76, 82, 85, 87, 89, 94, 100, 103, 104, 106–108, 110–117, 119, 121–123, 136, 140–142, 144, 155, 159, 161, 175,

		176, 179, 182, 183, 191,
		192, 198, 201
belief, 52, 85, 94, 190
belonging, 2, 3, 15, 22, 26, 32, 73,
		94, 173
benefit, 30
betrayal, 44, 168
betterment, 145
bias, 83, 93, 94, 154
bigotry, 2, 10, 52, 95–97, 106, 180,
		199, 205
binary, 3, 129, 151, 162, 165, 167,
		168
biographer, 147, 184
biography, 13, 49, 54, 97, 147–151,
		154–158, 184–187,
		189–195, 197–200,
		204–207
birth, 24, 25, 101
bisexuality, 183
Black, 197
blend, 192, 198
blueprint, 176
body, 24, 42, 113
boldness, 175
bond, 151, 152
book, 145, 149, 158, 181, 184, 185,
		189, 190, 192, 193, 195,
		196, 198–200, 204
bound, 116
boundary, 201
box, 72, 126
brainstorm, 63, 81
bravery, 45, 46, 101, 191
break, 11, 28, 68, 72, 100, 101, 120,
		127, 137, 169, 182–184,
		187, 189
bridge, 13, 23, 39, 55, 78, 84, 98, 99,
		101, 119, 127, 132, 134

bridging, 23, 71, 126
building, 6, 10, 11, 14, 29, 34, 35,
		38, 39, 54–56, 63, 64, 70,
		71, 76, 81, 94, 97, 99, 104,
		108, 116, 124–126, 129,
		134, 138, 141, 152, 169,
		195
bullying, 26, 83
burden, 13, 73, 74, 106
burnout, 29, 42, 43, 56, 58, 94, 105,
		106, 110–116, 144, 159,
		160, 191, 199, 201
business, 56, 126
button, 104

California, 196
call, 43, 138, 149, 180–182, 191
calling, 205
calm, 113
camaraderie, 11, 15, 141, 194
campaign, 21, 31, 68, 87, 124, 172
campus, 2, 12, 13, 17, 20–23,
		27–31, 38, 155, 156, 191
capacity, 176
care, 28–31, 42–45, 48, 50, 51, 57,
		58, 83, 86, 94, 95,
		102–108, 111–113,
		115–117, 120, 121, 136,
		138, 141, 142, 144,
		159–161, 176, 179, 182,
		188, 191, 199, 201, 205
career, 14
case, 46, 53, 79, 127, 167, 171,
		184–186
catalyst, 2, 5, 18, 24, 35, 36, 53, 61,
		140, 176, 200, 205, 208
catharsis, 114
cause, 10, 11, 14, 16, 17, 19, 22, 23,
		27, 31, 41–43, 45, 47, 49,

50, 52, 54, 56, 57, 75, 104, 105, 114–116, 121, 123, 128, 134, 144, 145, 163, 168, 171, 174, 176, 186, 187, 194
caution, 160
celebration, 13, 30, 36, 38, 165
celebrity, 124
center, 86
challenge, 2, 5, 9, 12, 17, 18, 21, 23, 24, 26, 28–31, 38–40, 52–54, 63, 66, 72, 73, 87, 89, 92–94, 98–101, 105, 118, 120, 121, 126, 127, 130, 132, 134, 140, 143–145, 148, 154, 157, 158, 161, 165, 169–172, 176, 177, 179, 180, 182–184, 188–190, 192–194, 198–200, 205–208
champion, 40, 42, 54, 120, 128, 143, 159, 161, 163, 181
chance, 192
change, 2–6, 10–13, 16–18, 23–27, 29–32, 34–36, 39–41, 43–48, 51–54, 56–58, 61, 62, 64, 66, 68, 70–72, 76–78, 81, 84, 85, 87–89, 92, 94, 95, 97, 98, 101, 104–106, 108, 110, 115, 117–121, 123–128, 132, 134–140, 142, 143, 145, 148, 149, 153, 156, 161–174, 177–184, 187–191, 193–195, 198–202, 204, 205
channel, 12, 108, 114
chaos, 45, 57, 113, 121

chapter, 6, 44, 49, 112, 147, 149, 190, 199, 204
character, 27, 49, 147, 158
charge, 160, 193
charisma, 6, 22, 40, 61
charm, 194, 198
check, 114
checking, 49, 154, 157, 158
child, 1, 12, 26, 155
childhood, 2, 8, 16, 155
chink, 119
choice, 68, 100
church, 127
circle, 9, 150, 154–156, 159, 195
cisgender, 128
city, 5, 30, 31, 35, 44, 46, 52, 58
clarity, 113
class, 1, 3, 137, 165
CLHA, 84
climate, 20, 27, 29, 87
close, 1, 9, 10, 112, 126, 137, 139, 155, 159, 185, 190, 193, 200, 204
closing, 149, 192, 199–201, 205
clothing, 24
club, 6
coalition, 52, 63, 78, 81, 94, 97, 195
cohesion, 135
collaboration, 10, 11, 38, 40, 47, 55, 56, 62–64, 66, 72, 76, 77, 79–81, 94, 124, 125, 132, 134, 135, 143, 162, 164, 169, 174, 178, 179, 191, 199, 205, 206
collaborator, 152
college, 2, 10, 19, 21–24, 27, 30, 31, 38, 155, 191
color, 24, 100, 165
combat, 41, 87, 100, 102, 104

combination, 68, 125, 154
comedy, 43, 115, 186
comfort, 43, 117, 153
comment, 160
commentary, 185–187, 198
commerce, 126
commitment, 6, 8, 10, 16–18, 23, 24, 27, 31, 36, 40, 42, 43, 45–48, 52, 55–57, 61, 77–79, 84, 94, 95, 97–99, 104, 105, 116, 125, 127, 129, 134, 137, 140, 144, 156, 162, 163, 167, 169, 172–178, 190, 193–195, 199, 200, 204, 205
communication, 19, 34, 63, 101, 102, 116, 134, 144, 162
community, 1–6, 8–10, 12, 13, 15, 16, 18, 19, 21–25, 27–31, 34–48, 50, 52–58, 62, 64, 66, 68, 70–74, 76–81, 83, 85, 88, 92, 94, 99–102, 104, 106, 109, 113, 115–117, 124–137, 139–144, 148, 152, 156, 159, 160, 162, 164, 165, 169, 171–176, 178–186, 189, 191, 193, 194, 196–199, 205, 206
companionship, 153
company, 196
compassion, 9, 10, 27, 44, 55, 98, 111, 112, 119, 120, 133, 169
competency, 83
competition, 129, 160
complexity, 8, 28, 115, 129, 148–150, 152, 156, 158, 179, 190

component, 113
compromise, 63, 134, 171, 172
concentration, 111
concept, 110, 148, 166, 207
conclusion, 16, 29, 31, 41, 58, 66, 74, 85, 99, 104, 116, 135, 142, 156, 161, 163, 164, 167, 168, 172, 174, 178, 179, 187, 188, 190, 198, 200, 208
conference, 5, 68
confidante, 155
confidence, 24
confirmation, 88
conflict, 144
conformity, 127, 133
confusion, 8
connection, 1, 8, 73, 74, 92, 153, 159, 182, 207
consensus, 40, 150
consent, 207
consequence, 163
conservative, 3, 5, 10, 13, 17, 20, 23, 27, 36–38, 41, 49, 50, 52, 55, 77, 83, 85, 86, 93, 98, 99, 124, 126, 127, 135, 136, 152, 205
consideration, 185
contact, 147
content, 68, 187, 196, 197
context, 9, 11, 26, 78, 98, 121, 158, 185, 186
control, 164, 167
controversy, 161, 162
conversation, 24, 30, 47, 80, 140, 180, 187
conversion, 38, 40, 76, 85–87, 93, 129, 140, 148, 174, 177, 205

Index 215

conviction, 52, 57, 136
cooperation, 128
coordination, 135
core, 127
correspondence, 71, 157, 185
corruption, 44, 46–48
cost, 13, 43, 48, 105, 175
council, 31, 40
counseling, 19, 26, 111
counter, 23, 36, 49, 50, 87, 93, 98
country, 39, 41, 47, 58, 60, 61, 66, 68, 79–81, 86, 178, 197
couple, 26, 96, 152, 160
courage, 11, 18, 25, 40, 43, 47, 48, 142, 143, 163, 173, 183, 192, 195, 198–200, 205
course, 205
court, 80
cover, 46, 88
coverage, 124, 150
creation, 135, 167
creativity, 51, 72, 155, 170
credibility, 49, 125, 157, 158
criticism, 6, 24, 28, 63, 94, 115, 119, 143, 144, 161–163, 167, 172
cross, 148, 150, 154, 157, 158
crowd, 56
cry, 176
cult, 167
culture, 24, 26, 68, 72, 94, 167, 169
cup, 201
curiosity, 1, 5, 16, 154
curricula, 40, 55, 70, 100, 132, 173
curriculum, 20
curtain, 161
cybersecurity, 93, 102
cynicism, 111

damage, 38, 57
dance, 184
dancing, 113
danger, 167, 168, 175
darkness, 118
day, 16, 45, 46, 111–113, 159
death, 104
debating, 152
debunking, 79, 99, 101, 148, 175, 205
decision, 40, 73, 111, 124, 162, 171, 174, 201
decline, 42
dedication, 10, 22, 23, 27, 31, 41–43, 57, 75, 77–79, 84, 104, 105, 121, 141, 144, 152, 163, 165, 174, 176, 178, 182, 189, 191, 193, 195, 196, 198–200, 204, 205
defeat, 169
defense, 50
defensiveness, 187
defiance, 3, 191
definition, 128, 168, 170
delay, 135
demand, 56, 205
demigod, 167
democracy, 3
demographic, 194
depiction, 156
depletion, 106
depression, 85
depth, 71, 105, 147, 150, 152, 154, 155, 195, 200
design, 197
desire, 1, 8, 39, 127, 151, 162
despair, 56, 116
destigmatization, 93

destination, 30
detail, 154
detective, 151
determination, 1, 2, 4, 5, 8, 10, 11, 13, 16–18, 22, 26, 35, 37–39, 41, 43–48, 51–54, 76, 77, 80, 81, 85, 92, 95, 99, 136, 139, 140, 142, 150, 154, 155, 159, 173, 176, 182, 183, 204
development, 145
dialogue, 6, 11, 27, 28, 30, 39, 47, 53, 55, 56, 63, 64, 79, 81, 84, 93, 98, 99, 101, 104, 124, 125, 127–129, 131, 133, 135, 152, 156, 161, 164, 165, 167, 170, 181, 188, 189, 196, 200, 208
diary, 154
diet, 113
difference, 1, 3, 5, 12, 13, 17, 18, 74, 136, 172, 174, 180, 181, 192, 204
difficulty, 116
dignity, 31, 52, 70, 80, 84, 87, 139, 175, 184, 190
dimension, 152
direction, 72, 137
disability, 29, 63
disagreement, 133
disappointment, 73, 135, 164
disbelief, 44
disclosure, 207
disconnection, 111
discourse, 100, 163
discovery, 1–4, 8, 9, 13, 151, 152, 156, 169, 183
discrimination, 1, 2, 4, 8, 9, 13, 19, 22, 26, 27, 29–32, 36–39, 41, 44–46, 48, 53, 55, 59, 66, 70, 71, 76, 78, 80–84, 86–89, 93, 94, 98, 100, 101, 106, 113, 127, 129, 134, 135, 138–140, 143, 159, 161, 163, 165, 169, 171, 174–183, 188, 191, 196, 199, 205
discussion, 125, 197, 208
disheartening, 106, 135, 136
disillusionment, 136, 164
disorder, 85
disruption, 4
dissent, 168
distraction, 144
distribution, 207
diversity, 3, 17, 18, 24, 28, 29, 34, 48, 70, 84, 99–101, 129, 131, 165, 171, 172, 184, 189, 195
divisiveness, 11, 131–133
document, 71, 151, 154, 197
documentation, 72
dog, 152
dogma, 170
donation, 197
dormitory, 22
doubt, 17, 52, 57, 105, 110, 143, 154, 159, 169
drag, 24, 196
drain, 110
dream, 139, 143, 199
dress, 26, 27
drink, 49
drive, 3, 10, 12, 23, 52, 119, 121
duo, 52
duty, 106, 156
dynamic, 52, 72

educating, 6, 89, 101, 132, 169, 200
education, 1, 4, 13, 16–22, 37, 40, 53, 55, 70, 72, 76, 79, 81, 83, 84, 87, 88, 97, 100, 128, 131, 133, 140, 142, 161, 166, 173, 174, 177, 204
effect, 6, 27, 29, 43, 44, 47, 62, 68, 77, 117, 124, 135, 145, 156, 162, 199, 205
effectiveness, 96
efficacy, 171
effort, 32, 35, 39, 43, 77, 132, 151, 164, 173, 182, 189, 195, 197, 204
electorate, 31
element, 24, 148, 155, 158, 184, 185, 192
elimination, 174
eloquence, 23, 66
email, 154
embodiment, 44
emergency, 50
Emma Thompson, 124
empathy, 1, 5, 11, 21, 23, 26, 28, 39, 54, 55, 70, 87, 88, 93, 99–101, 104, 115, 116, 119, 125–133, 137, 143, 164, 166, 178, 181, 182, 186, 188, 190, 207
emphasis, 169, 178
employment, 2, 37, 55, 59, 70, 76, 81, 82, 87–89, 92, 140, 171, 174
empowerment, 3, 20, 22, 25, 40, 72, 86, 133, 144
encounter, 27, 102, 180, 181
encouragement, 17, 20, 44, 48, 114, 117, 177

end, 22, 54, 71, 140, 149, 189, 190, 195, 199, 204–206
ENDA, 82, 84
endeavor, 29, 35, 95, 105, 117, 148, 167, 170, 189, 201
endorphin, 113
endorsement, 134
endurance, 42
energy, 14, 32, 57, 58, 104, 110, 113, 132, 135, 144, 163, 201
enforcement, 35, 46, 50
engage, 5, 11, 29, 42, 43, 55, 72, 77, 87, 101, 111, 114, 124, 130, 133, 135, 149, 165, 167, 170, 172, 181, 185–187, 189, 194, 195, 197, 198, 200, 207
engagement, 2, 6, 41, 89, 98, 104, 123, 162, 166, 177, 181, 202, 204, 208
entertainment, 68, 149, 158, 184–186, 192, 194
environment, 2, 3, 5, 17, 19, 22, 32, 34, 58, 63, 64, 83, 88, 99, 133, 168, 183
envy, 160
equality, 1, 2, 6, 9, 12–18, 20, 23, 27, 28, 30, 31, 34–41, 43–46, 48, 52, 54–56, 58, 60, 61, 63, 64, 66–71, 73–81, 84, 85, 87, 89, 92–95, 97–99, 104, 105, 112, 113, 115, 120, 121, 123–129, 133–140, 142, 143, 148, 149, 159, 161, 163, 165–167, 169, 171–178, 180–184, 190, 191, 193–200, 204
equilibrium, 145

equity, 135
eradication, 93, 174, 205
erasure, 129
error, 24, 164
escape, 3, 115, 141
essence, 154, 157, 184, 185, 192, 194
esteem, 26
evaluation, 151
evening, 5
event, 12, 13, 35, 36, 38, 46, 51, 55, 56, 181, 197
eviction, 82
evidence, 46, 47, 49, 76, 157–159, 162, 168
evil, 168
evolution, 155
exaggeration, 193, 194
examination, 172
example, 21, 48, 49, 51, 55, 56, 71, 72, 124, 125, 134, 135, 137, 138, 140, 165–167, 169, 171–174, 177, 182, 183, 188, 201
excellence, 22
exception, 31, 41, 56, 78, 118, 119, 156, 159, 189
exclusion, 87, 129
exercise, 51, 112, 113, 144
exhaustion, 31, 56, 58, 110, 111, 136
existence, 16, 128, 158
expansion, 89, 177
expectation, 73, 74
expense, 163
experience, 5, 18–20, 26, 29, 30, 38, 54, 55, 58, 71, 74, 81, 84, 87, 100, 106, 110, 112, 127, 159, 160, 165, 171, 189, 208

expertise, 125, 135, 181, 196
exploration, 1, 8, 24, 48, 92, 165, 167, 191, 198, 200
exposure, 47, 48, 110, 116
exposé, 47
expression, 22, 24–26, 67, 79, 88, 114, 133, 165
extent, 37
eye, 115, 116, 141, 150, 160, 176, 189, 208
eyeshadow, 24

face, 8, 10, 18, 24, 27–30, 41, 42, 44, 45, 48, 51, 53, 56, 70, 73, 78, 80, 82, 87–89, 93, 102, 104–107, 110, 111, 114, 116, 118, 119, 121, 128, 129, 135, 136, 140, 143, 152, 163, 164, 167–169, 171, 172, 174, 178, 182, 199, 200
fact, 49, 98, 148, 150, 154–158, 165, 189, 201
factor, 64, 137
faculty, 20, 22, 23
failure, 136
fairytale, 45
faith, 27, 127, 167
fallibility, 157
fame, 160
family, 1, 4, 5, 26, 41, 57, 81, 98, 104, 114, 127, 152, 163, 181, 195
farewell, 140, 149, 200, 204, 205
fashion, 22–25
fatigue, 42, 105, 110
favor, 79
façade, 167

Index 219

fear, 8, 13, 22, 39, 57, 70, 83, 86–88, 124, 129, 139, 140, 143, 167, 182, 205
feat, 27
feedback, 130
feeling, 41, 144
femininity, 165
fiction, 148, 150, 154–158, 189, 192
fictionalization, 194
field, 14, 193
fight, 1–3, 5, 6, 11–15, 17, 18, 20, 25, 28, 32, 36, 37, 40–45, 47, 48, 51, 53, 54, 57, 58, 60–62, 66, 68, 69, 71–73, 75, 77–81, 83–87, 89, 92–95, 97, 104–106, 108, 110, 113, 115, 118, 121, 124, 126, 129, 131, 135–138, 140, 141, 143, 148, 149, 155, 158, 163, 165–167, 169, 172, 173, 175–184, 190, 191, 193, 194, 196–201, 204, 205
fighting, 16, 17, 31, 34, 45, 46, 49, 56–58, 63, 71, 76, 85, 99, 112, 115, 128, 136, 140, 161, 169, 179, 189, 194, 197, 198, 201, 204, 205
figure, 10, 23, 28, 79, 105, 127, 158, 167, 189, 196
film, 29, 167
finding, 2, 15, 17–19, 24, 52, 57, 64, 94, 108, 114–116, 125, 129, 133, 141, 142, 145, 152, 153, 185, 191, 201
Fiona Lawson, 127
fire, 3, 5, 12, 44, 200
Flores, 147
fluidity, 3

focus, 29, 38, 43, 49, 55, 58, 70, 104, 105, 113, 115, 129, 144, 159, 163, 168, 175, 191
food, 113
foray, 39
force, 11, 27, 36, 48, 52, 53, 73, 85, 138, 159, 161, 183, 191, 196
forefront, 28, 44, 75, 205
forgiveness, 132, 133
form, 24, 28, 52, 114, 128, 169, 194, 195
format, 149, 158, 194
formation, 4, 56, 133
foster, 9, 19, 21, 35, 40, 52, 54–56, 63, 84, 99, 104, 107, 116, 119, 128, 130–133, 137, 143, 160, 170, 182, 184, 188, 191
foundation, 11, 18, 21, 35, 40, 66, 70, 76, 81, 133, 151, 155, 179, 195
framework, 165, 168
freedom, 4, 7, 9–11, 13, 18, 36, 41, 48, 54, 55, 58, 63, 79, 85, 98, 123, 189, 190, 192, 195, 199, 204
friend, 9, 151, 155
friendship, 151, 152, 155
front, 29, 42, 129, 134, 135
frugality, 42
fruition, 196
frustration, 56, 110
fulfillment, 110, 141, 142, 201
function, 110
funding, 42, 110
fundraising, 124, 162
fusion, 22

future, 5, 16, 18–20, 27, 36, 41, 43, 66, 71, 72, 80, 85, 87, 95, 128, 133, 136, 138–140, 142, 155, 161, 176, 178, 179, 182, 190–193, 196, 200, 205–208

gain, 5, 8, 75, 145, 150, 151, 153–155, 161, 162, 172, 183, 207
gap, 55, 98, 99, 101, 119, 127
gateway, 17, 194
gathering, 12, 46
gender, 1, 3, 5, 8, 11, 18, 20, 22, 24–26, 29, 38, 63, 67, 69, 76, 82, 83, 85, 86, 88, 98, 100, 101, 127, 137, 139, 140, 143, 165, 174, 176, 179, 183, 205
generation, 43, 71–73, 137, 138, 142, 143, 169, 173–175, 179, 191
genre, 193, 194, 206–208
glass, 193
glimpse, 147, 149, 150, 156
globe, 177
goal, 39, 52, 54, 55, 63, 94, 101, 134, 186
goldmine, 154
good, 13, 168
goodbye, 190
gossip, 158
governance, 40
government, 5, 44, 126
grace, 23
gradualism, 161, 163
gratitude, 149, 190, 192, 193, 195, 197, 198, 200, 205
gravity, 187

ground, 11, 40, 55, 63, 64, 94, 125, 129, 131, 133, 143, 152, 159
groundbreaking, 10, 59, 76–78, 176, 196
grounding, 113
groundswell, 80
groundwork, 43, 70, 72, 196
group, 22, 50, 56, 100, 129
grow, 13, 21, 36, 62, 70, 101, 117, 129, 133, 140, 166, 169, 196, 198, 199
growth, 6, 8, 18, 21, 43, 48, 114, 118–120, 133, 141–145, 151, 164, 166–170, 172, 176, 201
guest, 28, 55
guidance, 1, 20, 28, 32, 43, 51, 71, 73, 114, 117, 132, 152, 168, 173, 196
guide, 116, 178, 207

hair, 24
hall, 40, 124, 181
hand, 40, 52, 71, 134, 162, 171, 172, 182, 186, 204
happiness, 141
harassment, 28, 31, 45, 47, 48, 50, 57, 70, 81, 88, 93, 102–104, 106, 113, 136, 183, 205
harm, 85, 86, 130, 167, 168, 174, 187, 205
harmony, 145, 201
Harris, 10
Harvey Milk, 196
Harvey Weinstein, 167
hate, 36, 37, 41, 57, 93, 94, 102–104, 106, 119, 136

Index 221

head, 38, 49, 52, 53, 78, 131, 144
healing, 43, 47, 48, 54–56, 108, 114, 120, 132, 133, 182
health, 15, 16, 29, 31, 42, 45, 48, 51, 57, 58, 76, 83, 85, 86, 94, 103–108, 110–112, 117, 136, 138, 159, 163, 176, 191, 199, 201, 205
healthcare, 37, 38, 55, 59, 76, 81–83, 87–89, 129, 140, 177
hearing, 183
heart, 1, 3, 5, 21, 76, 182, 184, 204
heartland, 16
help, 19, 28, 29, 34, 50, 51, 71, 86, 87, 100, 103, 104, 108, 111–114, 116, 128, 130, 132, 136, 141, 159, 180–182, 202, 206
hero, 6, 144, 161, 167, 168, 189
heroism, 193
heteronormativity, 22
high, 3, 12, 44, 56, 110, 164
highlight, 29, 53, 92, 100, 121, 124, 136, 150, 153, 172, 180, 188, 189, 194, 196, 198–200
hike, 159
history, 4, 20, 21, 37, 71, 72, 78, 79, 83, 132, 164, 167, 180, 196, 197, 202, 205, 207, 208
hold, 42, 68, 98, 101, 128, 129, 167, 168, 192
Hollywood, 167
homage, 189, 198
home, 1, 5, 23, 50, 58, 66
homelessness, 26, 172
hometown, 12, 40

homophobia, 10, 41, 44, 46–48, 78, 93, 177, 196
homosexuality, 98, 135
hope, 25, 36, 40, 52, 56, 68, 73, 105, 108, 136, 143, 149, 159, 166, 167, 173, 177, 189, 190, 192–194, 198–200, 204, 205
hormone, 88
hostility, 53
housing, 37, 59, 70, 81, 82, 87–89, 92, 140, 174, 182
hub, 19
humanity, 75, 143, 164, 182
humility, 160, 161, 166
humor, 43, 68, 87, 93, 99, 115, 118, 158, 170, 185–187, 189, 192–194, 198
hunger, 150
hurdle, 17
hypocrisy, 44, 200

icon, 142, 193
idea, 100, 169, 201, 206
identification, 88, 175
identity, 1–4, 8, 9, 12, 16–19, 22, 24–26, 38, 52, 67, 69, 76, 82, 83, 85, 88, 98, 100, 101, 119, 139, 140, 143, 144, 151, 165, 174, 176, 183, 190, 205, 208
ideology, 5
ignorance, 17, 55, 100
illness, 42
illusion, 169
image, 24
imagery, 197
imbalance, 110

impact, 2, 4, 6, 12, 13, 18, 21, 25, 26, 29, 31, 34–36, 38, 40, 44, 45, 47, 53, 54, 57–59, 61, 64, 67, 70–74, 76, 84, 100, 101, 112, 116, 118, 123–126, 134, 135, 137, 139–143, 145, 147–149, 151–153, 155–157, 160, 166, 174–182, 184, 190–192, 197, 199, 200, 205
importance, 1, 6, 8, 9, 13, 17, 20, 24–26, 30–32, 34, 35, 38, 40, 42, 43, 45, 47, 48, 50, 53, 55–57, 63, 66, 70–72, 78, 79, 83, 86, 92, 94, 97–99, 102, 104, 105, 108, 113–116, 120, 121, 123–126, 129, 132, 133, 136–138, 141–145, 149, 155, 159–162, 165–169, 173, 174, 176, 178, 179, 189–191, 194, 197, 199, 201, 205
imposter, 159
imprint, 176
improvement, 39
in, 1–32, 34–61, 63, 64, 66–68, 70–89, 92–94, 97–102, 104, 105, 107, 108, 110–116, 119, 121, 123–128, 130, 133–137, 139–144, 147–169, 171–201, 204, 205, 207
incident, 53
inclusion, 20, 27, 28, 40, 67, 70, 125, 131, 152, 175, 177, 196, 206
inclusivity, 4, 9, 13, 19, 20, 29, 36, 38, 39, 53, 55, 71, 72, 80, 84, 98, 99, 126–128, 133, 135, 139, 142, 162, 171, 172, 178, 179, 206
income, 14
increase, 80, 113, 162, 178
indecisiveness, 183
independence, 14
individual, 4, 8, 9, 21, 26, 36, 39, 45, 64, 71, 73, 81, 94, 121, 122, 127, 139, 140, 143–145, 148, 149, 152, 160, 166, 168, 172, 176, 177, 182–184, 190, 191, 200, 201, 205
individuality, 26, 141
industry, 167
inequality, 1, 2, 45, 81, 92, 93, 161, 183
infamy, 148, 167, 168
infighting, 135
influence, 27, 49, 58, 59, 66, 67, 75, 79, 124–126, 134, 148, 151, 176, 177, 180, 191
inform, 184, 195
information, 46, 100, 147, 148, 150, 154, 157, 185, 189, 195, 201
injustice, 32, 155, 163, 169
innovation, 72, 126
insight, 8, 153, 183
inspiration, 20, 24, 31, 36, 41, 48, 51, 73, 87, 95, 99, 143, 144, 167, 173, 182, 191–193, 202, 205
instance, 70, 113, 134, 135, 160, 183
institution, 127
instrument, 141
integrity, 184, 185, 189, 207

Index

intelligence, 207
intensity, 141
intention, 149, 185, 192, 194
interconnectedness, 132, 173
interdisciplinarity, 207
interest, 1–3, 8, 12, 16, 80, 105, 186, 187, 190, 195
interpretation, 127
intersection, 144, 152
intersectionality, 6, 20, 29, 63, 71, 101, 132, 137, 138, 162, 167–174, 178, 179
intervention, 126
interview, 151, 155, 156
interviewee, 155, 156, 195
intimacy, 152
intimidation, 45–47, 104
introduction, 4, 10, 59, 125
introspection, 1, 201
invasion, 28, 73, 74
inventory, 201
investigation, 151–153
investment, 144
involvement, 2, 21, 23, 40, 41, 71, 162
invulnerability, 120
irony, 187, 198
irrationality, 188
irritability, 111
isolation, 54, 169
issue, 21, 26, 53, 54, 76, 79, 86, 92, 93, 98, 112, 127, 131, 160, 168, 179, 205

Jamie, 9, 26, 156
Jamie Thompson, 156
Jane Michaels, 145
jet, 42
job, 82, 182

John Krasinski, 189, 194, 198
John Thompson, 10
Jordan, 152, 160
Jordan Walker, 152
journaling, 29, 114
journalism, 147
journey, 1–6, 8–13, 15–18, 20–26, 30–32, 34, 37–39, 41, 44–46, 48, 51, 52, 55–58, 62, 64, 66, 70–72, 74, 75, 87, 89, 95, 98, 104, 105, 108, 111, 115, 116, 118, 119, 124–126, 128, 135, 137–140, 142–145, 147–157, 159–161, 163, 164, 166, 169, 171, 172, 176, 178–180, 182, 183, 189–191, 193–195, 198–202, 204, 205
joy, 29, 42, 57, 111, 112, 115, 136, 141, 201
judgment, 19, 22, 24, 111, 129
judiciary, 79
juggling, 14, 94
justice, 1–3, 5, 6, 8, 10, 12, 16, 22, 27, 29, 35–37, 40, 41, 44–48, 63, 66, 71, 74, 78–81, 84, 85, 97, 105, 113, 130–132, 136, 138, 141–145, 151, 159, 163–169, 173, 175, 187, 190, 193–195, 198–201
justification, 53

key, 8, 9, 18, 21, 24, 35, 51, 54, 56, 57, 64, 67, 68, 79, 82, 86, 92, 95, 96, 115, 116, 129, 131, 151, 154, 155, 158, 161, 184, 187, 189, 196

kind, 139
knowledge, 5, 6, 18, 20, 23, 66, 70, 74, 86, 118, 127, 132, 135, 142, 177, 193, 202

labor, 192
lack, 3, 8, 82, 87, 92, 110, 135, 163, 195
lag, 42
landmark, 40, 41, 48, 52, 75, 79, 88
landscape, 10, 36, 39, 40, 66, 72, 75, 76, 98, 104, 118, 120, 126, 140, 149, 174, 176, 179, 192, 206
language, 129, 181
laughter, 43, 115, 194
law, 35, 46, 50, 175
Lawson, 127
layer, 8, 28, 158, 186
leader, 47, 152, 156, 191
leadership, 19, 35, 36, 48, 72, 84, 85, 140, 143, 173, 174
learning, 6, 16, 18, 55, 80, 83, 117, 138, 143, 164, 166, 167, 172, 194, 200
legacy, 6, 36, 64, 66, 70–72, 80, 84, 85, 133, 138–143, 147, 148, 151, 155, 169, 174, 176, 178, 190–193, 196, 200
legalization, 75, 80, 174, 177
legislation, 10, 30, 36, 38–41, 52, 59, 70, 76, 77, 81–89, 92, 93, 124, 139, 143, 171, 174, 175, 177, 179, 181, 196, 204
legislature, 10
Leila, 9
lens, 158, 186, 190, 194

lesson, 126, 137, 160, 178, 179
letter, 43, 197
level, 27, 54, 63, 70, 93, 115, 132, 154, 161, 171, 173, 181, 182, 184, 194
levity, 118
liberation, 16, 18, 138
life, 2, 3, 9, 12, 13, 16, 17, 31, 37, 42, 44, 49, 57, 58, 70, 73, 75, 89, 93, 101, 104, 105, 110, 111, 114, 116, 128, 136, 140–142, 145, 147, 149–151, 153–158, 160, 163, 176, 180–182, 185, 186, 189, 192–195, 197, 199, 200, 204, 206, 207
lifeline, 50
lifestyle, 111
light, 6, 23, 44, 46, 48, 76, 78, 116, 147, 149, 150, 152, 154, 159, 161, 176, 177, 185, 192–194, 198, 200, 206
limelight, 70
line, 105, 123
lip, 24
Lisa, 156
Lisa Carlson, 156
list, 201
listener, 9
literature, 83, 150, 154, 180
living, 8, 9, 14, 105
lobbying, 26, 75, 81, 83, 92, 125, 139
loneliness, 73, 74, 111
look, 22–25, 141, 156, 166, 191
loss, 28
love, 13, 26, 27, 36, 75, 78, 93, 98, 119, 127, 141, 142, 152, 182, 192, 195, 205
low, 56

Index

loyalty, 116
luxury, 43, 105

magnitude, 180
mail, 36
mainstream, 26, 72, 197
majority, 80
makeup, 24
making, 10, 17, 18, 22, 40, 52, 68, 73, 74, 76, 105, 110–112, 124, 136, 147, 155, 162, 168, 171, 187, 193, 194, 197, 201
man, 101, 196
management, 111
manner, 99, 185–187, 194, 207
marathon, 94, 136
marching, 42
marginalization, 37, 82, 92, 129, 140, 171, 179
Maria Santiago, 151
mark, 6, 27, 39, 140, 143, 174, 178, 190, 191
marker, 88
marketing, 181, 196
marriage, 26, 27, 52, 70, 75, 76, 78–81, 92, 93, 129, 134, 135, 139, 148, 174, 177, 188, 204, 205
Marsha P. Johnson, 196
masculinity, 165
Matt, 9
matter, 39, 52, 66, 79, 104, 136, 166, 186, 187, 206
Maya, 10, 127, 155
Maya Patel, 155
Maya Sharma, 43
mean, 129, 133, 164

means, 22, 24, 28, 51, 57, 101, 108, 129, 140, 150, 162, 165, 168, 170, 171, 187, 190, 198, 205
mechanism, 113, 115
media, 20, 21, 26, 49, 51, 53, 61, 64, 66, 68, 70, 72, 75, 78, 83, 87, 88, 92, 93, 99–102, 105, 114, 124, 134, 135, 140, 143, 150, 160, 162, 173, 178, 180, 183, 191, 197, 207
meditation, 51, 111–113, 115, 144, 159
meeting, 53
member, 31, 76, 144, 156
meme, 170
memorabilia, 155
memory, 111, 157, 158
mentee, 152
mentor, 41, 142, 152
mentoring, 72
mentorship, 20, 26, 151
message, 20, 23, 26, 29, 58, 60, 64, 68, 70, 72, 124, 126, 161, 184–187, 197
messaging, 21, 162
messiness, 190
Michael Harris, 10
midst, 15, 22
milestone, 92, 174
mind, 112, 113, 167, 184, 185, 192, 198
mindedness, 1, 84, 128
mindfulness, 29, 42, 57, 111–113, 159
mindset, 113, 115, 168
misconception, 100

misinformation, 49, 55, 87, 88, 93, 148, 158
mission, 46, 47, 67, 104, 105, 116, 140, 154
misunderstanding, 24
mitigation, 50
mix, 12
mobilization, 125
model, 73, 74, 106
modesty, 26
moment, 5, 8, 18, 36, 43, 46, 80, 111, 113, 115, 143, 159, 189, 190, 196–198
momentum, 13, 31, 88, 180, 199
money, 22
monolith, 178
morality, 168
motion, 139
motivation, 32, 110, 136
move, 13, 54, 105, 112, 133, 149, 162, 164
movement, 6, 29, 36, 41–43, 45, 47, 48, 50, 58, 60, 63, 64, 71, 72, 84, 101, 118, 125, 126, 128–131, 133–135, 137, 139, 140, 144, 160–162, 166, 167, 171, 175, 176, 194, 196, 199, 201, 204, 205
multitude, 9
music, 3, 51, 55, 114
myriad, 95
myth, 148, 163, 164, 183, 189, 199

name, 198
narrative, 26, 49, 50, 66, 71, 72, 93, 137, 149, 154, 157, 158, 164, 167, 178, 184, 185, 189, 194, 197, 200, 207

nation, 44, 61, 174
nature, 6, 29, 31, 42, 51, 57, 77, 85, 98, 112, 115, 152, 155, 158, 159, 161, 166, 186, 187
necessity, 43, 76, 123, 124, 160
need, 4, 13, 14, 16, 22, 23, 31, 40, 45, 47, 54, 58, 71, 73, 76, 77, 82, 83, 127, 136, 142, 156, 168, 169, 171, 176, 179, 182, 191, 199, 201, 207
negativity, 36, 57, 106
network, 2, 4, 13, 15, 30–35, 38, 46, 50, 57, 60, 63, 86, 111, 116, 117, 138, 141, 151–153, 178, 191, 199, 201
networking, 66, 154
newfound, 4–6, 8, 127
news, 5, 44, 49, 154, 157
niece, 127
noise, 159
nondiscrimination, 20
norm, 5, 55
note, 54, 98, 128, 149, 156, 194, 198
notion, 26, 27, 100, 148, 167, 169, 189, 201, 206
nuance, 6, 118, 150, 163–167, 169, 170, 179, 189, 195, 199
number, 78
nutrition, 113

objective, 145, 150, 157, 158
obstacle, 10
ocean, 159
offer, 32, 43, 81, 114, 116, 155, 156, 197
office, 40

official, 44, 46, 150, 196
on, 1–6, 8, 9, 12, 13, 15, 17–23, 26–31, 35, 36, 38–46, 48–59, 61–64, 66–68, 70–74, 76–82, 84–89, 93, 94, 98, 100, 102, 104–106, 110, 112–117, 120, 121, 124–129, 131, 134, 136, 137, 139–144, 147–157, 159–169, 171, 173–178, 180–182, 184–186, 188–202, 204–207
one, 8–10, 15, 16, 18, 21, 28, 32, 35, 45, 52, 54–56, 98, 101, 106, 107, 110, 112, 119, 121, 127, 130, 131, 138–140, 142–145, 160, 162, 164, 165, 167, 169, 170, 172, 179, 184, 186, 189–191, 196, 199, 204, 205
op, 61
openness, 200
opinion, 64, 79, 80, 83, 97, 99, 104, 124, 126, 134, 160, 167, 177, 178
opponent, 10
opportunity, 21, 38, 45, 47, 53, 63, 101, 117, 128, 155, 160, 187, 192, 205
opposition, 2, 4, 5, 10, 11, 17, 20, 23, 28, 29, 31, 38, 41, 49, 51, 52, 70, 78, 83, 85, 93, 95–98, 106, 115, 128, 135, 136, 140, 174, 175, 179, 188, 205
oppression, 63, 71, 100, 138, 163, 169, 171
order, 26, 98, 100, 121, 124, 155, 163, 171, 186, 205
organization, 12, 13, 17–23, 30, 38, 43, 63, 94, 155, 172, 191
organizer, 10
organizing, 6, 8, 19, 21, 28, 30, 36, 38, 42, 51, 75, 81, 98, 124, 196, 197
orientation, 1, 8, 11, 18, 38, 67, 69, 76, 82, 85, 98, 100, 139, 140, 143, 174, 176, 182, 183, 205
other, 6, 9, 20, 23, 28, 29, 37, 38, 40, 41, 52, 54, 60, 62–64, 66, 68, 71, 76, 77, 84–86, 89, 92–94, 112–114, 131, 134, 138, 140, 145, 148, 151, 152, 157, 162, 164, 165, 169, 174, 175, 178, 191, 207
otherness, 3
outlet, 18, 114
outrage, 44, 53
outreach, 10, 40
owner, 53
ownership, 132

pace, 135, 161
page, 154
pain, 110
painting, 51, 114, 141, 150
panel, 6, 19, 27, 28, 63, 66, 86, 98
paper, 114
parade, 35, 52
parenting, 26
parodist, 149, 198, 200
Parody, 187, 198
parody, 148, 158, 184–187, 192, 194, 198, 200

part, 8, 17, 20, 23, 39, 51, 57, 64, 104, 143, 155, 193
participation, 19
partner, 116, 127, 141, 152, 156, 160
partnership, 11, 94, 124
party, 41, 127
passage, 59, 84, 148, 177
passing, 16, 86, 142
passion, 1–6, 8, 9, 12, 14, 16–18, 21, 22, 32, 35, 47, 60, 66, 77, 115, 116, 123, 136, 140–142, 151, 194
past, 71, 132, 133, 193
path, 3–6, 9, 13, 14, 21, 35, 43, 48, 52, 145, 163, 164, 172, 199
patience, 55, 125, 127, 167
pedestal, 163, 164, 167
pen, 190
people, 40, 42, 58, 61, 70, 73, 87–89, 93, 100, 101, 116, 124, 132, 140, 154, 161, 165, 170, 173, 181–183, 185, 187, 195–197
perception, 208
performance, 170
period, 1, 48
perpetuation, 167
persecution, 66
perseverance, 17, 45, 59, 76, 97, 136, 140
persistence, 55, 84, 93, 178, 179
person, 8, 82, 85, 139, 143, 145, 151, 166, 172, 174, 179, 182, 183, 186, 199, 204–206
persona, 148, 150, 159, 160
personality, 154, 167, 177
perspective, 6, 49, 72, 148–151, 155–157, 168, 180, 185, 193, 198

phase, 100, 183
phenomenon, 128
picture, 148, 150, 191
piece, 150, 154, 184, 189
pillar, 123
place, 5, 205
plan, 54, 56
planning, 19, 35, 68, 154, 172, 181
platform, 12, 18, 19, 22, 31, 35, 38, 40, 41, 44, 55, 60–63, 68, 86, 98, 124, 133, 162, 180, 191, 206
play, 2, 5, 19, 62, 126, 153, 167, 171, 183, 185
player, 196
playing, 114, 115, 141, 191
poetry, 63, 114
point, 26, 45, 47
police, 50
policy, 6, 22, 26, 45, 64, 66, 67, 76, 77, 97, 125, 143, 173, 184
policymaking, 31
politician, 40, 126
pop, 68
population, 39
portrait, 151
portrayal, 100, 147, 150, 158, 159, 164, 206, 207
position, 31, 73, 127, 167
positivity, 104
possibility, 201
poster, 197
potential, 2, 3, 8, 11, 20, 21, 35, 39, 50, 54, 56, 72, 94, 105, 124, 126, 128, 134, 144, 157, 161, 168, 172, 183, 186, 187, 189, 193, 197, 205, 206, 208

Index 229

power, 2–6, 10, 12, 17, 18, 22, 25, 31, 36, 39, 40, 45–48, 51–54, 56, 62, 63, 66–68, 71, 72, 74, 76, 77, 80, 89, 93, 97, 104, 105, 120, 123, 124, 126, 128, 133–135, 140, 142, 143, 148, 149, 152, 153, 156, 162, 164, 167, 172–174, 178, 179, 182–184, 187–195, 198, 200, 201, 204–206, 208
practice, 54, 85, 111, 113, 114, 121, 122, 136, 159
practicing, 28, 57, 104, 111, 115, 121
precedent, 175, 177
predictability, 50
prejudice, 12, 17, 23, 24, 32, 48, 52, 55, 78, 81, 86, 93, 95, 97, 99–101, 134, 140, 175, 176, 181
presence, 9, 12, 23, 68, 72, 101
present, 46, 111, 113, 115, 151, 155–157, 159, 175, 185, 187, 188, 193
presentation, 155
preservation, 50, 94, 108, 115, 121–123, 160, 176, 191, 201
press, 49
pressure, 30, 42, 45, 73, 74, 106, 110, 116, 159, 165
price, 140
pride, 30, 36, 73, 74, 180
principle, 29, 34
printing, 42
prioritization, 171
priority, 42, 129
privacy, 28, 29, 73, 74, 105

privilege, 6, 9, 156, 166, 169, 180
process, 1, 3, 8, 9, 17, 24, 46, 47, 51, 55, 83, 92, 108, 118, 123, 133, 154, 156–158, 166, 172, 181, 189, 200, 207
producer, 167
professional, 39, 50, 111, 116, 126
professionalism, 196
progress, 4, 9, 13, 17, 18, 43–45, 54, 56, 66, 68, 70, 71, 73, 77, 78, 81, 87, 89, 95, 98, 99, 110, 124, 126–128, 131, 133, 135–137, 140, 143, 161, 166, 168, 169, 171, 172, 175–179, 182, 190, 194, 196, 199, 204–206
progression, 9, 39, 161
project, 148, 156, 185, 189, 192, 196, 198
proliferation, 207
prominence, 48, 49, 105
promotion, 162
property, 73
proponent, 126
proposal, 56
protection, 39, 80, 92, 171
protest, 53
pseudoscience, 174
psychology, 207
public, 10, 27, 28, 45, 47, 49, 52, 55, 61–64, 70, 73, 76, 78–83, 86–89, 92, 93, 97, 99–101, 104, 105, 115, 116, 124, 126, 134, 141, 150, 158–160, 162, 167, 168, 174, 176–178
publicity, 196
publishing, 196

purpose, 6, 8, 74, 105, 108, 115, 116, 185, 194, 201
pursuit, 5, 6, 27, 36, 38, 43, 45, 47, 52, 54, 76, 77, 92, 94, 97, 104, 105, 110, 112, 114, 121, 123, 134, 136, 145, 163, 166, 168, 169, 171, 174, 191, 201, 204
push, 17, 30, 41, 45, 47, 52, 59, 68, 84, 86, 89, 93, 95, 134, 138, 140, 176, 177, 179, 183, 190, 191, 194, 200, 205, 206
pushback, 36
puzzle, 184

quality, 41, 51, 83, 114, 144
quantity, 34
queen, 196
queerness, 27
quest, 4, 26, 56, 147, 150, 151, 154, 157, 159, 171, 185, 190, 200
question, 5, 12, 18, 23, 45, 93, 139, 148, 149, 171, 179, 183, 187, 192, 198, 200, 206–208
quo, 1, 5, 9, 13, 17, 18, 21, 23, 26, 27, 40, 46, 52, 72, 97, 106, 118, 121, 127, 140, 161, 164, 176, 183, 187, 189–191, 198, 200, 205

race, 11, 29, 137, 165, 179
racism, 165, 169
radicalism, 161, 163
radio, 61
rally, 41, 44
Ramirez, 126, 127

range, 5, 19, 24, 63, 85, 96, 152, 168, 179, 187, 198, 206
reach, 20, 31, 35, 63, 99, 124, 134, 149, 175, 180, 186, 187, 194, 195, 197, 199
read, 189, 192, 194
reader, 182
reading, 12, 43, 145, 200, 201
reality, 3, 14, 16, 17, 22, 42, 52, 119, 158, 168, 199, 207
realization, 12
realm, 104, 142, 171, 187
Rebecca, 10
recognition, 23, 38, 54, 78, 82, 83, 87, 88, 135, 176, 177, 197
reconciliation, 47, 133
recounting, 155, 156, 195
red, 24
redemption, 11
reference, 148
reflection, 1, 3, 8, 17, 21, 24, 43, 54, 111, 112, 114, 116, 130, 160, 166, 169, 172, 192, 194, 201
reform, 80
refuge, 159
refusal, 47
region, 39
regression, 77
rejection, 8
rejuvenation, 57
relationship, 16, 116, 152, 156, 160
relaxation, 17, 111, 112
release, 114
reliability, 157
relief, 43
religion, 98, 127
reminder, 4, 6, 9, 16, 18, 25, 27, 31, 45, 48, 58, 64, 74, 84, 87,

Index 231

    94, 105, 112, 127, 136, 142, 143, 174, 176, 178–180, 182, 191, 194, 199, 205
repeal, 177
representation, 8, 22, 24, 40, 72, 73, 100, 149, 157, 171–174, 177, 183, 192, 206
reputation, 6, 49
research, 46, 66, 76, 87, 98, 125, 147, 148, 150–155, 157, 158, 185, 189, 195
residence, 50
resilience, 3, 5, 9–11, 13, 16, 18, 23, 25, 29, 36, 38, 41, 44, 45, 47, 48, 51–54, 57, 59, 71, 77, 84, 87, 92, 94, 95, 97, 102, 105, 107, 111–113, 115, 116, 118–120, 123, 136, 138, 140, 142, 143, 149, 151, 152, 156, 178, 179, 182, 183, 190, 195, 201
resistance, 6, 13, 27, 35, 38, 46, 51, 52, 55, 57, 83, 85, 94, 109, 125, 129, 130, 135, 136, 144, 187, 191
resolve, 4, 12, 20, 46, 51, 95
resource, 20, 34, 43
respect, 55, 64, 86, 88, 116, 130, 135, 139, 158, 181, 185, 186
respite, 42, 51, 73, 159
response, 22, 36, 50, 104
responsibility, 42, 45, 73, 74, 106, 110, 126, 128, 154, 204
rest, 111, 112, 114, 115, 163, 204
result, 94, 105, 170
retreat, 115

revelation, 127, 151
rhetoric, 180, 188
richness, 71, 129, 155, 200
right, 26, 38, 52, 69, 78, 79, 85, 139, 143, 168, 171, 174, 207
rise, 6, 48, 75, 143
risk, 50, 111, 161, 183
roadmap, 137, 143
role, 1, 2, 4, 8, 10, 15, 18, 19, 38, 40, 41, 47, 48, 52, 62, 66, 69, 70, 73–76, 78–81, 88, 92, 97, 106, 113, 119, 125, 126, 139–141, 149, 151–153, 155, 167, 171, 173–175, 183, 191, 194, 195
rollercoaster, 56
room, 8, 73, 154
root, 1, 13, 55
routine, 51, 112
Ruby, 152, 153
run, 31, 40, 201

sacrifice, 31, 41, 45, 95, 104, 105, 184
sacrilege, 167
safety, 28, 31, 35, 36, 46, 47, 50, 51, 57, 104, 163
sailing, 64
sake, 31
Santiago, 151, 152
Sarah, 152
Sarah Evans, 152
Saryn, 1–6, 8–27, 30–64, 66–68, 70–87, 92–99, 104–106, 110–116, 119–126, 131–133, 136–145, 147–163, 165–167, 169, 170, 172–180, 182, 185,

186, 189–196, 198–201, 204, 205
Saryn Brell, 2–4, 7, 8, 12, 14, 15, 18, 23, 25–27, 32, 34–37, 48, 49, 51, 54, 58, 62, 70, 72–74, 78, 85, 92, 94, 102–104, 106, 108, 110, 112, 113, 115, 116, 121, 123, 131, 135, 142–144, 147, 148, 150, 151, 154–156, 158, 159, 161, 162, 178, 182, 184–187, 189, 190, 192–195, 198–200, 205, 206
Saryn Brell's, 1, 5, 6, 9, 16, 31, 41, 44, 46, 48, 51, 56, 64, 66, 72, 78, 81, 85, 87, 89, 97, 98, 104, 119, 120, 124, 133, 137, 139–141, 148, 149, 154–156, 159–161, 163, 164, 167–170, 172, 174, 176, 178–180, 192, 194, 200, 204
Saryn, 10, 46, 47, 105, 125, 150, 162
satire, 99, 118, 148, 149, 185–189, 192–194, 198, 200
scale, 4, 13, 30, 35, 61, 66, 94, 124, 126, 140, 177
scandal, 44–47
schedule, 42
scholarship, 17, 71
school, 3, 5, 12, 26
science, 79, 85
scrutiny, 28, 31, 49, 116, 167, 168
seat, 162
section, 2, 4, 26, 31, 45, 49, 62, 73, 75, 78, 92, 108, 112, 119, 135, 141, 142, 144, 149, 151, 155, 156, 185, 189, 196, 197
security, 36, 43, 50, 93
self, 1, 3, 4, 8, 9, 13, 17, 18, 22, 24–26, 28, 29, 31, 42–45, 48, 50–52, 54, 57, 58, 85, 94, 95, 98, 102–106, 108, 110–117, 119–123, 130, 133, 136, 138, 141, 142, 144, 151, 156, 158–162, 166, 169, 172, 176, 179, 182, 183, 191, 196, 199, 201, 205
sensationalism, 158, 193
sense, 2, 3, 6, 8, 11, 15, 22, 26, 32, 35, 39, 73, 74, 94, 106–108, 110, 111, 113–115, 132, 136, 141, 149, 159, 160, 166, 169, 173, 184, 189, 190, 192, 201, 204
sensitivity, 130, 154, 186, 187, 207
sentiment, 47
series, 22, 147, 188
seriousness, 186
serve, 19, 24, 36, 43, 53, 77, 87, 95, 105, 116, 127, 136, 140, 181, 183, 191, 194, 201, 204
service, 134
session, 113
set, 3, 8, 16–18, 21, 23, 27, 29, 34, 43, 48, 85, 102, 110, 138, 139, 141, 144, 150, 158, 164, 166, 175, 177, 189, 201
setback, 54, 117
setting, 2, 43, 57, 58, 73, 108, 112–114, 116, 141, 144, 160, 201

Index 233

sex, 22, 26, 27, 52, 70, 75, 76, 78–81, 92, 101, 134, 135, 139, 148, 174, 177, 188, 204
sexism, 169
sexuality, 3, 8, 127
shape, 3, 5, 6, 8, 9, 16, 18, 36, 64, 72, 143, 148, 176, 177, 192, 193, 195, 200, 205, 207
share, 1, 15, 19, 28, 39, 41, 46, 63, 66, 70, 71, 75, 86, 100, 101, 106, 114, 116, 131, 135, 141, 161, 169, 172, 173, 178, 183, 189, 190, 192, 195, 196
sharing, 22, 32, 34, 39, 41, 49, 68, 86, 94, 98, 99, 101, 104, 118, 120, 125, 135, 137, 142, 174–179, 181–183, 190, 195
shielding, 167
shift, 56, 78, 99, 135, 168, 177
shoulder, 9
show, 38, 76, 93, 180
side, 4, 9, 17, 49, 150, 151, 154, 159, 161, 168, 191, 199
sight, 158, 201
sign, 108, 114
significance, 11, 21, 35, 45, 78, 81, 108, 121, 124, 143, 149, 153, 158, 178, 179, 182, 185, 191, 194
silence, 13, 44, 47, 104, 167
sin, 85, 98
sit, 22, 206
situation, 172
size, 145, 162, 164, 170
skepticism, 31, 156, 168
skin, 28

sleep, 42, 110
Smalltown, 1–3, 5, 8, 12, 13, 142, 151, 155, 190, 195
smear, 45, 49
smile, 189
society, 1, 3–5, 8, 10, 17–19, 25–27, 35, 36, 38, 39, 43, 48, 53, 55, 58, 61, 70, 72, 76, 77, 80, 81, 84, 85, 87–89, 95, 99–101, 105, 119, 128, 135, 136, 140, 142, 145, 163, 164, 167, 168, 173–175, 179, 182–184, 187, 189, 192, 194, 197, 198, 204, 208
sociology, 207
solace, 1–3, 9, 19, 57, 113, 114, 141, 153, 159, 173
solidarity, 22, 30, 32, 62, 71, 93, 111, 134, 140, 177, 180, 184
source, 20, 114, 129, 141, 144, 159, 178, 205
space, 4, 6, 8, 22, 32, 48, 54, 56, 58, 93, 101, 105, 114, 120, 125, 151, 159, 164, 169, 182
spark, 5, 6, 45, 63, 140, 170, 183, 186, 187, 194
speaking, 55, 62, 87, 93, 99, 101, 156, 160, 167, 175
spectrum, 24, 72, 137, 150, 165
speculation, 154, 158
speech, 41, 66, 93, 94, 106, 136
sphere, 169
spirit, 36, 43, 45, 64, 128, 162, 176, 184, 193, 194, 204, 205
sponsorship, 35
spotlight, 53, 68, 76, 115, 116, 160, 176, 191

spread, 44, 49, 58, 66, 68
sprint, 94, 136
stability, 14, 105
stage, 20, 66, 85, 175, 191
stance, 126
standard, 194
standing, 42, 43, 99, 176, 205
star, 6
state, 66, 110, 112, 181
statement, 22
status, 1, 5, 9, 13, 17, 18, 21, 23, 26, 27, 29, 40, 46, 52, 68, 72, 97, 106, 118, 121, 127, 140, 158, 161, 164, 167, 168, 176, 183, 187, 189–191, 198, 200, 205
step, 24, 32, 38, 39, 77, 106, 113, 115, 136, 168, 173, 175, 182
stereotype, 26, 100
stigma, 87, 88, 93
stone, 154
story, 1, 7, 18, 25, 26, 43, 48, 49, 56, 58, 94, 98, 101, 105, 112, 119, 120, 123, 137, 138, 143, 145, 147, 149, 150, 152, 154, 155, 158, 161, 172, 174, 177–180, 182–185, 187, 189–193, 195, 196, 199–201, 204, 205, 207
storytelling, 52, 68, 72, 97–99, 137, 143, 149, 185, 193–195, 198, 200, 206, 207
strain, 41–43, 116, 160
stranger, 37, 57
strategizing, 40
strategy, 46, 49, 135, 162
strength, 9, 17, 19, 28, 47, 52, 60, 71, 74, 87, 114, 119, 120, 129, 136, 152, 153, 156, 159, 191, 193, 200, 201
stress, 31, 42, 48, 105, 110–113, 159
stretch, 180
struggle, 4, 16, 37, 57, 70, 84, 85, 92, 94, 123, 130, 143, 177, 184, 190, 195, 197
student, 2, 5, 12, 17–23, 27, 28, 38, 155, 191
study, 53
style, 22, 24, 25, 173, 185, 189, 194, 198
sub, 129
subject, 105, 160, 184–187, 206, 207
subjectivity, 158
subsection, 8, 9, 13, 18, 21, 23, 26, 27, 30–32, 37, 41, 46, 49, 51, 54, 56, 70, 75–77, 81, 84, 85, 87, 89, 98, 99, 102, 104, 106, 110–112, 116, 121, 124, 126, 131, 137, 141, 149, 151, 153, 154, 159–161, 164, 168, 171, 172, 174, 176, 180, 182, 184, 186, 190, 194, 201, 206
subversion, 118
success, 35, 40, 56, 61, 64, 68, 78, 79, 82, 137, 151, 152, 167
suicide, 85
summary, 27
support, 1, 2, 4, 9, 10, 13–15, 17, 19, 21–23, 26–28, 30–36, 38, 40, 42–48, 50, 51, 55–60, 64, 72, 78, 80–82, 84, 86–89, 93, 94, 101, 102, 105, 110–112, 114–117,

120, 121, 124, 126, 127, 132, 134, 136, 138, 141, 151–153, 156, 159, 166, 169, 171, 173–176, 178, 180, 181, 186, 191, 195–199, 201, 205
supporter, 156
surface, 128, 154, 155
susceptibility, 42
sustainability, 44, 118, 122
sustenance, 201
Sylvia Rivera, 196
symbol, 24, 25, 30, 31, 38, 40, 73, 74, 149, 159, 191, 199
symbolism, 76
syndrome, 159
system, 42, 70, 114, 159, 162

table, 162
tailor, 27
take, 8, 16, 29–31, 37, 39, 41, 43, 54, 66, 72, 77, 100, 106, 110, 114, 135, 136, 138, 143, 148, 149, 160, 173, 176, 182, 183, 186, 189, 190, 192, 194, 196, 198, 200, 202
talent, 156
talk, 61, 85
tapestry, 153
target, 21, 45, 47, 93, 158
task, 35, 95, 112, 144, 147, 154, 156, 158, 184, 205
taste, 2, 5, 12
Tatyana, 148–155, 157–159
Tatyana Flores, 147, 150, 154, 155, 157, 158, 185, 198, 199
tea, 9
teacher, 117

team, 30, 35, 36, 49, 50, 79, 125, 196, 206
technique, 111
technology, 135, 207
television, 61
tenacity, 75, 86, 147
tendency, 163
tension, 115, 171
term, 70, 72, 108, 112, 114, 121, 123, 145, 160
terminology, 129
terrain, 49
territory, 204
testament, 25, 41, 45, 48, 80, 89, 93, 143, 190, 205
thank, 143, 193, 196, 198
the United States, 16, 21, 37
therapy, 29, 38, 40, 42, 51, 76, 85–88, 93, 111, 114, 129, 140, 148, 152, 174, 177, 205
thinking, 2, 72, 111, 148, 168, 170, 200
Thompson, 10
thought, 24, 63, 87, 149, 155, 186, 187, 192–194, 198
threat, 98, 104
time, 5, 12, 14–17, 20, 31, 32, 39–42, 45, 51, 54, 56, 57, 66, 104, 110, 113, 114, 116, 118, 136, 141–144, 148, 155, 157, 163, 166, 176, 179–182, 197, 201
toast, 142, 143, 193, 200
today, 20, 25, 43, 102, 163, 168, 196
tolerance, 83
toll, 15, 17, 29, 31, 41–43, 45, 48, 50, 56–58, 73, 78, 94, 105–108, 110, 112, 114,

120, 136, 138, 159, 163, 175, 179, 191
tone, 186
tool, 18, 20, 24, 25, 30, 41, 100, 101, 118, 137, 173, 186–188, 198, 206
top, 54, 132, 186
topic, 130, 145, 186
torch, 43, 138, 140, 142, 176, 205
touch, 87, 155
tourism, 126
town, 1, 4, 6, 8, 16, 17, 21, 37, 40, 53, 55, 56, 84, 124, 149, 181, 190, 199
traction, 21
training, 19, 20, 63, 83, 86, 88
transformation, 16–18, 23, 24, 36, 75, 127, 175
transgender, 38, 76, 77, 82, 83, 87–89, 100, 101, 127, 129, 140, 148, 162, 171, 175, 177, 183, 196, 205
transparency, 49, 73, 144, 185, 207
transphobia, 177
trap, 160
trauma, 51, 110
travel, 42
treasure, 154
treatment, 53, 78, 81, 175, 177, 207
trial, 24, 164
triumph, 5, 20, 41, 75, 178
trolling, 93, 102, 104, 205
trove, 154
trust, 34, 35, 49, 116, 125, 126, 132, 195
truth, 9, 46, 47, 52, 143, 147, 149–151, 154, 157, 158, 184, 185, 191, 193, 208
turbulence, 52

turn, 44, 45, 53, 116, 173
turning, 45, 47, 51, 163
turnout, 12

unaccountability, 168
uncertainty, 52, 105
understanding, 3–6, 9, 11, 12, 18, 19, 26–29, 35, 36, 39, 40, 47, 48, 53–56, 62–64, 70, 71, 76, 83, 84, 87, 88, 93, 98, 100, 101, 104, 111, 115, 119, 127–132, 141, 143, 148–151, 154–156, 158–161, 163–167, 172, 173, 175–178, 180–183, 185, 190, 195, 204, 206–208
unearthing, 189
uniformity, 129
unity, 10, 30, 36, 39, 47, 48, 53–56, 60, 63, 71, 78, 94, 95, 109, 118, 129, 131–135, 143, 162, 178, 184, 191, 205
university, 2, 22
unlearning, 166, 200
unreliability, 157
up, 1, 3, 5, 6, 8, 9, 12, 16, 36, 40, 42, 46, 63, 69, 99, 106, 138, 140, 143, 151, 155, 163, 164, 166, 173, 175, 176, 178, 179, 188, 205, 207
upbringing, 1, 13
update, 175
urgency, 83, 85, 92, 104, 149, 161, 162
USA, 1–5, 8, 12, 13, 16, 142, 151, 155, 190, 195, 199
usage, 129

use, 61, 68, 70, 72, 93, 162, 166, 180, 182, 186, 187, 192, 198, 205

vacation, 111, 115
validation, 73, 111
validity, 85
value, 26, 64, 94, 166, 186
vandalism, 20, 50
vehicle, 62
veracity, 47
version, 164
vibrancy, 24
victory, 31, 38, 75, 166, 169
video, 188
view, 98, 166
vigilance, 45, 77
violence, 42, 46, 50, 87, 104, 129, 135, 139, 183, 205
visibility, 23–25, 30, 35, 50, 52, 66, 72, 80, 162, 171, 173–175, 177, 178, 196
vision, 10, 13, 35, 36, 38, 39, 61, 63, 94, 133, 139, 142, 143, 166, 191
visionary, 85, 140
visual, 22, 24, 155
vitality, 115
voice, 2, 6, 7, 9, 12, 13, 18, 21, 31, 40, 42, 44, 45, 48, 49, 62, 71, 85, 124, 127, 134, 137, 144, 149, 159, 171, 177, 179–181, 191, 192, 204
vulnerability, 58, 98, 119, 120, 159, 183, 191, 200

wardrobe, 24
Washington, 196
wave, 30, 47, 174
way, 2, 8, 17, 19, 23–27, 30, 36, 42, 48, 49, 53, 54, 76, 78, 87, 104, 115, 119, 125, 126, 131, 135–139, 141, 142, 147, 151, 154, 161, 167, 174, 177, 179, 181–183, 186, 189–192, 194–196, 198–200
weakness, 108, 114, 119
weariness, 105
weight, 31, 42, 45, 56, 73, 74, 106, 111, 115, 121, 136, 159, 191
Weinstein, 167
well, 4, 6, 14, 15, 21, 28, 29, 31, 33, 37, 38, 41–44, 48, 50, 51, 56–58, 63, 66, 73, 76, 94, 103, 104, 106–117, 121–123, 136, 140–142, 144, 149, 151, 156, 158, 159, 161, 173, 175, 176, 178, 179, 182, 184, 189, 191, 201
wellbeing, 88
whirlwind, 121
whole, 76, 115, 125, 129, 171
wildfire, 44
willingness, 9, 24, 28, 48, 54, 55, 101, 115, 161, 166, 167, 172, 195, 196
wisdom, 30, 116
wit, 93, 115, 118, 185, 187, 194, 198
witness, 23, 48, 123
word, 46, 154
work, 1, 8, 15, 29, 38, 42, 43, 47–49, 54, 68, 70–72, 74, 76, 81, 85, 87, 89, 94, 101, 104–108, 110–112, 114, 115, 118, 120, 129, 133,

   136–138, 140–145, 148,
   151, 152, 157, 158, 164,
   166, 169, 173, 176, 179,
   185, 187, 189, 190, 192,
   193, 195–198, 205
workplace, 177
workshop, 21
world, 1–4, 9, 12, 16–18, 21, 25, 43,
   47, 63, 64, 66, 69, 72, 73,
   76, 87, 96, 101, 102, 105,
   120, 123, 124, 126, 127,
   136, 140–143, 147, 154,
   155, 159, 164, 165, 168,
   171, 173, 175, 176, 178,
   179, 182, 184, 190, 193,
   195, 196, 199–201, 204,
   205, 207, 208
worldview, 5, 18
worship, 167, 168
worth, 26, 27, 55, 105, 143, 145,
   185, 190, 201
writer, 198
writing, 51, 114, 141, 149, 157, 184,
   189, 194, 198
wrong, 160, 163, 167, 171

year, 36
yearning, 5
yoga, 113
youth, 26, 27, 71, 140, 172